It's a Dark World

A Primer of the Evil which Surrounds Christians Daily

In the Face of Evil – A Wakeup Call for Christians
And
Evil Defined – From a Christian Perspective

Roger J. Boehm, DCC, Ph.D.

Roger J. Boehm, Ph.D.

Titusville, FL

cfcc@lwol.com

Copyright 2007 by Roger J. Boehm

ISBN   978-0-6151-4590-7

About the Author

D r. Roger Boehm holds six earned degrees, all Summa Cum Laude, which include a Graduate of Biblical Studies and a Bachelor of Ministry in Christian Counseling from Bethany Bible College; a Master of Ministry in Christian Counseling, Doctor of Christian Counseling, and Ph.D. in Religion with a Christian Counseling Concentration from Bethany Theological Seminary; and a Ph.D. in Clinical Christian Psychology from Cornerstone University.

He is the Executive Director of the Center for Christian Counseling and Training in Titusville, Florida.

He has served as a chaplain in a 1200 prisoner facility, conducted mission work, evangelistic meetings, and pastoral training in the countries of Haiti, Cuba, and Cameroon, West Africa; pastored churches in 5 states; and conducted seminars evangelistic meetings and revivals in 14 states from California to Florida.

As a Christian Counselor Dr. Boehm is licensed through the National Christian Counselors Association as a Clinical Pastoral Counselor Advanced Certification. He is a Diplomat and Board certified as a Clinical Supervisor and Board certified in the areas of Sexual Therapy, Marriage and Family Therapy, and Child & Adolescent Therapy with the National Board of Christian Clinical Therapists.

Dr. Boehm has authored a number of other books and pamphlets including the books *Evil Defined – From a Christian Perspective* and *In the Face of Evil – A Wakeup Call for Christians*.

He and his wife Diane currently reside in Titusville, Florida.

I gratefully dedicate this book to my Lord Jesus Christ, my Savior and Redeemer – my friend, and my Wonderful Counselor.

I also dedicate this book to my wife, Diane, who I love very much. She is my wonderful partner, lover and my best earthly friend. She has been by my side through many of the counseling sessions and other incidents written of in this book. Without her support and encouragement this book would have been impossible to write.

I give a special acknowledgment to Rev. C.L. Powers who faithfully preached about the atoning blood and love of Jesus in a little country church in Georgia where I was born again. And who encouraged me in the early days of ministry.

And to other men of God who taught me the Holy Scriptures and encouraged me along the way.

Thank you all so very much.

**In Ephesians 6:10-17 we are taught that
in the believer's experience of union with the Lord Jesus
will be fought
the keenest and closest battles
with Satan and his hosts.**

*Finally, be strong in the Lord and in his mighty power.
Put on the full armor of God so that you can
take your stand against the devil's schemes.
For our struggle is not against flesh and blood,
but against the rulers,
against the authorities,
against the powers of this dark world
and against the spiritual forces of evil in the
heavenly realms.
Therefore put on the whole armor of God,
so that when the day of evil comes,
you may be able to stand your ground,
and after you have done everything,
to stand.
Stand firm then,
with the belt of truth buckled around your waist,
with the breastplate of righteousness in place,
and with your feet fitted with the readiness that comes
from the gospel of peace.
In addition to all this, take up the shield of faith,
with which you can extinguish all the flaming arrows
of the evil one.
Take the helmet of salvation and the sword of the Spirit,
which is the word of God.*

Contents

Facing Evil in the Town

Facing Evil in the Church

Facing Evil in Counseling

Facing Evil in Buildings

Facing Evil in Foreign Countries

Dealing with Evil in Everyday Life

Appendix

Bibliography

Forward

L et me stick my neck out along with Roger Boehm.

His book is important, for he says things many of us would be reluctant to say because we cling so desperately to the good opinion of our colleagues in the ministry. We believe we must be careful not to express ourselves too freely. It is risky to depart very far from what current intellectual and religious fashions dictate to be prudent. We fear for our reputations. This book could easily win disbelief and scorn for Roger. To many readers it will sound wild, far out. For those who have no experience with the things he writes about in this book and who perhaps have doubted occasional news reports, it is understandable that this would be so. Nevertheless, Roger has had the courage to put duty before personal ambition. I am therefore glad to stick my neck out and join him, for I, too, have both encountered some of the horror he writes about and joined him in some of the sessions discussed.

Quite correctly, Roger has shared with us his personal journey as he has come into contact with the activity of the powers of darkness and the treatment of multiple personality disorder (DID) in the ministry. The history of his inner and outer struggle during this period of time becomes an open book for us to read. It is better this way. There are two breeds of writers: those who dig up facts and theories and describe them, and others who, from the depths of their personal struggle with truth, speak from their living experience. Roger Boehm is the latter. He knows whereof he speaks.

Among the issues he discusses is satanic ritual abuse, which is difficult to do without opening oneself to the accusation of sensationalism. Some news is by its very nature appalling and sickening. Yet how can one convince the public of the horror without describing it – at least to some extent? Description of satanic ritual abuse is nauseating and horrendous. However, unless we are willing to grasp the horror, we will never understand, much less be able to help heal, the pitifully damaged victims.

There are many reasons Roger's descriptions will sound incredible. We have heard false reports, so we tend to be skeptical of all reports. Another reason for skepticism is that we have no idea how dark the darkness of evil really is. In fact, we do not want to know. Faced with it we shake our heads. Many pastors do not want to know. But now, little by little, the evidence mounts, and ministerial disbelief gives place to horrified recognition of reality. Sadly, even police officials, lawyers, judges, doctors, and psychologists are found among the perpetrators of unmentionable ritual evils. Community leaders can be active agents of the spreading of darkness.

Roger faces not only the disbelief of the public but also the dismissal of his views by some of his ministry colleagues. For too long, pastors and those in the ministry have buried their heads in the sand regarding the supernatural.

It is my hope that the Holy Spirit will use this book to enlighten all Christians, especially Church leaders, to the reality of spiritual warfare being encountered daily by countless individuals whom they never would suspect are having problems with the forces of evil.

I am delighted, therefore, that this book will be available to the public. It goes with my own prayers that Christ will triumph as the powers of evil are exposed and put to flight.

Rev. David Cotner

Missionary Church, Inc.

Senior Pastor

Retired

Introduction

This is not a novel but a book of **facts.** The happenings are accurate but the names have been changed to protect those whose experiences are related in this book.

Many shocking facts are presented which should serve to awake the Christian community throughout our country to the evils that surround us. The Bible says much about evil spirits and the spiritual warfare in which we find ourselves, but all too often we choose to ignore what it says and pretend evil doesn't exist around us. It does!

In Ephesians 6:12 we are warned that as Christians we are not struggling with flesh and blood, but against the spiritual forces of evil in the heavenly realms. In this book the author shares his experiences standing in the face of evil.

In 1995 I received a letter from a Southern Baptist pastor in Ohio. Following is a copy of his letter with the italics and bold print **he** used.

Dear Roger:

I received your newsletter with joy. I continue to pray for the Lord's best to fall on you and that your ministry will bear wondrous and voluminous fruit for our Lord Jesus.

I want to comment on your concern with ministry to Satanic Ritual Abuse, and how people will perceive your efforts. **They won't like it.** They will *insult you persecute you and falsely say all kinds of evil against you because of me.* (Matthew 5:11) *Rejoice and be glad, because great is your reward in heaven, for in the same way they persecuted the prophets who were before you.* (vs. 12).

My first encounter with the Satanic and Occult rituals was in the Mediterranean. If any culture should know more about spiritual warfare, surely it would be those close to where the great ministries of spiritual warfare by the disciples occurred. It was very common. I encountered it in North Africa, in Ethiopia, in South America, in the Caribbean, and in the Far East. It was there and it was obvious, but in all those places believers were afraid to deal with it. Believers in America would like to ignore the influence and spiritual power of Satan. They don't know how to live life on a spiritual plane, nor how to conduct spiritual warfare with knowledge of Satan and experience with God. We readily acknowledge the existence of God and His power. We readily admit that Satan exists and that he has power, but because so many Christians are spiritual babies they have never learned to defend themselves nor to defend the helpless. Some mature Christians do it, but don't talk about it, because the less mature find it *frightening and absurd*. For seven years in Arizona, the heart of Satan worship and the occult in the Southwest, I worked to gain a foothold in the minds of Christians to spiritual warfare. Some progress has been made. You are not alone my brother. Do not fear what man can say or do. Do not fear if they stop sending money, trust God that the releasing of the captive heart from the bonds of ritual abuse and ritual worship will produce revenue enough to continue, and produce great peace. Cast out the devils, and set the captives free, throw Satan's influence into the consuming fire of the Holy Spirit, he will run from you, and people will support you.

Let me also share a letter I received from a missionary friend in the Philippians who wrote:

I received your letter this week and was awed as I read of God's power being manifested through the ministry there. I realize that you are in the thick of the battle, and it made me ashamed that my prayers for you have not been as regular as they should be. I shared your prayer letter with my colleagues and I plan to Xerox it to send to some national (Filipino) pastors. I think some Filipinos are under the mistaken impression that there is no overt demonic activity in the United States and that they are the only ones who deal with it.

It breaks my heart when I think of the pastors, church leaders, and even denominational leaders today who don't realize they are in a battle with the forces of evil. So many pastors do not know how to recognize and deal with the forces of evil today because of the lack of training in this area in our schools and seminaries. So often they learn only about the existence of the forces of evil but not how they manifest in our lives and how we can deal with them.

And then there are the countless Christians who do not realize that they are struggling daily with evil and therefore allow their lives and marriages to be destroyed when they could have had the victory in Christ.

We have **got to wake up,** realize there is a lion in the street, and then learn how to successfully battle it.

There are Lions in the Streets

Proverbs 22:13 states that the sluggard says, "There is a lion outside!" or, "I will be murdered in the streets!" Proverbs 26:13 says that the sluggard says, "There is a lion in the road, a fierce lion roaming the streets!"

This man would not go outside because there was a lion in the streets. But let me say that God would have us go out in the streets anyway. "But." You say, "The lion may get me." No, no, there's definitely a lion in our streets but we Christians need to learn how to lick it and go on. You might say, "But what if the lion licks me?" Then it would be better to be licked by the lion in the will of God than to be outside His will.

The most dangerous place in the world is outside the will of God. It would have been more dangerous for Daniel to be "safe" than to have been in the lion's den. It would have been more dangerous for Shadrach, Meshach, and Abednego to be at home in bed than to have been in the fiery furnace. The safest place in the world for the Israelites when they came to the Red Sea was to go through it. No place is safe unless it is nestled right in the middle of God's will. God's will for us is to fight the lion in the street, so let's stop being disobedient, put on the armor of God, and start doing battle. After all, we're supposed to be soldiers in spiritual warfare.

Be aware that when anyone goes forward for God he will always find a lion in the street. However, the safest place in the world is where you have to fight a lion if that is the will of God for your life. Time and again this author has learned that lions are highly overrated. So if there is a lion in your street keep on going.

What does the lion symbolize? Well, in the New Testament we are told that Satan is a roaring lion seeking whom he may devour. It means that if you decide to do anything for God there will be a lion in your way. It will be your adversary the devil. When you see him don't run. When there is a lion in the street keep on going.

The man in this passage was not only lazy but selfish. He was afraid he would be slain because there was a lion in the street. I ask the reader, wasn't that a selfish way to look at it? Think how many folks were out in the street who needed help. But all he was worried about was that he might be killed. He didn't appear to be concerned about the little children who might be playing in that same street or the little old lady walking by. He was only concerned about himself.

There are lions running loose in our towns, cities, churches, and schools today, and we are not suppose to stay in the luxury and comfort of our homes and do nothing. We are to get outside where the lion is and help the people who are about to be ensnared by the wicked lion in the street who is walking about and seeking whom he may devour.

We as Christians need to move beyond the comfort and luxury of our services and get out there where the people are in danger of being destroyed by the lion. If I could recommend one thing to the reader it would be to forget yourself and bathe your life in service to others. There is no person as wretched as a selfish one, nor one more miserable.

If we as Christians don't immediately do whatever God tells is to do because there is difficulty, the difficulty will be definitely greater when we later decide to do it. I mean the time to attack Satan and his evil spirits is the first time they stick their heads up. We need to make up our minds that when God says to do something the best and safest time is immediately before the lions begin to multiply. James IV rebelled against his father and brought an army against him. James was so remorseful later that he wore an iron belt around his waist. It represented his burden of remorse and shame. It is said that in every succeeding year he added another iron link to that belt so that in his old age he could barely walk. The belt was heavier than it had ever been before. And that's the way it is when you let the forces of evil have just one little inch, the burden will be heavier as time goes on.

What are we suppose to do with lions? ***Tread on them.*** In Psalm 91:13 we are told *you will tread upon the lion and the cobra; you will trample the great lion and the serpent.* The most dangerous place when there is a lion in the street is also the safest place. In doing God's will we are in the safest place.

What should we do with the lion? Tread on it, march over it, defeat it. I think back on my past ministry and the lions that have lurked in the way. When God first called me into the ministry, people said, "Surely not." There was a lion in the way, but I preached anyway. Tread on the lion! Years ago when denominational leaders tried to ruin the ministry I was involved in, there was a lion in the way. But they didn't ruin it and I pastored churches in that denomination, was appointed a missionary, and served on the mission board of that denomination. Tread on the lion! When I pastored my first church, and the head deacon called me to his home and told me I wouldn't preach anymore if I didn't change my sermons, there was a lion in the way. I didn't change my sermons. Tread on the lion! When I pastored in Missouri, and we were threatened repeatedly in the middle of the night and would have to leave our home because of taking a biblical stand, there was a lion in the way. I didn't change my stand. Tread on the lion! When a man came to the church with a gun to shoot me and the church was full of children in vacation Bible school, there was a lion in the way. I'm still alive and the Lord took him. Tread on the lion!

Why can we tread on lions if we will? Philippians 4:13 says that *I can do everything through him who gives me strength.* And then we are told in 1 John 4:4 that *the one who is in you is greater than the one who is in the world.* What does it mean? It means that in every believer there is something greater than the roaring lion outside. And what is it?

The Lion of the Tribe of Judah

Let's awake from our slumber and get in the battle, after all we are told in Ephesians 6:12-13 that our struggle is not against flesh and blood, but against the rulers, against the authorities, against the powers of this dark world and against the spiritual forces of evil in the heavenly realms. Therefore put on the full armor of God, so that when the day of evil comes, you may be able to stand your ground, and after you have done everything, to stand.

Oh Christians, lets fight the forces of evil around us and regain our communities and our country. And never forget that the people in the streets are not our enemy. The lion is the enemy. We need to get out there and love the people and fight the lion.

Roger J. Boehm

D ear Dr. Boehm:

Life has been a cold and empty place for sometime now. Eighteen months to be exact. All the beauty and color of life has faded no matter which direction I've turned. **I am trapped in this thick, heavy darkness.**

I've felt lost and all alone even abandoned by God and others. Either my loved ones aren't able to reach me or they further plunge me into despair, hopelessness, self hatred. **I've felt as if this darkness has had its hands around my neck choking out my very life**, to the point at times it hasn't been worth living and I find myself frequently considering suicide..

My relationship with God has ceased to exist, as I have been convinced that my life is cursed rather than blessed regardless of any of my efforts to live by God's Word. My prayers seem to have fallen flat. My faith washed away by my tears and replaced with pain.

My life has been unmanageable. My family nearly destroyed. My children in desperate need of a strong mother. And the place we all call home is nothing more than what feels like a prison.

Unfortunately our family, which consists of two adults married for just 8 years and two very hurt children, are trying to work together in what seems to be a cocktail of disaster.

All that we have tried has failed. The only relief I've found or ray of hope I've seen is when I remove myself and my children from the home in which we live.

That's the only time I can see reality, or past my own pain. That's the only time I seem to be able to thrive or sense that the Lord's presence really exists. How can it be that I'm only able to function as a person apart from my husband?

I don't understand how we got here, but can't deny if we continue as it is then it will surely be the end of me and all I was intended to be.

I've gotten a lot of input from people I've turned to for spiritual direction and basically I've been told that I must remain in the situation, submit to my husband, and be obedient to God's Word making myself the wife and mother I need to be. I don't want my marriage to end but have been incapable of doing that, and if I continue to take that advice I fear for my own sanity.

I don't know what to do or where to turn, but felt led to write you this letter. I'm not sure if you remember me but we did meet once.

If you wish to contact me please feel free,

(321) ***-**** anytime

Joan

Chapter One

EARLY EXPERIENCES WITH THE DEMONIC

I trusted Jesus Christ as my Savior in October 1978 while attending Pine Ridge First Congregational Methodist Church near Dallas, Georgia. By early 1979 I knew the Lord was clearly calling me into the ministry. Little did I know then what lay ahead.

Meeting one Sunday after church, I shared with our pastor Preacher Powers, as we used to call him, concerning my calling to the ministry. I still recall how he tried to discourage me, and it was not till later that he explained that he felt if he could have talked me out of entering the ministry that day, then I probably wasn't called by God to the ministry and shouldn't be entering it. But if he couldn't, then he felt God had called me into the ministry. He couldn't, and I began my journey.

Within months a door opened in the local county jail for me to do some ministry work. Later I would be a member of the chaplain corps of the Atlanta Fulton County Jail and be assigned a cellblock of African Americans (many of whom were black Muslims), a set of solitary confinement cells, and the "gay" cell. This early ministry opened doors to my understanding of the demonic.

The Hitchhiker

In the smaller county jail I would be locked up with the prisoners to spend as much time with them as I chose. There was a man named Bill, about 40 years of age, who when I would try to strike up a conversation with him, would walk away and ignore me.

One afternoon as I tried once again to establish a relationship, Bill showed a willingness to talk. He shared how he had been convicted of murder and was awaiting transfer to the state penitentiary. As we spoke, he began to share the circumstances leading up to his murder conviction.

Bill was married and lived with his wife and two small children in a neighboring town. They owned a home and had a family car. One night he woke up about three in the morning, took a gun out of his nightstand, got dressed, and went hitchhiking. The family car was parked in the drive. An elderly man pick him up and at gunpoint was forced by Bill to drive him out of town. In a sparsely populated area he shot the driver, drove the car back within two blocks of his home, set the car on fire, and went back to bed.

I questioned why he had committed such an act. His reply was that he wasn't on any alcohol or drugs, but at times there was something that seemed to take control of him, and it was during one of those times this incident occurred.

About a week later I was awakened sometime after midnight by a call from the jailer. He stated Bill was asking that I come up to the jail immediately because he needed to talk to me.

After dressing quickly and driving to the jail I found that Bill had been put in an interrogation room and was awaiting my arrival. Locked in the interrogation room with him, I asked Bill why he had me come there at that time.

Bill was sitting about five feet from me on another chair smoking a cigarette as we faced each other. He slowly raised his head toward me and stated slowly and in a reduced voice "it's back." "What's back?" I asked. He went on to say, "Whatever it is that takes control of me and does these awful things."

Wondering if this weren't something in the spirit realm I instructed him to tell it to go away in the name of the Lord Jesus Christ. He couldn't! At that point I started reading verses of Scripture that I had previously underlined in my Bible relating to how Jesus had power and authority over spirits. As I was quoting the Scriptures I noticed Bill's facial features change to that of pure hate. He took the cigarette out of his mouth, crushed it out in the palm of his hand, looked up at me while positioning his hands as though they were around a throat and said, "If I could I'd kill you right now."

I knew without a doubt that an evil spirit was manifesting, and I no longer was dealing with Bill. As every hair on my body stood at attention I immediately stated, "But you can't because greater is He who is in me," putting every ounce of faith I could muster in God's Holy Word.

Continuing to read Scriptures the evil spirit started speaking in some unknown tongue. I then began commanding the evil spirit in the name of the Lord Jesus Christ and by His authority to come out of Bill, and when it did Bill immediately hit the floor on his knees, trusted Christ as Savior, and was truly a new creation in the Lord.

As we talked and shared Scripture, and I shared with Bill what had happened he was rubbing the palm of his hand. I asked him if something was wrong, and he stated that his palm was sore. He had no knowledge of what had taken place while the evil spirit was manifesting. I also questioned him on whether he knew any other languages or knew what it meant to "speak in tongues," and he said no.

I left the jail later that night and went home, but I couldn't get back to sleep. I was too busy rejoicing in all that God in His graciousness had taught me that evening, and in Bill's conversion experience.

Later that week returning to the jail I was surprised to find that Bill had been made a trustee. He had been convicted of murder and awaited room in the state penitentiary to serve a life sentence, but the change the jailers had seen in Bill led them to make him a trustee for the brief time he had remaining with them. As a trustee he had the run of the jail and spent much of his time witnessing to others about Jesus and passing out tracts.

The House of Evil

My first pastorate was that of a small country church outside Pell City, Alabama. About six months into the ministry there I preached one Sunday morning on the spirit realm and the existence of evil spirits. After the service a young couple who had begun attending the church asked if they could have a word with me.

The young husband shared how they were currently living in his deceased grandfather's house and were having some problems. They had not mentioned what they were about to tell me to anyone before because they felt they might be considered crazy, or sick, or mentally deranged. Both shared how there was "a presence" in the house. They called it a ghost but really thought it was an evil spirit. There were many continuing manifestations of doors closing at night and other strange happenings. The young wife told how recently she had gone to the bathroom in the middle of the night and saw a faint figure standing in the corner of the bathtub. The husband stated that he had seen the same figure in other parts of the house.

I questioned him about his grandfather and was told that the man had been involved in occult activity in the house for many years prior to his death. These activities included Tarot Card reading and levitation, but the grandson did not know the full extent of his grandfather's involvement. Clearly this was an evil spirit that was in the home probably as a result of the activities of the grandfather.

That afternoon Diane and I went over to the home and had prayer with this young family. The four of us then went from room to room claiming each as a place where Christians could dwell in peace and commanding any evil spirits that inhabited the place to leave in the name of the Lord Jesus Christ and by His power. Over the doorpost of each room was placed a small cross in oil.[1]

God in His graciousness honored the efforts that afternoon, and the young family was not plagued by these beings again.

---

[1]Although olive oil carries no magical power, throughout biblical times it has been a fitting symbol of the Spirit. In the Old Testament the anointing oil, which was prepared according to divine instructions, was a symbol of the Spirit of God. It is used here as an outward sign of Who are faith has been place in.

"He's Here to Shoot You Pastor"

A couple years into my second pastorate in the foothills of the Ozarks in southern Missouri a false doctrine started to make its way into the church. The teachings were entering through a Sunday school teacher who was part of the controlling family in the church. In my effort to stop this teaching I went to the individuals involved but they would not agree to stop having been deceived[2] into believing the false doctrine was biblical.

Shortly thereafter on a Sunday morning I preached a message condemning this doctrine and warning the church against it. About a dozen members got up and left the church during the service. The woman who had introduced the doctrine into the church through her Sunday school class got out of her pew and came forward during the message wanting to speak on the doctrine's behalf. At that point I instructed the deacons to show her to her seat, and she left.

In the parking lot after church those who had left gathered around my car to talk to me again and to see if they could win me over to their line of thought. When I opened up my Bible and told them that we needed to see what God's Word had to say about the subject they said they didn't care what God's Word had to say because they had the experience.

In the weeks to come the church stood with me and the family was voted out of the church, but the problem didn't end there. We started receiving threats and would have to leave our home in the middle of the night at times for our own safety. Then I received a letter with a pentagram drawn on it with the words written "your future." There was no return address on the envelope, but there was the zip code. Going through some books at the library I found that the color, etc. of the drawing meant death, and the zip code was from the town in Michigan where a family member lived who had introduced these misguided Christians to the false doctrine.

The next summer we had a friend visit us from out of town. On Friday evening, the last night of Vacation Bible School, we were to take our friend to the bus station after the evening commencement and fellowship. We had

---

[2]Let us not forget the Bible clearly teaches that Satan is the great deceiver.

begun the service, and the church was crowded with children and their parents who were going to witness the commencement exercise and then go to the fellowship hall for cookies and drinks before dismissing.

As I was busy passing out VBS diplomas one of the deacons came up to the bookstand and waited for a pause. As I stopped and leaned over to him he stated that an individual was outside with a gun and wanted to shoot me. This was a direct result of the problem we had experienced months before concerning the false doctrine. There was no phone in the church, so we moved everyone to the fellowship hall, and the deacons and myself went out to talk with the man.

He did leave the churchyard but later was waiting at our home so that we couldn't get the visiting friend's suitcase. I had to have the county sheriff drive with us to the house to get her bags as well as some clothes for our family so we could spend the night, once again, in the safety of a deacon's home.

Satan and his forces tried to destroy that church through the entrance of false doctrine, but he did not succeed. The church membership stood behind us and we pastored for two more years.

There were other battles with the forces of evil as we continued to place ourselves under God's direction to be used as He saw fit. However, the largest battle was yet to be waged.

And that battle began in 1990 when we were assigned by our Home Mission Board to a mission church in the northern plains.

Facing Evil
In the Town

Chapter Two

THE TOWN WITH PROBLEMS

It all began in August of 1990 when Diane and I arrived in the northern plains to begin our assignment as Mission Service Corps missionaries at a small church. The town itself is a community of approximately 13,000 people and appeared on the surface to be a conservative Christian town in the upper Midwest. The type of town one would feel comfortable raising a family in and calling home. Little did I realize then that it was about to become the seat of Satanism in the state, have six active Satanic covens, a cult library housed in a subbasement below a prominent building in town, and have much Satanic activity, including human sacrifice, going on regularly. Later I would also find out, much to my surprise, that there were individuals spanning the whole social ladder, including professionals, involved in Satanism. One area pastor of a traditional Protestant church was also a Satanist unbeknownst to his congregation, or at least most of them.

I wanted this to be a ministry and a pastorate that was pleasing to the Lord, and I felt that I needed to begin by seeking His will.

Shortly after arriving at our assignment I met another Southern Baptist pastor who was then pastoring a mission church in a town about 30 miles south of us. Upon getting acquainted with him I realized that he also was seeking God's will for his life and ministry, so we agreed to begin praying together to seek guidance for our ministries.

We began to meet for all night prayer meetings every two weeks on a Friday evening. Rotating between the two churches, we would begin about 10:00pm and would pray until about 6:00am the next morning. During the night we would go out into the community and pray at various locations where pornography, alcohol, and other sin was being tolerated in the community.

By March of 1991 I felt the Holy Spirit was showing me it was His will that prayer should be offered for Spiritual Awakening in our community, and that this should be a joint effort with other churches since we were not the only church of Jesus Christ in town. He wanted His people uniting in prayer for our community and beyond, not only in our community but in other communities as well. To this end I asked the Lord in prayer to put me in a position to accomplish His will for the community.

In May of 1991, He did just that. I accepted the position of chairman of the local Evangelical Ministerial Association. Since the group does not meet during the summer months, it was not until the fall that I was able to share what God was leading us to do.

In November of that year it was agreed that we would begin bi-weekly prayer meetings for Spiritual Awakening. These meetings would rotate to various Evangelical Churches in the community, and the host pastor would conduct the meeting. Guidelines were set so that the meetings would remain focused on their intent. The meetings were held on the 2nd and 4th Monday evenings of the month. Generally speaking Baptists, Wesleyans, Mennonites, First Missionary, Christian & Missionary Alliance, and Nazarenes attended the meetings. We began with the motto "Unity but not Uniformity." We agreed that we could meet as Christians and leave our peculiar theologies behind as we prayed together.

As I think back on those times, we were able to come together as Christians and unite in unified prayer for a common purpose, that being Spiritual Awakening for our community and beyond. The love for one another that grew out of that experience is one I shall never forget and will cherish the rest of my life.

Looking back we now know that the forces of evil were not at all content with what was happening. On several occasions there were those under the influence of the demonic who cunningly attended the prayer meetings and tried to disrupt. Ultimately the attack would become stronger and more obvious as we stayed united and continued to pray.

In early 1992 all night prayer meetings for Revival and Spiritual Awakening in our community and beyond were begun at our church. These meetings were held once a month on a Friday evening beginning at 10:00pm and lasting until between 5:00am and 6:00am. Members of the Baptist, Mennonite, Christian & Missionary Alliance, and First Missionary Churches usually attended them, although there also was representation, at times, from the Wesleyan and Nazarene Churches.[3]

During 1992 we saw a definite blessing of the Holy Spirit in our community. There were two large, extremely liberal churches in our community that were not interested in what the Evangelicals were doing as it related to prayer. Both churches ended up calling pastors who were evangelical, and they immediately became a part of the prayer for Spiritual Awakening and started leading their churches in that direction.

In May of 1992 the Lord arranged for me to be contacted by the state Sunday School Association, an interdenominational group of which neither our church nor I was a part, and I was asked to conduct two seminars at their annual state convention in September on community prayer for Spiritual Awakening. I gladly accepted because I saw this as the Lord opening a door to encourage other communities to also begin praying for Spiritual Awakening.

During this period the pastors began to meet regularly at the Christian & Missionary Alliance Church for speakerphone conversations with Dr. Henry Blackaby, writer of "Experiencing God" and director of the office of Spiritual Awakening at the Home Mission Board. He had been actively involved in the 1970's in the awakening that broke out in Saskatoon, Canada. Dr. Blackaby gave us a lot of encouragement, direction, and wisdom as we continued on.

---

[3] We must remember that the Awakenings of the past were always preceded by a season of prayer crossing denominational lines. For instance, when awakening broke out in Saskatoon, Canada in the 1970's the meetings started at Ebenezer Baptist, then to the Anglican, then to the Christian and Missionary Alliance, then to the Third Avenue United Church as the crowds grew & thousands of lives were touched.

Oh yes, one other event that occurred in May of 1992 was that bi-weekly prayer meetings were expanded to include a noon prayer meeting the Tuesday after the Monday night meetings in a meeting room in the Central Business District for those who might want to come and pray for Spiritual Awakening during their noon lunch break.

In June of 1992, as our family visited supporting churches in the South, several interesting things happened as the Holy Spirit moved in our lives. First of all I felt that God would have us begin praying for every household in our town weekly. This was a big order considering the fact there were well over 3000 households. But along with the leading came the guidance on how to conduct the prayer campaign house-by-house, and later upon returning to our home the plans were instituted.

I consider the other remarkable event to be what happened once we arrived at the home of Diane's mother in Georgia. Let me state here that there were actually three areas that I felt the Lord leading us into out of the original all night prayer meetings as far as the ministry of the church was concerned. First of all, prayer for Spiritual Awakening, secondly, the development of a youth program, and thirdly, a Christian counseling outreach ministry. I have been explaining how the Holy Spirit was guiding the development of community prayer, but he was also leading in these other two areas. I had begun for instance, under His guidance, to obtain a degree in Christian Counseling. But *I also made a commitment before leaving for the south that while there I would visit any church that would have me. The Lord used that commitment mightily.* One evening while at Diane's mother's home in Dallas, Georgia, I received a call from a small church in South Central Louisiana. The woman on the phone told me that they had received my name and telephone number, and they were asking me to come to their church and speak for 30 minutes to the children concerning missions the last night of their Vacation Bible School. To this day I do not know how they got my mother-in-law's number in Georgia as we have no ties in Louisiana. To fulfill this request I would be gone for three days, drive hundreds of miles, and with no promise of any financial assistance. I asked if the pastor of the church was aware that she was calling me and she said he was and would expect me to stay overnight at the parsonage when I arrived. *Remembering the commitment I had made in prayer, I told her I'd be there. Little did I realize then the far-reaching affect on the ministry this phone call and trip would have and how marvelously God was working.*

Accepting the call, I decided to go alone in order to keep the expenses to a minimum. The appointment to speak to the children was for Thursday evening, and since I would be driving through Birmingham Alabama I decided to leave on Wednesday morning and stop to visit the Women's Missionary Union Building in Birmingham, as I had never been there before.

Arriving at the WMU building I was given a tour and while speaking to the editor of Contempo Magazine I was invited to attend services that evening at a new church that was temporarily meeting in the building. I accepted and found a motel nearby. How I now look back and see the almighty hand of God at work planning for what was to come.

That evening I became acquainted with the Church at Brookhills, an acquaintance that would never have happened had I not stepped through the door the Lord had opened in Louisiana. Little did I know then that this new relationship with a church would have far reaching ramifications.

The next morning I continued on to Louisiana and, although I spoke to the children on Thursday evening, God's primary reason for my being there, as it turned out, was to minister to a hurting pastor who had lost his wife to cancer just four months prior, then had his teenage son hospitalized, then had his own gall bladder removed, and all without hospitalization insurance

On Friday morning, before I left the pastor's home, the church treasurer came over and gave me $70.00 for coming. The pastor needed the money as much as I did and so we split it, and I left never to see or hear from him again. But my heart cried out for him as I drove away.

Arriving back home the first part of July, and still not realizing what the Lord had set up, I began planning the task of seeing that each household was prayed for weekly. To accomplish this a letter was sent to every pastor in our community explaining how I felt the Holy Spirit was leading and called for a meeting of the pastors at our church. At that meeting the pastors of the Wesleyan, Nazarene, two Mennonite Churches, Christian & Missionary Alliance, First Missionary, and Presbyterian churches were present. I explained that I felt God was leading us to pray for every household in town weekly, and in addition I felt that we needed to schedule Evangelistic Tent Meetings on the State Fairgrounds in our town the next summer (the summer of 1993). Out of that meeting was formed a prayer group into which later the State Child Evangelism Fellowship leadership became a part.

In August of 1992 a Baptist church in Missouri came to do some work on our building as a missions project and while they were at the church the ladies of their Women's Missionary Union group helped to complete the mapping of our community. The entire city was divided into six block areas and mapped on 8 1/2 x 11 sheets of paper showing the location of all the homes and apartments in each area.

We then wrote "Letters to the Editors" of all our denominational state newspapers, some 35 in all, explaining what we were doing and asking for churches with prayer groups that would be willing to take a section of our town and faithfully pray for each household weekly, to please get in contact with us. Many of the newspapers did print the article, and out of this request we had churches with prayer groups in California, Wyoming, Louisiana, Mississippi, Alabama, Georgia, Florida, the Carolinas, Tennessee, Virginia, and Indiana who responded. These churches each received a section, and the campaign began. Other pastors in the community notified their denominational newspapers also and had churches with prayer groups praying.

However, the forces of evil were at work to try to bring discouragement to what was happening. Our state denominational leadership informed us that they would not print the letter because they considered it controversial. I questioned how asking for prayer could be controversial and did not receive an answer. Additionally I was told that the leadership in the state did not like the idea that I was working with other churches in our community. Why not? Were we not all working toward the same end? Also I noticed much passiveness within our church as to what was going on. The membership could not be encouraged to enter into involvement in the bi-weekly prayer meetings, the all night prayer meetings, or prayer for individual homes in the community. Why not? What was the hindrance? Little did I know at the time that one of the hindrances was a point of contact with the demonic which was displayed proudly in the church building. An explanation will come later in this book.

It was decided that we would divide the city up among the participating churches and begin praying for our respective areas.

The large tent owned by the Baptist state organization was reserved for July 15 to August 3, 1993. The tent was capable of seating about 300 people. Additionally, a portion of the State Fairgrounds was reserved for the meetings.

In September I conducted the two seminars on community prayer for Spiritual Awakening during the state Sunday School Association's annual State Convention. Shortly thereafter a deacon from a First Missionary church in a neighboring town called and asked if I would speak to their church on a

Wednesday evening concerning community prayer and then to a prayer breakfast the following morning to churches in their town on the same subject. I accepted, and since the town was about 100 miles from us, arrangements were made for me to stay overnight at a bed and breakfast.

In November of 1992 the Mennonite Churches north of town joined in with the prayer group and mapped the area from the city limit north to the County line. I was then asked to preach at the Mennonite Church on a Sunday evening out on the prairie to kick off their campaign as they began praying for Spiritual Awakening.

Remember the Church at Brookhills in the National WMU Building in Birmingham? Well, when we started the prayer campaign they contacted us and were willing to take one of the sections of our town and pray weekly for those households. During November I was contacted by their Minister of Discipleship and was asked if we had any work needing to be done at our church that they could do as a missions project during the summer of 1993. In trying to fulfill the leading of the Lord to start a youth ministry I said that it would be helpful if they would come and construct a youth facility in the church basement and a 30' x 60' concrete basketball court outside as we begin to prepare for a youth ministry. They agreed to do the project almost immediately. (But this was just the beginning.)

As 1993 began, letters were prepared and passed out to every residence in our town explaining the prayer campaign and asking for any particular prayer requests that a family might want to share. The requests were then shared with the local church whose area the family was located in as well as the prayer group out of state praying for that particular section and home in our town. In this manner the prayer became more specific, and the community realized, as did the Satanists, that there were churches of different denominations united together in prayer.

We pastors involved began meeting to plan the Evangelistic Tent Meetings and to search for an evangelist. We searched our denominations, contacted the Billy Graham Evangelistic Association, and the more we hunted the more we kept running into seeming brick walls. For a time it seemed there was no evangelist to be attained. And then, remember the Church at Brookhills? Their Minister of Discipleship called and said that their pastor had offered his services as an evangelist for the tent meetings if we so desired. And **God** gave us an evangelist. One who was given a heart and a burden through prayer for our community. It was immediately recognized by all the area pastors that God was at work, and we accepted his offer to be the evangelist.

As we continued to prepare for the meetings the responsibilities were delegated. The Nazarene pastor was in charge of the altar workers, the First Missionary pastor was in charge of the finances and paying the bills, I was in charge of the prayer for the meetings as well as seeing that there was proper follow-up on any decisions that were made during the altar calls, the Open Bible pastor was in charge of taking up the nightly love offerings and the Christian & Missionary Alliance pastor was in charge of the music.

Meeting in early July, a couple weeks before the meetings were to begin, we pastors discussed the need for advertising and the rental of a good sound system. The only funds available were about $450.00 (remember that amount) in love offerings that we had taken up in our various churches several months before. We had earlier decided to finance these meetings by having each church take up a love offering, and we would trust God for the rest. Trusting God for the "rest" was a major mistake on our part that will be explained later in this chapter. Now we started to be concerned that the love offerings already taken would not be enough for music equipment rental, insurance, advertising, and, although the evangelist had said nothing about money, we felt we should give him at least a $500.00 honorarium. What were we to do? We came to a crisis of belief and had to decide if we were doing this in the flesh or if God was truly leading and guiding in this endeavor. It was unanimously decided that God was in charge, and so He was. We therefore went ahead and did what we needed to do and trusted God for the needed funds.

The time was quickly approaching, and a member of the C.M.A. church went to pull the trailer containing the Baptist tent to our community, a trip of about 280 miles, a few days before we were to erect it on a Saturday.

When Saturday morning came there were men from seven different denominations on the fairgrounds to erect the tent. When we pulled the pieces out of its trailer it was quickly realized that there were no instructions, but we figured out quickly how to lace the main pieces of the tent together and had it up and ready in a little over three hours.

On Sunday morning at 6:00am the chartered bus with 45 people from the Church at Brookhills arrived at our church to begin a week of construction of a youth facility and ministry in our town that will not be soon forgotten by the entire community. I felt it would be good to have a joint Lord's Supper service at the evening service on Sunday for our congregation and the folks from

Birmingham. However, when I shared my plans with the other pastors they wanted to be a part, and the Lord's Supper service quickly outgrew our small mission church. So, that Sunday evening we had a joint Lord's Supper service at the Christian & Missionary Alliance Church that was attended by all the churches involved in the prayer campaign. What a blessed time we all had as we shared together as Christians and as His children. This also included a "commissioning service" for the members of the Brookhills group, a group of Baptists, conducted by the Nazarene and Christian & Missionary Alliance pastors.

All was going well, but the forces of evil were going to try to stop the meetings. Pastor Rick Ousley, the evangelist, was to fly into Sioux Falls on Monday morning. Diane and Rick's wife, who had come the previous day on the chartered bus, left early Monday morning to pick him up at the airport. Interestingly enough we were to later find out that when he arrived at the airport in Birmingham to fly to Minneapolis he found the flight had been canceled. Making arrangements on a later flight he arrived in Minneapolis only to find the flight to Sioux Falls had been canceled. He finally boarded another flight to Sioux Falls, and when the landing gear was extended for the landing at Sioux Falls it was thought there were landing gear problems, and the plane was directed back to Minneapolis. Arriving back in Minneapolis he finally flew on to Sioux Falls again and arrived just in time to be driven to our town arriving at the tent just five minutes before the service was to begin at 7:00pm.

What a week it was! The first night the services were good, but they only got better. The attendance on Monday was 193. On Tuesday the attendance rose to 268 in a tent that was equipped for a little over 300. The meetings were growing and lives were being touched. Satan's forces had to do something to try to stop the meetings, so on Wednesday morning there was a storm which blew the tent down and with the soggy ground and the wind continuing to blow we were unable to put it back up. If my thoughts here are correct, that the forces of evil took down the tent, then it must be pointed out that God who is Sovereign over all allowed the tent to be taken down in order to move us into larger facilities. Although I didn't realize it then, I do know now that the forces of evil have some control over the forces of nature. This showed up many times in the years following these meetings and will be pointed out later in this book. Quickly people arrived from the various churches, and we packed up the tent in the trailer, returned the chairs to the various churches, and said, "What do we do now." It appeared that Satan had won a battle. The pastors gathered, and after prayer we all agreed to move to the Christian & Missionary Alliance Church since that church would hold 330 and was air-conditioned. As Satan was moving so was the Holy Spirit and that evening there were 350 adults with an additional 70 in the children's meetings. There was excitement among the

Christian community. That evening there was an "after meeting" to praise and worship God which ended about 10:00pm. On Thursday we moved to a large building on the State Fairgrounds that holds 600 in theater style seating and God gave 450 adults plus the children's meeting. On Friday the attendance rose to close to 500 with an after meeting for prayer following the service.

We had been concerned about advertising especially since the local newspaper, which was extremely liberal, would not even print a revival notice without cash in advance. But God took charge and gave us 1/3 of the front page for advertising. He is so gracious!

To share just a few of the many things that were happening and show the love that was abounding I received a call from a woman, a member of the C.M.A. Church, who ran a Laundromat. She told me that if any of the folks from Birmingham had laundry they should just drop it off, and it would be done free of charge. On another occasion a local doctor, a Nazarene, took care of two of the Birmingham folks and refused to charge a cent.

What were the concrete results? There were salvation decisions from 10 cities in our state as well as the states of Alabama, Arizona, and Nebraska. However, much more took place and continued to take place than showed up in concrete numbers.

Did we have Revival? No! But God had given us a taste and encouragement to continue praying and seeking a Spiritual Awakening. Dr. Blackaby helped us to realize after the meetings that had God blessed us with hundreds of rededications and salvation decisions our churches would not have been ready so we needed to begin to prepare our congregations with a sharp sense of what the Holy Spirit would have us do and where He was working.

After the meetings we had calls from California, Texas, and Ohio wanting more information.

Remember the $450.00 in love offerings and our concern for the finances of the meetings? The evangelist would not take a dime, not even for expenses, because he felt that he was in the middle of God's will in preaching those meetings. We took up a love offering each night. When all the bills were paid, guess what, we had $450.00 still remaining for future evangelistic work in our community. When I said we made a mistake by trusting God for the "rest" what I meant is that we should have trusted Him for all of it. Isn't God great! Isn't He marvelous! Oh that we would pray as we've never prayed before. Remember what He says in 2 Chronicles 7:14, *If my people, who are called by my name, will humble themselves and pray and seek my face and turn from their wicked ways, then will I hear from heaven and will forgive their sin and will heal their land.*

We had had a taste of the battle as we watched the forces of evil mount a pitiful and unsuccessful attempt to try to stop the meetings, but soon, we would look them straight in the face, literally.

Facing Evil
In the Church

Chapter Three
THE INFILTRATED CHURCH

When we first arrived in this small northern plains town in 1990 we were greeted by a church family of approximately 25 members which appeared to be in solidarity and wanting to see the ministry of the church growing and doing the Lord's will in ministry.

The church building was built with Home Mission Board monies in approximately 1969 with the congregation assuming a mortgage on the property with the Board. By the time we had arrived in 1990 they had lost the church building once because of their inability to pay the mortgage, had then rented the building from the Board, and finally had bought back the building with a $321.00 monthly mortgage payment to the Board.

A very adequate facility, the church building housed on the main floor a nursery, office, Sunday school room, bathrooms and the sanctuary which also had a baptistry. In the basement were the kitchen, fellowship hall, library, and at the time four additional Sunday school rooms. Two of these rooms later would be combined into one large youth room. The grounds allowed plenty of room for parking as the church grew, as well as a large garden plot in which the church grew vegetables in the summer to be consumed by anyone who wanted them.

A parsonage was located about 3/4 mile from the church which, although it had no garage, was adequate consisting of a three bedroom house with a basement.

Although small, this church and congregation appeared on the surface to be just what a pastor needed to see growth and the salvation of souls. As we were to later learn, the forces of evil had a stronghold in this church, and our efforts and God's blessings would be challenged as we moved forward in the direction our heavenly Father would show us through prayer.

Finances for both the church and our family were a problem from the outset. However, God always provided.

Shortly after arriving in August of 1990 the church entered a crisis because it was unable to pay the mortgage payment on the parsonage. After prayer I felt that God would have us pay the parsonage mortgage off by the next Easter. I shared this with the church and told them that we would have no official fund-raiser. We would simply trust God and any Sunday that monies were put in the offering specifically for the mortgage payoff, we would praise God in the next Sunday service for it, no matter whether it was $500.00 or .50 cents. Immediately there were people problems. Some openly accused me of trying to squeeze money out of the membership and others openly stated that it couldn't be done. However, any monies that would come in we would praise God for the next Sunday. In November of 1990 we owed $2,100.00, and as we approached Easter 1991 the amount had dropped to $1799.23.

Two weeks before Easter the telephone rang as I was praying about the balance needed. It was the State office calling. The director stated he had heard that we were trying to pay off the parsonage and asked if that was so? I assured him we were. He went on to say that someone, he didn't know who, from either Texas or Oklahoma had sent the Home Mission Board some undesignated monies and told them to pray about it and use it as God directed. They prayed and felt that God was leading them to send the monies to the upper Midwest. When the state office received the monies, prayer was offered, resulting in the monies being sent to our church. When I asked how much it was, guess what, $1800.00. Within a dollar of what we still needed, so the mortgage was burned the week before Easter, right on God's schedule. God is so gracious. Some might say this was a coincidence. I say it most surely was God's hand at work.

So God was faithful, but it was clear whenever God would bless in some special way that evil was always **very** present.

About a year later we arrived at another financial crisis, the mortgage on the church. Our note called for a monthly payment of $321.00, but for some time the church had been only able to pay $100.00 a month which went toward the interest payment. We had received several letters of concern from the Church Loans department of the Home Mission Board, and I realized it was just a matter of time before all this would come to a head. I also knew the possibility existed that we would lose our building again.

One Monday, while I was on my face in prayer at the church concerning the financial situation, the phone rang. It was the Church Loans Department of the Home Mission Board. The voice on the other end of the receiver asked if we would be willing to extend our loan one more year with the Board lowering our interest rate and if so, the monthly payment would be just $97.00 a month. I stated that I knew the church's answer would be yes. He then told me that the Board was meeting on Friday, and I needed to have a request in by then on church letterhead asking for the changes he had discussed with me. I got details from him, sat down immediately and composed a letter, and sent it out express mail so it would be sure to get there by Friday. The change to the loan was approved and once again God was gracious and helped in our time of need. I knew we were in His will with all that He was doing to aid the ministry.

Even though God was clearly blessing us in many ways, something was happening in the church. When we would come in the church on winter days there would be windows in the basement that would be open causing the church to be extremely cold. We would close the windows, and the next day they would be open again. Finally the basement windows were nailed shut to take care of the problem. Then, much to our surprise the upstairs windows would start being open. I would come into the church in the morning to work in the office and shut the windows only to find later that windows would once again be open even though no one else was in the building. What was happening? No one knew for sure.

In 1994 it was determined that a new roof was needed for the church. Again I led the church to start praying for a new roof and just trust God for the monies. I explained that since this was His ministry, He would provide both the money for the shingles and the laborers. During our yearly trip south we shared the need for a roof with various churches and asked them to pray to

God to see if He would have them involved in this need. A church in Florida later contacted us and said they would be willing to come on a missions trip with some men during the summer of 1995 and put the roof on.

Once again the church membership agreed that a new roof was needed, the old one was already leaking. There was a lot of apprehension as to whether the money could be raised, but God came through again. We ordered the material still needing $500.00 and the Sunday after the roof was installed a deacon from a church in the south stopped by on his way home from a missions trip to a neighboring state and presented our church with a check for, guess how much, yes, $500.00. God was so gracious once again.

But all of this was not without some surprising problems. On the first day of reroofing, Monday, the crew removed old shingles from the building. For most of the afternoon it was apparent that a dark cloud was sitting in the sky just west of the church. Comments were made during the afternoon by the roofing crew from Florida of how strange and ominous the cloud looked. Around mid afternoon it was decided to buy some large rolls of plastic, just in case of rain, to protect the building.

Roofing work continued until dark at which time the plastic was spread on the roof and securely fastened down. About eleven o'clock that evening the cloud moved over the vicinity of the church as a thunderstorm which blew so hard the plastic was blown off the roof and into some high voltage power lines at which time the rain started to pour down. The roofing crew was in the church taking showers and preparing to go to bed when the rain and wind began. Water started coming into the sanctuary, dripping down into ceiling tiles and then onto the carpet. The crew's initial reaction was to quickly do what they could about the water that was pouring in. However, they realized that the problem was much greater than the physical water, so they gathered at the alter to pray. The rain stopped but not before the sanctuary sustained quite a bit of water damage everywhere except strangely the northeast corner of the room where an associational Women's Missionary Union anniversary quilt hung on the wall.

Later one of the men present wrote the following concerning that evening: "We realized what was happening with the roof leaking and water pouring in throughout the church except for the northeast corner. When we began praying at the altar, spiritual darkness was everywhere and water was everywhere. As we prayed, confessing, worshipping, and singing, the evil fled not to return the rest of the week with "minor" exceptions. We prayed for an hour or so. When we finished, what was wet in the sanctuary was now dry. The damage was nowhere near as severe as we anticipated. Satan, I am convinced, did not want us there. After that evening, we all sensed God's protection. Many times we'd slip on the steep roof and all I can say is that God stopped the fall. Greater is He!"

The church needed much work if we were going to attract people. There was the need for a new roof, a handicap ramp, and new steps and landings as the old ones were rotted. The steeple was rotted and needed to be either replaced or have major repairs. There was also work that would need to be done on the interior of the building, and it needed to be air-conditioned. God's original direction included youth facilities also. Where would this come from?

We continued to make yearly trips in June to the Southeast for two reasons: first, to reinforce our support so we could stay on the field that God directed us to and secondly, to seek out churches that would be willing to help better the facility in the future. These trips involved a month away, 8000 miles on a car, and several thousand dollars in expenses. God was gracious.

During these trips arrangements were made to also have the steeple repaired, install a wheelchair ramp, replace outside steps and landings, install central air conditioning, and prepare youth facilities in the basement and a concrete basketball court outside to prepare for youth activities. These projects were all completed thanks to the efforts of various churches in Missouri, Georgia, and Alabama.

Personal needs continued to be a problem, although not one God couldn't handle. To show how gracious God is, one fall Diane hit a deer and did major damage to one of our vehicles. We needed a replacement. God touched a godly man in a church in Georgia, and he informed me that the church would have a car for us the next June. We were eventually presented with a brand new 1994 Ford Taurus and the story behind it was very interesting.

This church leader later told me when he started to share his vision with the church concerning a car for us there were several old cars that were donated for the project. These cars were fixed up and sold. Later the church held a silent auction and a barbecue and raised the remaining funds needed to buy the new car. Our heavenly Father knows our needs and once again proved so very gracious.

As was discussed in a previous chapter, God was leading us to include Christian counseling as part of the church ministry. To that end I began taking counseling courses in order to obtain a seminary degree in counseling and be licensed in the Christian counseling arena. I felt that once I had a degree and was licensed that God would begin using the counseling ministry to help others. But our timing is not God's timing, and He didn't wait. The counseling began to my great surprise in remarkable ways.

Chapter Four
THE QUILT

As previously stated, I had wondered for a long time if there might be evil spirits dwelling within the walls of our church. On most Sunday mornings I would try to be at church around 8:00 in order to have time to not only review my message and pray but also to work on cleansing the church from the forces of evil that I knew were present but didn't know exactly why.

When I would spiritually cleanse the church prior to morning services it would be apparent that the congregation was more attentive and active in the service, but when I did not, a gloom seemed to hang over the congregation. During those times I would wonder if many of those attending were actually hearing what I was preaching.

Let me stop and interject a thought here. While counseling with individuals who were heavily demonized there have been times when I have wondered if they were hearing what I was saying.

I recall one evening I was sharing some Scripture with a woman during counseling who kept looking blankly at me and finally said, "You'll have to talk to my husband about that because I don't fish." I had been talking to her about Jesus, and she had been hearing about fishing. I then took a piece of paper and printed in large print "Jesus Christ." Holding the paper up in front of her I asked her to read what the two words said. She replied, "blue jeans." When an individual is demonized to any degree the evil spirits can block what is coming in through the ear and eye gates to the mind and insert whatever they want.

Every person who has ever witnessed to someone about Christ has at times wondered if they heard what was said. In reality they may not have. When this happens in the counseling session we have to stop and bind the evil spirits from further activity through the power of Jesus Christ.

Often, while working with a victim of satanic ritual abuse, sessions would be held in the church sanctuary with a team of strong Christians acting as a prayer group. The team consisted of local pastors and some spiritually strong lay Christians both male and female.

At the beginning of these sessions an alter personality[4] of the client would always tell us where the evil spirits were so that they could be dealt with before proceeding. Of the churches in which these sessions were held, ours by far had the most demonic activity. At the beginning of every session we would spend time dealing with the evil. One location where the spirits always appeared to be in numbers was in the northeast corner of the sanctuary near a Women's Missionary Union patchwork quilt that had been made by ladies in our association of churches a number of years ago commemorating the hundredth anniversary of the WMU. That quilt had hung for a number of years in our sanctuary. You might also recall from Chapter Three that during the cloudburst that occurred while reroofing the building, this was the only corner of the sanctuary that was undamaged.

One evening as we began one of these team sessions, we once again were told by an alter of heavy spirit activity in that corner of the sanctuary. I suggested to another pastor who was part of the team that evening that we take

---

[4] A victim of Satanic Ritual Abuse suffers from a disorder known as Dissociative Identity Disorder. In the Diagnostic and Statistical Manual of Mental Disorders fourth edition text revision of the American Psychiatric Association the diagnostic criteria is described on page 529 *as the presence of two or more distinct identities or personality states (each with its own relatively enduring pattern of perceiving, relating to, and thinking about the environment and self). At least two of these identities or personality states recurrently take control of the person's behavior....* These "personality states" are known as "alter" or "alternate" personalities. Often the alter personalities are able to see the spirit realm around them when they are in control of the person's behavior.

down the quilt and move it to a Sunday school room. He and I got up on a pew, which was just below the quilt, took it down and put it in the Sunday school room at the other end of the hallway. At the time I had every intention of putting it back after the session but was just curious as to whether it might for some reason be part of the problem.

Later that evening as we continued the session, the client stated that she felt like walking to the back of the sanctuary for some reason but didn't know why. She wanted to know if it was OK with me if she go. Not knowing what was about to happen I told her to go ahead and the team followed her.

As she neared the back door between the sanctuary and the hall an evil spirit manifested itself, taking control of the client's body, and began running to the Sunday school room knocking a table over and pulling hangers off the coat rack as it ran. In the Sunday school room it quickly grabbed the quilt that we had laid on one of the tables and clung tightly to it.

As I entered the room I sensed that our client's body was going to be thrown backward by the evil spirit onto one of the tables and fearing she would be hurt I immediately grabbed the back of her neck to stop the thrust of her body backward onto the table. As the others entered the room right behind me they too saw the problem and braced her back to protect her.

The evil spirit was very upset as I held the back of the client's neck with one hand and tried to free the quilt with the other. The spirit would not let go but immediately stated very emphatically, "You had no right to take down this quilt." I commanded it in the name of the Lord Jesus Christ to tell us why it thought we had no right and it strongly replied, "Because it belongs to Satan."

We struggled for about five minutes with the evil spirit as we pleaded the blood and protection of the Lord Jesus in our lives. Finally we stopped, had prayer again and sang "There is Power in the Blood," while still bracing the client in order to protect her from physical harm. Then, once again we issued several commands to the evil spirit in the name of Jesus to cease its work and to leave her and it finally did.

During our dealings with this evil spirit it was revealed that apparently one of the women who originally made the quilt was not a Christian but rather an infiltrator. In other words she was a Satanist who had become part of one of the associational churches, had even involved herself in the Women's

Missionary Union group of that church, but had dedicated one of the patches to Satan. From that point on the quilt became a very strong point of contact for evil spirits, and when it was hung many years ago in the sanctuary the evil spirits came with it.

With the client back in control of her body she felt very weak. We took a short break in the session during which time we removed the quilt from the church and temporarily put it in the trunk of my car. As we continued the session in the sanctuary there was no longer any spirit activity in that corner of the room.

The next evening during Wednesday evening Bible Study I shared what had happened to those present, a small group making up the core of the church. As they thought back on when the quilt was hung in the church they determined that it was about the same time the church started having some problems. All present agreed the quilt should not be put back in the church but instead should be burned, as is the case with any point of contact.

The following night I took the quilt out of town to a farmer's home. As he answered the door I told him I had a quilt that needed to be burned and was instructed to put it on his burn pile for burning the next day. I told him that this quilt needed to be burned right away and didn't need to be lying around his property. I sensed he had some idea what was going on because without saying another word he put on his coat and burned the quilt.

Spiritual warfare in and for the church had been going on for several years but this event was the "last straw" for the devil. About a week later I found a dead frog hanging from a string attached to the dome light of my car one afternoon as I left the counseling office. I knew immediately that a drive was on by the forces of evil in the town to see us gone. However, Diane and I were called by the Lord to minister in that town and our intentions were not to leave until we would be in God's will in doing so. Ultimately I was to leave the pastorate and begin full time counseling ministry in the town.

Chapter Five
THE CHURCH SATANISTS ATTENDED

S peaking of evil in a church. For a period of time I found myself working with two women who had been ritually abused in childhood. Neither was familiar with the other, but both had similar experiences and events while children in generational Satanist families.

Both women were in their forties with fathers who were Satanists and mothers who had been raised Baptist. In both instances the mothers were not aware the fathers were involved in Satanism when they married and later chose to ignore the problem rather than face it.

Both families were members of a large Baptist church while the girls were in elementary and high school. In fact, one of the fathers was elected and served as a deacon. Both fathers were also active in a men's Sunday School class.

Interestingly enough neither man was saved but in fact both worshipped the devil. They were satanic plants in a church that never realized the enormity of the problem, both spiritual and physical, these men presented.

Both women, as children, were ritually abused by their fathers and the satanic covens of which they were members. Regularly, and especially on satanic holidays, the men would take their girls to a home near the beach and ritually abuse them sexually and in other manners that are best not discussed in this book.

Both women reported separately that as children they would be taken to Saturday evening Sunday School Class parties attended by the men in the particular class at church and be sexually molested over and over by the "class."

The women each reported separately there were times when one of the fathers would remove his daughter from the Sunday School class and take her to an unused office on the second floor. As the father would stand at the door another man would sexually molest the daughter in the office. Keep in mind this was on Sunday morning during Sunday School. One of the women reported she finally told her Sunday School teacher only to be told she was lying and should be ashamed of herself. One such incident reportedly took place on Easter Sunday.

The pastor of the church at that time was a man who later would become a prominent denominational leader. He never realized what was happening in the church, quite possibly partially because the church was so large it wasn't difficult for the Satanists to hide their activities. And then possibly because in our Christian culture in the United States we care not to recognize the enormity of the spiritual warfare in which we are engaged.

Facing Evil
In Counseling

Chapter Six

DISSOLVING A MARRIAGE TO AN EVIL SPIRIT

One day I received a call from a pastor friend in the upper Midwest. He explained that he had been working with an ex-Satanist for quite some time and that the woman had been married to an evil spirit a number of years before during the annual September 7th Marriage to the Beast rituals. This evil spirit was refusing to give up what he had considered so long to be his. The plan was to schedule a time with this woman to deal with the apparently higher principality or power to which she was married.

For many Christians this may seem unbelievable, but let me introduce you to Illinois State Law #87-1167[5] effective January 1, 1993 which states in part

---

[5] The State of Illinois, Public Act #87-1167, Effective January 1, 1993. Be it Enacted by the Legislature of the State of Illinois RITUALIZED ABUSE OF A CHILD-EXCLUSIONS-PENALTIES-DEFINITION.

(a) A person is guilty of a felony when he commits any of the following acts with, upon, or in the presence of a child as part of a ceremony, rite, or similar observance.

(1) **Actually** or in simulation, tortures, mutilates, or **sacrifices** any warm-blooded animal or **human being:**

(2) Forces injection, ingestion, or other application of any narcotic drug, hallucinogen or anesthetic for the purpose of dulling sensitivity, cognition, recollection of, or resistance to any criminal activity:

(3) Forces ingestion or external application of human or animal urine, feces, flesh, blood, bones, body

that it is a felony to *"**involve a child** in a mock, unauthorized or **unlawful marriage ceremony** with another person **or representation of any force or deity,** followed by sexual contact with the child."*

Additionally the Satanic Ritual Calendar clearly sets September 7th of each year as the "Marriage to the Beast" during which satanic marriages occur. The type of ceremony is sexual, usually with a sacrifice or dismemberment of a female human being any age from infant to 21 years.[6]

The woman in question was raised in a generational Satanist family in a very large city in the upper Midwest. As a child she was married to this evil spirit. Her job within the coven as she grew to adulthood was to join evangelical churches and ultimately seduce the pastor and destroy the ministry of the church. She had been successful in several churches until she became involved in a church where the pastor was preaching hard the atonement of Jesus for our sins and His great love for each of us. She came under conviction and was saved. She then found herself in a battle none of us ever want to be involved in.

Because of her new found faith in Jesus Christ this woman had to give up her family (who were Satanists), her friends (who were Satanists), quit her job and move out of her community legally changing her name. She had to literally

---

secretions, non-prescribed drugs or chemical compounds;

(4) **Involves a child** in a mock, unauthorized or **unlawful marriage ceremony** with another person or **representation of any force or deity, followed by sexual contact with the child:**   *(Continued on bottom of next page)*

(5) Places a living child into a coffin or open grave containing a human corpse or remains:

(6) Threatens death or serious harm to a child, his or per parents, family, pets, or friends which instills a well-founded fear in the child that the threat will be carried out, or:

(7) Unlawfully dissects, mutilates or incinerates a human corpse.

(Bold print added by author)

[6] Satanic covens have young female "breeders" who, several months prior to a required human sacrifice, are impregnated. The night of the ritual the infant is aborted and immediately offered as a human sacrifice. In this manner there are no records of a birth. Isn't it interesting that we accept the unborn as just so much fetal tissue which can be aborted at will, when in reality even Satan recognizes the fetus as a human being and acceptable as a human sacrifice. We are doing Satan's "dirty work" in legalizing abortion in our country.

give up all because of her new found Christianity. Moving to another town she broke off all contact with the past.

She sought Christian counseling because there were the issues concerning her Dissociative Identity Disorder and demonization[7], both caused by her involvement, abuse, and trauma in Satanism, which needed to be dealt with.

---

[7] **Contrary to popular belief a born-again believer can be demonized.** The word "demonized" comes from the Greek word "daimonizomai" which means, "Have a demon." It is improper to say a person is demon possessed; the proper terminology is "demonized." The result of demonization is control not ownership. Satan and evil spirits cannot own a Christian. The reason for this is because Christ has purchased us for God *(Revelation 5:9)* The areas of control by the evil spirit are not in the person's spirit, but in the person's soul (mind, emotions, will, affections) occasionally resulting in physical manifestations. Scripture references that teach about the trichotomy of the human nature plus the warfare against the soul are: *1 Thessalonians 5:23; Hebrews 4:12; 1 Peter 2:11; Psalm 71:13; John 3:3-6; Romans 7:22-23; 8:10-16; 1 Corinthians 5:5; 6:17-20; and Galatians 5:16-25.* What evidence is there that a born-again believer can be demonized? (It is assumed that all Christians accept the fact that an unbeliever can be demonized.) The Scriptures do not conclusively prove a born-again believer can or cannot be demonized. However, the Scriptures do conclusively prove that people can be demonized. In the Old Testament *1 Samuel 15:1-35; 16:14; 18:10;* the demon was sent by God to torment Saul because of his disobedience to God (see also Matthew 18:34-35) The demon caused great changes in Saul's nature and controlled his physical behavior. In the Gospels there were two violent men in the country of the Gadarenes in *Matthew 8:23-32*; the man who could not speak in *Matthew 9:32-33*; the man in the synagogue at Capernaum in *Mark 1:23-27*; and the woman who had been healed of evil spirits and followed Jesus in *Luke 8:1-3.* There are also many other examples found in the four Gospels.

In *Acts 5:1-4* the word for "filled" in verse 3 is the same word Paul uses in *Ephesians 5:18* for a believer to "be filled" or controlled "with the Spirit." Satan or an evil spirit had taken control of Ananias' heart and produced the greed and lie. In the Epistles we find in *1 Corinthians 5:1,5* that this believer in the Corinthian church was living in an open, unrepentant incestuous relationship. Paul's only option was to turn the man over to Satan for discipline. He would be killed but at least his spirit would be saved. In *Ephesians 4:26-27* Paul warns the Ephesian believers not to give the devil a "place" (KJV) or "foothold" (NIV). The common sense of the word in Greek is "place" or "location," but it can also have the transferred sense of "opportunity." Unchecked anger gives the devil an opportunity to control a place in the believer's life. In *1 Peter 5:8* the word "devour" in Greek means, "drink down, swallow, digest." The Septuagint uses this word to translate the word "swallow" where the great fish "swallowed" Jonah. Satan would like nothing better than to "devour" believers and destroy them. He does not have the power to do that, but he does have the power to control believer's lives to the point where their relationship with God is seriously hindered, they are in bondage to sin, and their lives are ineffective in service to Christ.

This woman was saved and the Holy Spirit was living within her spirit. She had renounced and dealt with the other evil spirits. However, this spirit claimed her as its bride and refused to give her up[8].

The woman was instructed to pray and fast, and a time was set to meet at the church my friend was pastoring. As the time arrived those present at the meeting were the woman we shall call Jill, two other pastors and myself. Jill wanted desperately to get rid of this and any other remaining spirits and to give her soul fully over to the Lord Jesus Christ. She had prepared and was now ready.

With Jill sitting on a chair we stood around her and began to pray as her forehead was anointed with oil[9]. At that point the evil spirit manifested through Jill's facial features and vocal cords and insisted that he would not give her up. Fearing that she might be hurt if her body was thrown to the floor we slowly lowered her out of the chair and unto the floor positioning her in a cross position. When she was laid with her arms outstretched the spirit began to rebel hating the position. He tried to thrash her body around on the floor but our gracious loving heavenly Father intervened and we were able to contain her. The spirit kept insisting she was his bride but after about 45 minutes during which time commanding in the name of the Lord Jesus Christ and by His shed blood, was mixed with prayer, the spirit came out of her, and she was delivered[10]. There were still some weaker demons that were commanded in the name and by the authority of the Lord Jesus Christ to come out of her and as they did there was a very foul stench to her breath. Once they were removed Jill was sick to her stomach and vomited several times into a wastebasket.

---

[8] **How can an evil spirit live in the same body with the Holy Spirit?** Two biblical answers: 1. In the same way that the Holy Spirit can live in the same body with our sin and sinful nature (*Romans 7:15-25*) so the Holy Spirit can live in the same body with a demon squatter. 2. Our bodies are temples of the Holy Spirit. (*1 Corinthians 3:16-17; 6:19-20; 2 Corinthians 6:16-18*) The Old Testament temple was a "type" of the New Testament temple that is our body. (*John 2:19-20*). In the Old Testament the temple could be defiled yet the presence of God was still there. (*2 Kings 23:4-8*)

[9] See *James 5:14-16*

[10] **For the born-again believer who is demonized victory is guaranteed.** The Lord Jesus Christ through his death and resurrection has defeated Satan and all his evil hosts. (*Genesis 3:15; 1 Corinthians 15:24-27; Colossians 1:15-23; 2:13-15; Hebrews 2:14-18; 1 Peter 3:22; 1 John 3:8; Revelation 19:11-16; 20:1-15.*) The believer is in complete authority over Satan and his hosts because we share in Christ's authority over them. (*Psalm 108:12-13; Matthew 12:28-29; 18:18; 28:18-20; Luke 10:17-19; 2 Corinthians 10:4; Ephesians 1:17-2:6; Colossians 1:12-14; James 4:7; 1 John 4:4.*)

However, she was delivered by God that day, the marriage was dissolved, and she now lives in freedom.

Chapter Seven

"HELP ME, SHE'S GOT DEMONS"

As the counseling ministry began to grow I received a call from Bill, a licensed professional counselor who had a private practice in the eastern part of the state. He is a Christian. Bill asked if I might consider sitting in on a session at his office with a client whom he felt might be demonized and was suicidal. I agreed to do so. An appointment was scheduled, and with the prior permission of the client the three of us met at Bill's office. Marie was a 42-year-old female raised in a mixed Lutheran/Methodist family. She had been married several times and had one son out of wedlock. She indicated that she was trusting Christ as her Savior.

Bill began the session asking Marie how her week had gone since their last session. She stated that she was still having severe headaches, some of which extended down the back of her head to the base of her skull. (Neurological tests had been performed and indicated there were no problems physiologically.) Marie also stated she had heard voices in her head over the weekend as well as footsteps in her hallway at home. Additionally she stated that at one point over the weekend she was held down on her bed by an unseen force and unable to get up.

When I began talking with her about God's love for her and quoting some Scriptures she started getting a worse headache and was close to dissociating herself from what was going on in the room. Bill finally had to ask her to rub her hands and arms and slap her own face in order to get back to reality. She said she felt like running out of the room.

As the session closed Bill asked Marie if she would promise him that she would not do anything to harm herself until we met again. She would not promise. Bill then scheduled another appointment for the two of them to meet the following morning so that he could keep a close check on her with the possibility of hospitalization. We had prayer and she left.

Bill and I discussed the situation concerning Marie. We agreed the cause of the suicidal thoughts were probably demonic and needed to be dealt with immediately. It was decided that Bill would speak to Marie's husband about the possibility of meeting at the church on Friday evening to deal at least with the evil spirits we suspected were causing the suicidal thoughts.

On Friday evening Bill, Marie, her husband and I met at church to deal with the evil spirit activity we felt were causing her suicidal and depressive moods. (This is not to say that evil spirits cause all depression. Depression can have many sources.) I explained to the three of them that there was nothing to fear because our blessed Savior would be in charge and greater is He that is in us than he that is in the world. We then had prayer claiming protection through the shed blood of Jesus Christ our Savior and asking our loving heavenly Father to protect us from the forces of evil in this session and to give the needed victory to Marie.

I explained to Marie that we would ask any evil spirit that manifested itself during the session to state its name, how it gained entry, and what its job was within her so that she could be alerted to guard against future reinfestation. As we progressed with the session and called the demons to attention there were nine evil spirits who so fully controlled Marie that they spoke through her lips more or less uncontrollably. Their names were Sickness, Self Hate, Hate, Adultery, Fornication, Death, Unbelief, No Name and Self Hate. When asked, several stated that they entered as a result of illicit sex and even on occasion named the sexual partner. Unbelief specifically stated that he entered because she went a few times to a particular church that claimed to teach the Bible but in reality were actually teaching falsehoods. He named the church. Hate stated he entered when her father beat her. No Name was there to cause depression and to kill, and it took some 20 to 30 minutes to finally see this one expelled. Adultery was a sexual spirit whose job it was to keep her from being sexually active with her husband. It took some time of praying, commanding, and anointing before this spirit finally released itself from her. This spirit stated that he had had sexual relations with Marie in the past himself.[11]

At any rate, as each spirit manifested, stated its name, how it gained entry, and its function, Marie would then need to confess the sin and renounce the evil spirit before she could be delivered from it.

At the beginning of the session Marie was experiencing a severe headache and wheezing, but both problems subsided with the removal of the evil spirit named Sickness. As the session concluded she felt tired but relieved and happy. The session lasted two hours.

Bill was excited. He knew what the Bible had to say about evil spirits but never dealt directly with them. His concerns of suicide were also relieved. As Marie left, Bill told her that he would check with her in the morning for an update. Both Bill and I agreed that another session probably was in order.

The next day Bill called and said that he hadn't gotten much sleep the night before because he couldn't stop thinking about what great things he had seen the Lord do in delivering Marie from the evil spirits. He went on to say that he had called Marie earlier and she was doing fine. There were no suicidal thoughts, no wheezing, and no headaches. She went on to tell Bill that her greatest problems now were her upcoming doctor appointments. How was she going to explain to her neurologist that she no longer had headaches? How would she explain to her family doctor that she no longer was wheezing?

It was amazing. God had done in two hours what a licensed professional counselor, a neurologist, and a family doctor were unable to do over a long period of time. (Again I want to emphasize that all sickness is not demonic in

---

[11] This evil spirit brought up a very important question. Can an evil spirit have sexual relations with a human being? The answer is yes. There have been reported throughout history untold instances of women and men who were sexually assaulted or molested by an invisible evil spirit. The incubus is a male evil spirit which assaults women for the purpose of gratifying its sexual appetite, and the succubus is its female counterpart that preys on men for the same purpose. These experiences cannot be dismissed merely as sexual dreams, hallucinations, or delusions by mentally ill individuals. Instances such as these are generally reported by normal, rational persons, including some Christians. Such assaults by demons and other spirit entities have long been investigated and reported by the Church as well as by other investigators.

The spirits are usually invisible; however, at times they actually appear as beautiful young women or handsome young men. Even when invisible the victims report that the entity has form and weight that can be felt, and that their method of sexual relations is precisely that of a human being.

I have personally counseled with women who have been sexually assaulted by spirits. Generally such oppression comes as a result of previous occult involvement and/or much promiscuity from which the counselee had to be set free, but not always.

origin and I myself go to the family doctor or to a specialist when the need arises.)

At the second session scheduled later there were four additional evil spirits dealt with. Their names were Deception/Lies, Escape, Gluttony, and Drunkenness. Deception/Lies stated that his job was to keep her from growing in Christ. Escape said he entered in childhood and was there to help her flee when necessary. He had tried to get her to leave the room before we had started the deliverance portion of the session. Gluttony was there so that she would hate herself. Drunkenness was there to dull her emotions and required some time of prayer, commanding, and anointing before it finally released itself from her.

Marie continued to see Bill for her Multiple Personality Disorder. Yes, there were a few more demons but because of Bill's experience in the two sessions at church he was able to both recognize and deal with the problem. Oh that there would be more "Christian counselors" who would seek the training needed to deal with the demonic.

Chapter Eight

A SUNDAY SCHOOL TEACHER
WITH MORE THAN A MARRIAGE
PROBLEM

"It's the 21st and I've been thinking a lot today about who I am and wondering what will change about me when this Dissociative Identity Disorder[12] is over. Will I notice the change? Will others? Will I like this new person? There are characteristics about Cathy that I admire and wish I was more like that, and things about Brenda that are fun. But when we are all joined together which traits will I have and will I want them? I am comfortable with where the alters are at and how far we've come. I can't see beyond this point. I don't know what else to do. It seems we're all just maintaining and although I want the alters to experience God's peace now I don't want them too satisfied that they don't want to leave the state they are in."

Written by Paula five weeks before full integration

occurred to the glory of God

It was a Sunday afternoon when I first came in contact with Paula by way

---

[12] Originally known as Multiple Personality Disorder. The American Psychiatric Association changed the name to Dissociative Identity Disorder with the publication of the DSM-IV.

of a telephone call. She stated that she was attending a nearby church and was very active as a Sunday school teacher and youth leader but had a problem that she felt she was unable to go to her pastor about. A friend had recommended she discuss the matter with me. We scheduled an appointment for the next morning.

Paula came to the church office the next morning, and before me sat a very attractive young woman in her 30's who was a married homemaker with four children. She met her husband while attending a Christian College, and they later were married. The marriage was described as basically a happy one with some minor problems from time to time. Paula stated she loved her husband.

Recently Paula had gone out of state to visit her family and while there met an old friend named Fred. Fred was still single. Affectionate feelings started to erupt, and Paula found herself comparing Fred with her husband Jim and began to feel that Fred was everything she had ever wanted in a husband. She and Fred had only talked briefly on a few occasions while Paula was visiting her parents. Shortly before returning to her home she told her husband Jim on the phone one evening that she really didn't want to come back because she found love and acceptance while she was at home with her family (and with Fred.)

During further discussions that first session Paula stated that she realized that marriage is forever and she didn't want a divorce.[13] In fact, she stated the way she was feeling was wrong. She didn't want to feel the way she did, and couldn't understand why the feelings persisted or even where they were coming from.

I asked Paula if her husband Jim would be willing to come in and speak with me. She thought he would. Jim called later the same day and made an appointment. He told me that he knew about Fred but he wanted the marriage to stay together. He stated that there are times when he feels he doesn't even know Paula. Before the marriage, he explained, they were both very close romantically. But once they left town on the honeymoon things radically changed. He said Paula didn't want to spend any time with him at the motel and required him to keep his distance when they were alone together. He said all she wanted to do was go sightseeing. Jim said he had thought the honeymoon would be a romantic time away with just the two of them, but in

---

[13] Unfortunately many pastors at this point would have told Paula to confess her sin, and just decide to do what is right. But the problem went much deeper.

reality it wasn't, and Paula was the one who just shut down romantically. Furthermore, she later stated she didn't know why.

As I continued counseling with the two of them I asked Paula to do some daily journaling. Differences in her handwriting started to appear. Then one day Paula was late for her session, and she told me she had to stop by the bank to verify that a signature on a check was hers. I asked her if that happened often and she indicated that it was an occasional happening.

It came to light that she played with the Ouija Board in High School. The board stated it's name was Antichrist, and it predicted the initials of the person she was going to marry (correctly) as well as giving the exact date when her cousin died, which Paula later confirmed. There also had been suicidal thoughts from time to time in Paula's life. During her sophomore year in high school, after breaking up with a boyfriend, she had taken an overdose of aspirin that only made her extremely sick. There were also suicidal thoughts while in college.

A month into the counseling there were indications that Paula may be suffering from Dissociative Identity Disorder[14]. I discussed my thoughts with Jim that this possibly could be due to some traumatic experience earlier in her life and how this could be affecting their relationship. Jim again stated that sometimes he feels he doesn't even know her, that she is a different person. In Paula's journaling that week was written:

> "I might call Fred tonight. I can't stand this. I just want to talk. Fred respects me and I think he always has. When I didn't care about him he loved me, **the me that so many people never see.**" *(bold print added)*

This was written in handwriting different than Paula's usual script. In all that day, I saw four different handwritings in her journaling.

During the next session Paula told me how a friend of hers quite candidly told her there are times when she feels she doesn't know Paula. After prayer and some preliminary discussion I gave Paula a pencil and paper and told her to

---

[14] See footnote #4 on page 30.

draw herself however she felt best pictured her, and then I left the room for about ten minutes. When I returned she had drawn what appeared to be six distinct personality states and two sets of hands. The first was friendly, outgoing, helping and happy. The second was stubborn, skeptical, manipulative, lonely, and misunderstood. Number three apparently liked to sing and be in front of people. Four was angry, hurt, misunderstood, envied, quiet, thinking, concerned, exhausted, and demanding. Number five was giving and self-sacrificing. The last, number six, apparently was a small child and was portrayed by the hands. When I questioned Paula she stated "I feel sometimes there's a child inside me who is one or two years old." I asked which part of her was sitting and talking to me right then and she pointed to the one I labeled as number two.

Sharing with Paula my belief that she was suffering from Dissociative Identity Disorder, I assured her that God was going to heal her soul as only He could do. After all, Jesus stated that he came to heal the brokenhearted.[15]

Trying to rule out any satanic ritual abuse, my wife Diane and I checked Paula's hands, lips, and eyebrows for scarring and asked if she had any other scars on her body. She had none that she knew of. How about tattoos? Were there any triangles, 666, upside down crosses, black widow spiders, roses, etc.? She answered no. I had her go to her gynecologist to have a vaginal and anal exam checking for old scaring. The report came back that there was none. So I decided to proceed with the thought that the Dissociative Identity Disorder was

---

[15] Does the Bible allow for Multiple Personalities? The answer is yes. While it is true that the Bible does not use the terminology, Scripture does allow for the possibility that the soul can be broken or shattered. In Isaiah 61:1 the prophet speaks of Jesus' ministry and states that He was going to be anointed by the Holy Spirit to do four things: (1) preach the Gospel to the poor; (2) heal the broken hearted; (3) proclaim liberty to the captives; (4) open the prison (release from the darkness) those who are bound.

As we deal with those suffering from Dissociative Identity Disorder, we find that they are poor, brokenhearted, often held captive against their will by evil forces, and are in need of being set free from the forces of evil. The "broken hearted" are literally "the shattered in heart." And since the word heart (lav - Hebrew) is sometimes used interchangeably with the word soul (nephesh - Hebrew), then the broken hearted are those whose souls have been shattered by severe trauma, which is usually deliberate. The concept of a shattered mind is a very good description of a person suffering from Dissociative Identity Disorder.

not caused by ritual abuse.

Beginning each session with prayer asking the Lord to reveal anything that needed to be known, in the following weeks I was to meet four alter personalities and one evil spirit.

Carla was the first alternate personality (alter) who took control of Paula's body and introduced herself to me. She appeared friendly enough at first, but it didn't take long to find out that I wasn't speaking to an alter personality at all. I commanded Carla in the name of the Lord Jesus Christ to tell me who she served. As Paula's facial features changed to one of very deep hate she exclaimed "Satan." I commanded her to answer yes or no, was she an evil spirit. An emphatic "yes" was the response. I asked it how it gained entry to Paula's soul, and it exclaimed, "through her use of the Ouija Board."[16]

By the authority of Jesus I commanded the evil spirit to tell me what its job was within Paula, and it stated, "to make trouble and destroy their marriage." Lastly I commanded it to tell me in the name of the Lord Jesus Christ if these statements would stand as true before the throne of Almighty God, and it got very upset and emphatically stated "yes."

Binding the evil spirit I then talked with Paula who immediately confessed her sin and renounced her involvement with the Ouija Board and the evil spirit. The evil spirit was then commanded to leave since it no longer had any right in the spirit realm to be there, and it left. The mighty power of Jesus Christ had once again conquered evil and set this captive free. Paula felt a sense of relief.

Brenda had never been abused but was a protector alter (alternate personality). The first time she took executive control of Paula's body I met a nineteen year old who stated her job was to make everybody happy. She also stated that she existed to protect Paula from thinking and knowing too much. Brenda said she really was what Paula wanted to be: happy and bubbly. She thanked me for getting rid of Carla the evil spirit, and that gave me the

---

[16] When are people going to learn that dabbling with occult objects is nothing less than an open door for the demonic to gain entry to their souls? When will involvement with such occult activities as astrology, horoscopes, astral projection, automatic writing, channeling, clairvoyance, palm reading, crystal ball, hypnotism, Ouija Boards, Dungeons & Dragons, and Tarot Card laying, just to name a few, be recognized as dabbling with evil spirits and the distinct possibility that exists with demonization.

opportunity to ask if she knew Jesus Christ. Brenda told me that she did know Jesus Christ and had a personal relationship with Him, recognizing Him as the Son of the living God and her Lord and Savior.[17]

Brenda told me about three other alters, Cathy, Lee, and the Little Girl. She said that she didn't think any would be willing to speak to me and that Little Girl was not old enough to talk yet. It was also pointed out to me that both Cathy and the Little Girl were upset that Brenda was talking to me.

I asked Brenda if she liked Paula's husband Jim and she stated that part of her job was to try to make Jim happy and that she was the one who actually exchanged vows with him when they got married.

Brenda also pointed out to me which of the handwritings in the journaling being turned in was hers. She told me that Paula's was more printing style, hers was very neat script and Cathy's was more scribbly. This information helped immeasurably in the weeks to come as I read the journaling that was being handed in each week.

The next week Jim came in with Paula, and during our session I asked **Cathy** if she would take executive control of Paula's body and speak with the three of us. (Diane, Jim and myself) Cathy agreed to come forward and speak to us. When Cathy took executive control of Paula's body she had a noticeably different posture, was very arrogant, and would not even look at Jim. She crossed her arms, looked at me, and said, "What do you want?" In the moments that followed she somewhat hesitantly shared that she was seventeen years old and that she carried pain. When asked about the pain she was unwilling to share any information.

I asked her if she liked Paula's husband Jim, and she replied she didn't like him and that Paula didn't need him and would be better off without any man. Furthermore, she stated that she couldn't understand why Paula wanted another

---

[17] Paula, the original personality, was saved and active in her church. Because of her trust in Jesus Christ in reality the entire system of alter personalities were under the blood, for our name is only written once in the Lamb's Book of Life. However, many times alters need to be introduced to Jesus and helped to build a personal relationship with our risen Lord. Bear in mind that most alter personalities have been horribly traumatized through abuse and are very distrusting of everyone at first.

baby because the world is not always safe, and parents can't always be with their children.[18]

Later while talking to Brenda she stated that it was Cathy who went on the honeymoon with Jim and not Paula. She said that all Cathy wanted to do was go sight seeing and experience some new things. Brenda pointed out that since Cathy distrusted men she wouldn't let Jim get anywhere near her or touch her on the honeymoon.[19]

It was becoming obvious that Cathy was definitely a problem in this marriage. When she would take executive control of the body Jim would not be treated well, and he certainly could not have a loving, affectionate relationship with his wife. On the other hand, Brenda felt that it was her duty to try to keep Jim happy for the sake of Paula and the marriage. With this in mind and the fact that there had been an evil spirit trying to destroy the marriage it is a wonder that Jim and Paula were still together. (But for the grace of God . . .)

In the weeks to come I began talking to Cathy about Jesus Christ but she stated she didn't trust anyone. Finally, she was willing to at least learn more about Him and so in prayer we asked God to give Cathy a Bible, in the realm in which she lived (Paula's soul), so that she could read about Jesus and His love for her. Immediately after praying Cathy told us that she did indeed now possess a Bible in her realm with her name on it. I encouraged her to start reading in the book of John.

Paula was confused. She asked if that meant that now she would have to start reading the book of John for Cathy. I told her no that Cathy would read it with the Bible God had furnished to Cathy in her realm. Paula could not believe this was possible. But God did exactly what we asked Him to do.

I had encouraged Paula to talk daily to her alter personalities so she would get to know them better, and she did so documenting on sheets we furnished

---

[18] This was a clue that something had happened to Paula while away from her parents that caused the trauma.

[19] This was the reason why the honeymoon had gone so wrong. This was the reason Jim stated that he felt like he went on the honeymoon with another woman. In reality he did, same body, different personality. In fact, one that didn't like or trust him.

her called "Alter Communication Sheets."

The week after God had given Cathy a Bible to read, when Paula came in for the counseling session one of her first comments was "well you were right." She went on to say that one evening she was talking to Cathy and asked if Cathy was reading the book of John, thinking all the while it was a dumb question. Cathy replied that she had been and Paula told her that was impossible. Paula told me at that point her mind was flooded with information contained in the book of John, and then Cathy said, "See, I have been reading." Paula was amazed at what God was doing in her life. Little did she know that the best was yet to come.

Wanting to meet all the alters and get acquainted with them, as well as have them feel more at ease with us and begin building trust, it was time to meet the **Little Girl**. I talked to Cathy and Brenda about their helping the Little Girl alter take executive control of Paula's body. They agreed to encourage the little girl alter and to help her gain executive control. During our discussion, as trust was building, Cathy stated that Little Girl's pain was by one person whereas Cathy's was by a group.

It was decided the best place to meet Little Girl was in the Church nursery, in a setting where she would be more comfortable. Paula, Jim, Diane, and myself sat down on the floor in the nursery and waited while Cathy and Brenda helped Little Girl take control. As she took control before us sat a grown woman's body with all the characteristics of a toddler.

The Little Girl was very afraid and sat looking around the room. She saw a doll near the corner wall and crawled over to get it. She then sat there hugging the doll in fear of us. Diane took some very simple nursery toys and started playing with her. Little Girl, although still very cautious especially of Jim and myself, started playing with Diane. She was nonverbal and after about ten minutes left us as Paula once again assumed control of her body.

Lee turned out to be a young boy of grade school age stating he was nine years old. When he first took executive control of Paula's body he had all the mannerisms and the speech of a nine year old. He appeared to be a sad little boy and stated that his job was to hurt and have pain. He has seen love. Later after Cathy placed her trust in Jesus so did Lee.

In discussions with Cathy we found she had many questions. As she read more about Jesus and His love she finally placed her trust in Him. Concerning Jim, she said he was a wimp and didn't like him. I explained that he is a gentle man and God created him like he is. We discussed her possibly cutting Jim some slack and she agreed to think about it. Additionally I encouraged Cathy to share her trauma, which she had absorbed for Paula, but she was reluctant because she felt if she did there would no longer be a purpose for her existence, and she would die. I assured her she would not and once again explained how God loved her.[20]

In order to help Cathy and the others sense God's great love for them we asked God in prayer to give each of the alters a gold chain and cross as a token of His love and concern for them. God did that in their realm, and they all were excited as they shared what each cross and chain looked like. Cathy got what she described as a "hip cross," Brenda a dainty one and the Little Girl got a little one appropriate for her. Oh how God was moving. But the best was still yet to come.

One day in a counseling session Cathy asked if it would be possible for her to be baptized. Cathy was appearing to be a new person. She was a lot more humble but just couldn't understand why God would love her. Enjoying the things God had given her she still was amazed and began crying when discussing His love for her. She recognized yielding to baptism as an act of obedience on her part.

Now obviously Paula had been saved years ago and was baptized. But allowing Cathy to be baptized as her act of obedience to a loving God whom she now knew couldn't hurt anything. Could it? In fact it might help!

I discussed the idea of baptizing Cathy with Jim and Paula. They both agreed that we would schedule a time for just the four of us, Diane, myself, Jim and Paula, to meet at the church. I would fill the baptistery with water and, after Cathy took executive control of Paula's body, I would baptize Cathy. We

---

[20] I might add at this point that we had run Temperament Analysis Profiles known as APS's on Paula and Jim as well as Lee, Brenda and Cathy. We use a test put out through the National Christian Counselor's Association and find that it is very helpful in determining which of the alters is strongest in the area of control. Although all the alters and the original person inhabit the same body, they all have different temperaments. Cathy was found to have the strongest temperament, so we felt that she would be the key to integration back into one complete soul as God had made Paula originally.

set a date, and the plan sounded good and right but God had a better idea.

On the appointed day I filled the baptistery with a thousand gallons of water in the morning. About one o'clock Paula and Jim showed up ready for the baptism, carrying a change of clothes for Paula/Cathy. Meeting in my office first, we prayed that the Will of God would be done in this matter of baptism. All of a sudden Paula looked at me in amazement and said, "It's happening." I said, "What's happening?" And she said, "the baptism!"

God allowed the baptism to occur but not in the way we had planned, proving once again that His ways are not our ways.

Paula began explaining how she was seeing in her mind that God had set up a beautiful grove of trees with a stream running through it. He had sent an angel who was inviting all the alters and Paula to witness Cathy's baptism. She went on describing how all were gathered around the stream with the angel and Cathy now in the water. She said the angel was now baptizing Cathy in the name of the Father, and of the Son, and of the Holy Spirit. After the baptism Paula described how when they came out of the water the angel was dry, but Cathy was wet. The angel then gathered all the alters around him and put his arms around them and told them how much God loved them. As Paula described what had happened we were all amazed. Oh how great our loving, gracious heavenly Father is in His love for us. This was to be the turning point in the healing process.

I instructed Paula sometime during the next few days to allow each of the alters to take executive control and describe in their own words what they had experienced. The next week she brought in the tape, and I listened to each, in their own voice, describe what had happened. Let me share with you now what each stated in their own words:

Cathy stated: The first thing that comes to my mind is that it was extremely humbling and it made you weep because of how little your faith is. When I saw this angel I didn't question anything. I knew that God was an awesome God and that every one of us is undeserving of His love, of His power, and of His grace. The presence of this angel was extremely peaceful. He is extremely gentle and holy, incredibly holy. And he doesn't have to speak and you want to get down on your knees. You want to give everything that you have, everything that you are, to this person and trust with all.

I remember that he took me to the water where I was to be baptized. And I remember feeling extremely warm inside. The water was warm. His touch was warm. It was incredible. And when he spoke I felt no anxiety and no sadness. I felt no pain, just incredible, complete peace. And I wanted him to take me with him wherever he came from. I wanted to serve whoever made him.[21]

It took a lot of fear out of my life, that experience did, the whole experience, because I was not afraid of what I didn't know. Because like Jesus said, 'They saw and they believed,' and that's how it was with me.

When I'm looking back on it all, I wish that I had felt the same way about Jesus before seeing this angel as I did afterwards because this convinces me how small my faith is. He said how blessed are those who will believe and have not seen. I have no reason now not to trust in Jesus Christ,[22] because I saw the angel with my own eyes. I touched him, and he was real, and it was awesome."

Brenda stated: About the experience with the angel, I'll tell you one thing, I think about this experience every day because it was incredible and it was awesome. There were so many things that I believed about Jesus, that I read about Jesus Christ, that I wondered. And yet, being around this angel with the others and just being in that righteous presence, I didn't feel like there was anything I didn't know. There were real simple details. I just knew that I believed that only God could make this being. And that God is most wise, and all-powerful.

I don't know how to describe it. When I saw the angel taking Cathy down to the water, I wasn't jealous, I wasn't envious because I was there too. And it didn't feel like this angel loved her more than the rest of us. I felt like he had so much love that there would be enough for everyone in this world, enough to go around. There was enough to go around. And I remember just smiling, seeing, and watching this happen. And I was holding the little girl. And she was looking at me and smiling because of Cathy's peace.

---

[21] Notice the thought was on serving the angel's Master, not the angel.

[22] Again the emphasis is on Jesus, not the angel.

As I looked around, in the eyes of the others there was no sadness, and I began to feel things that I never experienced before. To be honest with you I try not to consider the situation that much because it's convicting. It's very convicting to know that this God who knows everything that I am, everything that I've done, everything that I will be, took His time to be in the presence of us and to send this angel. And I think how can I forget this. This wonderful experience, how can this not change my life forever and make me want to be completely holy and completely righteous.

This angel, there was a warmth about him physically; there was a warmth emotionally. There was a warmth about him. He was very tall. He had a very gentle, gentle peaceful look on his face. He looked like he had all the time in the world. He was very, very patient. He looked very blessed.

And you know, I never really thought about this before, but when he walked into the water his gown, his clothes did not get wet. They didn't get wet. He walked out and he was not wet. And when he walked it was like gliding. He was so incredibly smooth and graceful. And he put his arms around all of us. And you know how sometimes when you put your arm around a group of people, and you just get the tips of their fingers or the sides of their arms? But no one was out of place. When he put his arms around us we all felt like we were as close to him as we could be. We were all within the circle and no one was getting left out I guess you could say. And he touched us and we listened to him, and we hung on to every single tiny word that he said. His voice would make you believe just listening to his voice. I can't believe God did that for us. It's unbelievable.

David stated: What can I say. This tall, kind man dressed in a white or light blue something very, very bright, very soft. He took Cathy into the water and he baptized her and he said: 'I baptize you in the name of the Father, and of the Son, and of the Holy Spirit.' And he put her under water and brought her back up. And she was wet, and he was dry. And then he guided her to the edge of the water on the bank and he spoke to us and he put his arms around us. And I felt something I had never felt before but I don't know what the word is.[23]

---

[23] Could it be that David felt the peace that passes understanding?

I remember I never wanted that feeling to leave me. I felt so protected, so safe. And I didn't care about anything else. I wanted him to take me with him. And I'll live in that moment. But it's not like the moment itself the way it was. Before he left he said "God is with you," and how could you not believe him. But those words were comforting and they made me feel good. It all made me feel good. It was the first time I saw an angel and the first time I felt like I was part of the family. Everyone accepted me. Everyone accepted me. And I knew things would be different from then on. And I wanted to learn more about this person Jesus Christ and this God. I wanted to know more.

Paula journaled after the baptism: Wow, what a day! It's Tuesday and today I witnessed a baptism performed by an angel. I remember seeing him and feeling no worry, no pain, and no questions. I remember feeling very humbled that I ever questioned this one's maker.[24] That I was not worthy to stand there in his presence. At the same time as feeling intense joy, I felt ashamed for my little faith.

The baptism significantly accelerated the healing process and integration of the alter personalities into one core personality.

When asked, Lee, the nine year old male alter, would reluctantly take executive control of Paula's body. He was very sad, but apparently God had given him a Bible also, and he had been reading in the book of Genesis. He asked many questions about God and why the events in Genesis occurred. We spoke to him about love, and I encouraged him regarding how God's love and the love of Paula and the alter family would help him as time progressed. He was somewhat afraid of my wife Diane and was concerned because Diane was in the room but was willing to "come out" because he noticed the other alters were not afraid of her. Could the perpetrator of the trauma he had endured be a female?

Because of what God had done in showing His love for them through the baptism, the Bible, the chain with a cross, and His holy Word in the Scriptures, the alters quickly moved to the point of sharing their abuse with Paula. They now knew they could get some relief and start living life more abundantly, not die.

---

[24] Once again note that in each case the presence of the angel caused the different personalities to think about God, not the angel.

I instructed Paula that when the alters shared their trauma with her, she had to be ready to forgive the perpetrators as Christ has forgiven us. She was not to hold the trauma inflicted upon her against those who offended her. For several weeks she prayed and wondered what the alters would share. Who were the perpetrators? Where did it happen? Was it family? What could have been so bad that an alter personality needed to be created to handle the trauma? Paula had much apprehension and many questions but was willing to forgive especially after all that she had recently experienced her loving heavenly Father do for her realizing that she too had sinned, and He had forgiven her.

I shared with the alters their need to share their abuse with Paula and to integrate, but at first they were hesitant wondering if it would really help them or Paula. I assured the alters that they weren't alone in their suffering because Jesus had suffered on the cross to atone for those very acts that were committed against them. They appeared relieved that Jesus had shared in their sufferings, hurt, and trauma. Finally it was agreed that Cathy would share her trauma with Paula first, and then possibly the others would follow her example. Before starting the process we all shared the Lord's Supper as we remembered Jesus and His sufferings and sought to keep Christ right in the center of the process. Additionally, I asked God if He would consider sending the angel back to comfort the alters while the exchange of information was taking place. He was gracious.

The process began as Diane, Jim and I watched Paula's lowered head. On her face started to come expressions of hurt, unbelief, and pain concerning what she was being shown by Cathy. Paula was at first shocked that her sister was in the scene and also recognized a boy from her high school years. (She told me later she always had a fear of him but didn't know why.) Paula continued to share with us what Cathy was showing her. She saw herself at a party her older sister had taken her to in high school. There was a lot of drinking taking place. During the party she saw herself tied naked to a bed with a number of people standing there laughing at her. Then she said that Cathy shared more which she chose not to share with me.

Paula was upset but stated that she and Cathy met on a grassy spot near the place where the angel had earlier baptized Cathy and that God did in fact send the angel back who then sat there with them and gave them comfort.[25]

We then discussed the need for forgiveness and to have the mind of Christ

---

[25] Realize this was talking place in her soul as she sat in the counseling office.

in this matter. I told Paula we were going to leave the room for a few minutes, and she was to be there alone with God, and ask His forgiveness for her being at the party, and then be willing to tell the Lord that she was in fact forgiving her perpetrators. When we returned to the room Paula said that she asked God to somehow show her if what she had seen was really true and really happened and she said that almost immediately He gave her an almost audible answer that He only dealt in truth, and then she knew for sure. She did ask for forgiveness and forgave.

When Cathy took over she said that sharing with Paula was easier than she thought it would be and that Paula had handled it better than she thought. She also confirmed the presence of the angel. All in all it was a very emotional afternoon session.

This trauma, which had been brought to light, occurred when Paula was a teenager and thus Cathy's age and teenage actions. At the time Paula was unable to handle the trauma of the abuse, but now she was an adult and also much stronger in her relationship to her heavenly Father. Now she could handle the truth of the abuse in an adult Christian manner. There was no longer any reason for Cathy to continue carrying the pain.

The other alters now were ready to follow Cathy's lead and share their hurt and trauma with Paula.

I spoke with Lee, and although he was a bit afraid, after prayer agreed to share his pain and the abuse he had hidden, with Paula. In answer to the prayer God had sent an angel to comfort him. Lee started to share with Paula, but she was unable to get a clear picture of the abuse. We paused, and I had a few words with Lee assuring him everything was all right and this was the right thing to do and prayed again. This time Paula had a clear picture. The abuse took place when she was nine years old (thus Lee's age). Apparently Paula was sexually abused after school one day by her female teacher in a one-room schoolhouse she was attending at the time.

Next Little Girl shared her abuse. In the picture Paula was shown in her soul, she stated that she did not know the perpetrator but that it was a man who was staying at the neighboring farm. Her mother and she apparently went to the farm to visit one day and while the two women talked in the kitchen, Paula, just an infant, crawled into the other room. The man then abused her in the next room. She went on to say that apparently he was a relative of the lady they were visiting, and neither woman knew what had happened. The baby didn't cry during the ordeal.

After each sharing Paula told the Lord in prayer that she forgave the perpetrators. Once her final prayer was completed after the baby had shared, Paula said that she could see angels who started singing, "It Is Well With Your Soul."

Remember that only Lee, Cathy, and Little Girl had suffered trauma. Brenda was what is known as a protector alter and had not been traumatized.

After the abuse had been shared I called upon Brenda to take executive control. She was a bit perturbed because she said everybody was celebrating and the nine-year-old boy was ready to integrate. After discussing integration for a few minutes all four alters were ready to integrate in order to produce the one soul that God had created originally as the "broken heart" became healed.

Paula described how she saw it occur in her soul. The alters formed a circle with Paula in the middle. She then thanked each of them and told them she had appreciated them. When they were ready, in the presence of several angels, the alters moved toward Paula and integrated. What an awesome God we serve! The great healer! Jesus truly did come in part to heal the broken in heart.

The next week Paula and her husband Jim came for their scheduled appointment. Paula appeared in very good spirits with both indicating that things were much better in their marriage. Paula stated that she is so happy that the alters had integrated. I told her we needed to check for any alters on a "lower level," and as we did two additional alter personalities were discovered.

One alter was a fairly heavy seventeen year old teenager named Cristy. She stated that her job was to hurt and that she was created during a date. The other was a little boy age three to four, dark hair, whose name was Billy. He stated that he didn't know why he was created but stated, "just to be here I guess."

While Christy was in executive control of Paula's body she was very bouncy and stated that she knew who I was and was familiar with all that had happened with the other alters. She stated that she was ready to share with

Paula and integrate if Paula was ready. Furthermore she said that she was in a layer below the original alter group, and they were not aware of her presence. As she began sharing, Paula related that she was being shown an older man that she went to a party with. While she was away from the man she got cornered once again by one of the perpetrators in Cathy's abuse but this time nothing happened because there were a lot of people around. However, she did feel very uncomfortable and it frightened her.

When Billy shared Paula was shown at a neighbor's home at a young age, and when she saw two young boys exploring each other it freaked her out. Paula said it was good that this was hidden from her because she went to the small country school with those two boys, and her thoughts of them would have been somewhat different.

After prayer, integration occurred without a problem. Paula stated that just before integrating Christy said, "Eat a few fries for me once in a while"

With the alters all dealt with, a check was made for any other evil spirits that still might be inhabiting Paula's soul. An evil spirit did manifest through Paula's vocal cords and facial features. It stated that its name was Darkness, and it gained entry through an open door with the alter Billy. When asked what its job was it stated that it was deceptiveness and then stated, "I know no truth." Its job was to keep a person in darkness so they couldn't tell the truth from a lie. When commanded in the name of Jesus Christ and by His shed blood to answer yes or no whether the answers would stand as truth before the throne of Almighty God, it answered "yes." Paula felt very uneasy about this evil spirit, and Jesus Christ delivered her from it, and she stated, "it's gone."

Both Paula and Jim appeared happy and content upon leaving the office, and I shared once again with them how much God loves both of them. Jim made the comment that they were both raised in Christian families and went to church regularly but were never really educated as to the spirit realm and demons.

I continued to see Paula for about six months on a regular basis to check for any new alters, and there were none. She also scheduled an appointment for me to discuss what had happened with her parents, and they commented that this helped explain many thoughts, actions, and events that previously they could not understand.

Today, Paula and Jim are happily married and have had another child. Fred is no longer a threat as it was Debbie who was infatuated with him, not Paula.

One final note! The Diagnostic and Statistical Manual of Mental Disorders, known as the DSM-IV-TR, published by the American Psychiatric Association states on page 528 that the average time period for this disorder from first symptom presentation to **diagnosis** is 6-7 years. In Paula's case, keeping our loving heavenly Father, His son Jesus Christ, and the Holy Spirit right in the middle of counseling, the total time to complete integration and resolution of the problem, not just diagnosis, was five months.

To God be the glory, great things He has done.

Chapter Nine

THE DEMONIZED FOREIGN
MISSIONARY

I received a call from a woman named Ann. She identified herself as a Foreign Missionary who had been on furlough along with her husband and family and was about to leave the states to go back to the South American country where they was assigned. Their Mission Board wanted both she and her husband to see me, and then I was to submit a report on their spiritual and marital well being.

Ann and Jeff had been married for thirteen years and were in generally good health. They had three children ages seven, five, and three. I questioned both at length, and there was nothing that stood out concerning Jeff, although I felt that Ann might be holding back some things. After a few sessions during which I did some testing, and we worked on the art of communication in their marriage, I concluded the relationship between them was in good shape.

I did find myself, however, still bothered concerning Ann. Something wasn't right, and I asked if she would mind seeing me one more time. Both agreed it would be OK, so an appointment was made.

The day I saw Ann without Jeff, my wife Diane was in the counseling room with me. I told Ann that I felt something wasn't right with her and asked her a few questions to get started. Ann stated she has been suffering from depression which she attributed to low blood sugar. Ann completed a questionnaire on which she indicated that she did play with an Ouija Board once when she was in the fifth or sixth grade, and it did answer one of her questions that no one else would have known the answer to. Her father, a deacon in their local church, told her the Ouija Board[26] was evil, and she shouldn't play with it ever again. Ann then told her girl friends they shouldn't be playing with it either because it was evil. She went on to say the other girls kept playing with it but that the Board wouldn't answer their questions when she was around. Ann said she had experienced suicidal thoughts going into the seventh grade, and after their third child was born she tearfully admitted to having continuing thoughts about killing all of her children. Additionally, she stated that Jeff didn't really love her, which was anything but the impression I had of him.

As we began discussing the possibility of demonic problems, she related an incident that happened while she was on the mission field. She said that one night, while her husband was away, she woke up being held down in bed by an unseen force that was choking her around the neck. She said she immediately pleaded the blood of Jesus in her life and the unseen force stopped the choking.

I gave her a doctrinal affirmation and a prayer for eviction of controlling wicked spirits to read daily aloud for a week. If she had problems while doing the procedure she was to call, otherwise I would consider the matter closed.

Several days later Ann called and said that when she would read the prayer and the doctrinal affirmation aloud she would get a lot of intrusive thoughts and a headache at the base of her skull in the back of her head. She was very concerned and wanted to see me in the office again.

---

[26] "Ouija Board" is the English name for a spiritualistic fortune-telling game, known in France as *planchette* and in Germany as *psychograph*. It is mainly girls between the ages of eleven and seventeen who seek to satisfy their curiosity in this way. People claim they have made contact with the dead through the use of the Ouija Board when in reality they have fallen victim to a great and sinister deception. It is not the dead who answer them, but demons, who have sometimes appropriated dead people's knowledge in order to give an impression of authenticity. Let me insert at this point that it does make me wonder what may be happening to the other girls who continued to play with the Ouija Board and continued to have their questions answered. Did they become demonized? Quite likely! Are they having some problems today because of the demonic? Possibly!

Ann came in and met with Diane and myself as scheduled. After some discussion it was decided to do confrontation work with any evil spirits that may be present. Apparently these spirits had maintained a foothold in her life for some years. By the way, Ann was now thirty-two years old. I explained to Ann that she would need to renounce any activities, confess any sin, and renounce the spirit before it would leave. She agreed

The first evil spirit was "Terror," and he stated that there were a total of five. He said that he had entered by way of her open door through the use of the Ouija Board. His job was to take away her joy in living. He also stated there was one greater than he named "Holy." Ann renounced her usage of the Ouija Board and this evil spirit, and Jesus delivered Ann from the spirit.

"Sharon" was the second evil spirit to manifest itself through Ann's vocal cords and facial features. After quite a bit of commanding he reluctantly stated that he had entered Ann when the wires crossed. I wondered what the

spirit meant by that. Ann quickly told me she knew exactly what it meant.

She said when she was a small child the church they attended was about to add on an educational wing. One Saturday her father and the other men of the church gathered to find the water lines before digging would begin. They agreed that they would not use a forked stick because that was water divining or water witching and was evil. However, one of them said two wires could be used in much the same way to find the water and that was OK. *(In reality it was just another form of water divining)* The men of the church did find the water lines that day using the wires. When the wires would cross they would be over the lines.[27]

---

[27] Although they thought it was some kind of magnetic force that would cause the wires to cross, in reality it was evil spirits who were "working with them that day" unbeknownst to them. The spirits would see that the wires crossed at the appropriate time.

Water divining is also known as water witching, water dowsing, radiesthesia, water switching (using a switch), doodlebugging, rhabdomancy, and so on. It is an ancient occult art practiced throughout the world from the United States to the Orient.

As a form of *divination*, which has its roots in heathenism, the practice is condemned by the Scriptures in the prohibition against all divination (Deut. 18:9-12). Divining with a rod is likewise condemned in Hosea 4:12. God declared: *"of my people. They consult a wooden idol and are answered by a stick of wood. A spirit of prostitution leads them astray;"*

Divining is not limited merely to locating water, but many dowsers are able to locate almost any other object

Ann was there and was fascinated by the procedure. Her father let her try using the wires, and she remembered when she crossed the water line the wires in her hands crossed. At that point the door was open for entry of an evil spirit into her soul.[28] Its name was "Sharon." *(When are we as Christians going to wake up?)*

The evil spirit named "Sharon" stated that his job was to deceive her by making her feel worthless and since she was married to tell her that her husband didn't love her. He also stated he makes her feel sick more often.

After Ann renounced her participation in the water witching and renounced the evil spirit, Jesus Christ delivered her from it.

"Holy" was next. He stated he served Satan, gained entry through the Ouija Board, and said his job was to destroy her by trying to get Ann to commit suicide. He also stated he was trying to destroy her through her diabetes. Ann told me she had decided the best way to commit suicide was to take an overdose of Insulin and just slowly go to sleep. *(We don't have to wonder where that thought came from)* Ann renounced this evil spirit and Jesus delivered her from it.

Then there was "Destroyer." He stated he served Satan, also gained entry through the Ouija Board, and his job was to destroy her witness for Christ and to destroy her marriage. Ann renounced him and he left, thanks to the power of the Lord Jesus.

"Demon" stated he gained entry during a time of her doubting the

---

desired, as well as diagnose diseases, which is also evidence of the occult nature of the rod and pendulum. The rod has been used in such things as crime detection, locating missing persons or corpses, sexing of chicks, finding lost objects, diagnosing human and animal ailments, determining blood types, forecasting the weather, locating military objectives, prescribing the necessary medicine for a patient, and determining from a photograph whether or not a missing person is dead or alive.

It is clear that the practice of water witching, or use of the rod and pendulum for any reason, places an individual under the influence and control of the forces of darkness and is in disobedience to the prohibitions against divination in the Word of God (Deut. 18:9-12)

[28] What about the men who were at the church that day doing the water witching? Are they demonized and oppressed by evil spirits because of their participation in this forbidden activity? Possibly! Oh that we would more fully understand the spirit world around us as Christians! Come on Christians, it's wake up time!

goodness of God. His job was to sow seeds of additional doubt. She was delivered from him.

"Legion" stated he was the spokesman for a group of demons. He said they served Satan and were servants to the other stronger spirits that she had been delivered from. Jesus Christ delivered Ann from them.

In all there were five evil spirits plus the group of serving spirits who were removed from Ann through the power of the name and shed blood of Jesus Christ on the cross of Calvary. Ann began experiencing the joy of her salvation and was a happy woman again.

Her problems were mainly due to spirit activity, and now she was free and ready to return to the mission field with a new joy and a new hope thanks to Jesus.

Chapter Ten

THE REFERRAL

"I CAN'T HANDLE THE DEMONS, YOU TRY"

How do we live with demons praytell
with their knowing and evil ways.
How do we live with demons praytell
with their lusty and painful ways.

How do we live with demons praytell
with their colors and leering eyes.
How do we live with demons praytell
with their touch and magnifying eyes.

How do we live with demons praytell
when it is to God in heaven we turn.
How do we live with demons praytell
when it is to prayer we turn.

How do we live with demons praytell

    when it is to God and us they seem to ignore.

How do we live with demons praytell

    when they increase their numbers more.

How do we live with demons praytell

    when our voices rise in prayer.

How do we live with demons praytell

    when it becomes too hard to care.

The day started out quite normally, but before it was over I would be taking on one of the most complex cases of Satanic Ritual Abuse and Satanism I had ever encountered.

About two o'clock I received a call from yet another Licensed Professional Counselor who stated he had been working with an individual for some time who had been diagnosed with Dissociative Identity Disorder[29]. However, he was starting to encounter what he thought were evil spirits which at times would take executive control of his client's body and threaten, curse, and growl at him. He wanted to refer her on to me because he felt he had come to a stand still and felt unable to cope with the evil spirits. I agreed to set up an appointment at my office to meet his client and her husband and review the case history. The counselor also agreed to be present.

The day they arrived for the initial session I was introduced to a 35-year-old female named Gayle and her husband Dick. They had been married only about eight years. Gayle is an office manager. It quickly became very obvious that a young alter personality was in executive control at the time. I asked who I was talking to and the alter replied "Kala." Kala was a 14 year old alter who obviously did not want to be there and was not overly cooperative.

---

[29] Originally known as Multiple Personality Disorder. The American Psychiatric Association changed the name to Dissociative Identity Disorder with the publication of the DSM-IV.

The counselor told me there were several alter personalities[30] who did most of the daily office work and were also fairly active in the counseling arena. The alters specialized in different activities. One would answer the phone, another was good at filing, still another at organizational activities, and yet another who was the bookkeeper. As the need arose the alters would switch and do their work therefore making the core personality look very skilled as an office manager.

He stated there was a male alter named Guardian who acted as an overall protector. Kala said when she went to church she saw Guardian in front at the alter with the pastor. Immediately red flags started going up in my mind. Wait a minute! If Guardian is an alter personality then how is it that Kala sees him in front of the altar with the pastor at church?[31]

I suspected right away that Guardian was not an alter personality as the counselor had suspected but was in fact an evil spirit who was pretending to be an alter and in reality could leave Gayle at times and be seen outside the body by the alter personalities, in this case standing with the pastor.

---

[30] See footnote #4 on page 30.

[31] It is going to be **very important** that the reader understand that alter personalities operate in the spirit realm within the soul. In fact, they are part of the soul that has been broken through trauma. When an alter personality is in executive control of the body, often they are able to see any spirits, good or evil, who may be in the room at the time.

Let me give an example. One morning before I was to see two ritual abuse victims who were heavily demonized, I asked God in prayer to protect both the clients and myself in the counseling sessions. I asked Him to do this any way He chose since He is sovereign.

Later, as I worked with an alter personality of one of the clients I noticed she kept looking over to one corner of the room. I asked her if she saw any other beings in the room except for the two of us. She said "yes" and then stated, "That angel in the corner." I asked her to describe him, and she said he was about seven feet tall, very slender, and looked peaceful, but one could tell he had great strength. He had on a long gown that was either a very pale blue or white and had something in his hand. I asked her what it was, and she said she wasn't sure, but there was a flame shooting out from it. She was describing the flaming sword of a warrior angel. God had sent an angel to protect in answer to prayer. I didn't say one word about the angel as the session continued but thanked the Lord privately in prayer for His protection..

Later that day as I worked with an alter personality of the other client I noticed this alter kept looking in the same corner of the room. Again I asked this alter if she saw any other beings in the room except for the two of us. She answered yes and then described the angel in the corner exactly as the other alter personality had described it earlier in the day.

The same is true with evil spirits. Alters can see them when they are present in the room. I recall one afternoon I sensed there were evil spirits in the room as Diane and I worked with a client. I asked the alter if there were any evil spirits in the room, and she said "Yes." She pointed to several locations and then said, "And there's one just behind Diane's right shoulder." Diane said later every hair on her body started to rise as she heard that tidbit of information. We dealt with the evil spirits, and they departed.

Agreeing to work with Gayle I spoke for a few minutes with Dick alone. He described some of the problems he was having at present with Gayle at night. He shared how quite often during the night evil spirits would take over Gayle's body, and he would wake up with them growling and hissing at him. He said he didn't know how to handle the situation, and things were getting worse. He also told me he didn't think Gayle was trusting Christ as her Savior. I suggested he come in and allow me to teach him some spiritual warfare techniques so he could help out at home. He agreed and within a week had learned how to handle the evil spirits through the power of the Lord Jesus Christ, and felt more prepared to enter the spiritual battle for his wife.

About a week later Dick called and said the last several days had been extremely rough and that an evil spirit had been manifesting and was hissing and growling at him. Additionally he said the spirit told him that nothing was going to get Gayle's soul because it belonged to him. Dick said that lately when encountering an evil spirit, along with taking authority in the name of the Lord Jesus, he had been saying the Lord's Prayer which would cause the spirit a lot of anxiety.[32]

During the first few sessions with Gayle I learned about her past. She had been raised in a Christian family in a conservative farming community. The family attended church regularly and worked very hard in the family business. She stated that when she was very young her parents would be out of town a lot on business and would have a baby-sitter stay in the house with her. She talked about having a rather normal childhood.

Childhood, yes! Normal, no! I had been talking to the original person during these first few sessions who had all the abuse blocked from her by the alter personalities.

Later I was to learn that in reality the baby-sitter whom the parents trusted was a Satanist. When the parents would leave town the baby-sitter would invite the coven over at night, and they would ritually abuse Gayle in the basement of her own home. The parents never knew because along with the ritual abuse, the Satanists programmed Gayle through fear and threats so that she would never reveal what was happening.[33] Alter personalities were formed to take the

---

[32] The Lord's Prayer would cause a spirit anxiety since it is Scripture, and part of the wording is a plea to the Lord to "deliver us from evil (or the evil one)."

[33] See footnote #5, page 37.

extreme trauma because the original person, a very young child, was unable to cope with it. And since the alter personalities took the abuse it was blocked out from the original person. She also came under the influence of demons very early on.

As Gayle grew, because of the early programming, the Satanists were able to keep their hold on her through the alter personalities. As a teenager not only did she suffer ritual abuse, but she was involved in Satan worship.

Gayle was a breeder in her teen years for human sacrifice. Four months or so prior to a required human sacrifice, according to the Satanic calendar, she would be impregnated by her coven. When the night of the sacrifice came, the infant was aborted and immediately sacrificed as a human sacrifice.[34]

Gayle had been involved in a satanic baptism in blood, had taken satanic communion in the past that consisted of eating human flesh and drinking human blood, and was married to an evil spirit during the annual Marriage of the Beast ceremonies in September.

I was also to find out that at least one of her alter personalities was used during her teenage years to lure vagrants from near the railroad in her town to where her coven was meeting. After "enjoying" sex, to the man's surprise he was then sacrificed to Satan and dismembered.

Interestingly, when I finally met her parents they told me that during those teen years they would sometimes realize she was getting in at four and five in the morning and would confront her about it the next day. She would completely deny it and tell her parents that she was home by 11:30 pm, her curfew time. They would accuse her of lying, which would hurt her feelings.

In reality Gayle was telling the truth. What happens in instances such as this is that the original person does get home by curfew. However, later a

---

[34] I find this very interesting because the god of this world, Satan, has our society in the United States convinced that what we abort is just so much fetal tissue when in reality he himself recognizes an aborted infant as a human sacrifice. We're just doing his dirty work when an unborn human being is aborted. And what's even more unbelievable is that there are many "Christians" who state they are pro choice. Then we wonder why God doesn't bless.

programmed alter personality gets up and goes to a meeting and returns home in the early morning pre-dawn hours and goes back to bed with the original person completely amnesiac to what had taken place.

Gayle's parents had seen an alter personality returning, when as far as Gayle was concerned she had been home on time.[35]

This is what Gayle and her parents had experienced and had much confusion and hurt in their family relationship because of. Now for the first time they were beginning to more fully understand their daughter.

Shortly after I began counseling with Gayle, she started cutting on herself. We were starting to get some understanding of the alter system as well as the system of evil spirits. With the evil spirits being pressured and fearful of being uncovered, they started to cut using alter personalities who had been previously programmed by the Satanists. Cuts were starting to show up all over Gayle's body under her clothing. A demonized alter would take executive control and use whatever was handy, a knife, pin, nail file, nail, etc. to cut on the body.

As the cutting got worse Dick feared that infection could set in. I called the doctor who was my medical supervisor and told him I wanted to send Gayle to be checked because she had been cutting on herself, and we were concerned about infection. He inquired as to why she was cutting herself, and I replied that actually alter personalities were doing the cutting under the direction of evil

---

[35] Let me give another example. I had been working with a professional woman who was raised a generational Satanist. Her parents were Satanists. One day during counseling she told me she had woke up that morning feeling like she hadn't gotten a good night's sleep and when she went to get in the car to go to work it was parked out in the drive rather than in the garage where she usually kept it at night. The woman lived by herself.

What had happened in reality was that sometime during the night the phone had rung. When she answered it, half asleep, a programmed word or other signal was given by a coven member which caused a particular alter to take control causing the original person to be totally amnesiac. The alter, now in executive control of the body, got dressed and drove to the meeting. Coming home much later she parked the car in the drive and went back to bed. When the alarm went off the original person got up, feeling like she hadn't gotten a lot of sleep the night before (which she hadn't), got dressed, found the car in the yard, and went to work.

spirits. There was a pause, and he said, "I don't want to know any more. Just send her over to me and I'll check the cuts." He did treat some that were getting infected. The evil spirits were trying to destroy Gayle, and the spiritual battle was raging. The cutting got worse and started to show up on the face and hands.

Shortly thereafter Gayle received Jesus Christ as her Savior, but the battle continued. Now she was saved. Now she had the Holy Spirit living in her spirit. Now Jesus, the only answer for healing the broken in heart was part of her life. Now there was hope for the future.

Counseling continued for over a year. During that period there were 124 alters identified. They are all different personalities. They perceived themselves as having different weights, color, and lengths of hair, ages, etc. Many were formed because of severe trauma inflicted during ritual abuse.

Let me introduce you to a few:

Gayle Age 45, 160 lbs, long blonde hair - was actually the original personality God created. She was a sexual assault victim, was alcohol dependent, and had severe marital problems with her new husband Dick. Gayle was extremely depressed, had suicidal thoughts, and really had a problem accepting the reality of the alters and the ritual abuse.

Alice Age 16, 5'2", 110 lbs, long blondish-brown hair, hazel eyes - a protector alter. She took care of most of the office work and was a peacekeeper and referee in the alter system. Always happy.

Gayle 10 Age 10, short brown hair. She was molested on horseback and was a carrier of guilt.

Baby The baby-sitter and other members of the coven abused her in the green room in the basement of her parents' home.

Pearl Age 22. She had many memories of being sexually abused by the coven. Also was sexually abused by a counselor she was seeing.

Luba Age 28. Carried guilt and remorse concerning the abortions for sacrifice.

Vida Age 3. She had previous memories of ceremonies, being attacked by a dog while tied to a tree, and being drugged.

Louella Age 16, 110 lbs, blue eyes, long brunette hair. She had open sex with evil spirits in the past and was involved in dismemberment of victims.

Emerald Age 17, 114 lbs. She would tease and tempt men (vagrants) to go with her for sex when in reality they were to be used for human sacrifice.

Eve Age 17. She performed all the duties of high priestess and was married to an evil spirit during the "Marriage of the Beast" ritual.

Obviously this is only a sampling. As was previously stated there were 124 alters in this system.

Dick had grown to know many of the alters and their different characteristics and needs. He once told me when he was in high school he always wondered what it would be like to have a harem, but now he's decided that wasn't a good idea after all. He rightly called the different alters by their correct names when speaking to them.

I recall early in the counseling process a call I received from Dick one Saturday morning. He said that they were having some relational problems, and could I please see them that day. When they came into the office I quickly realized what the problem was. Apparently one of the alter personalities had been in executive control, and Dick didn't realize it. Thinking he was speaking to Gayle he said something that was meant to just be silly about the size of her behind. The alter he was actually speaking to saw herself as weighing only 110 lbs and very slim and took severe offense to Dick's statement. A battle raged. I explained what had happened to both Dick and the alter and then had the alter system make a list for Dick stating what each of them looked like including their weight and other features. They couldn't realize that Dick was seeing only one body, and Dick didn't realize they all look different as far as they were concerned. In fact, when an alter looks into a mirror they see the body as they perceive it not as we see it. As time progressed Dick got to know each of them separately.

The system of evil spirits was yet another issue. There were 95 known by name that we personally dealt with thanks to the name and power of the Lord Jesus and His shed blood on the cross of Calvary. The spirits were fully defeated and Gayle saw victory in her life through Jesus her Savior.

I remember one day Dick shared with me how he had just entered Gayle's office, when the phone rang. The evil spirits were upset that he was present since he knew how to deal with them. Gayle (actually Alice) answered the phone, and as the conversation began an evil spirit manifested and began growling and hissing at Dick while the receiver was still up at Gayle's face. As quickly as it came, it left, and the alter named Alice was back in control. The individual on the other end of the line was still for a moment and finally said, "What was THAT!" How could you tell a customer, or most anyone for that matter, that they had just had an evil spirit growling and hissing in their ear??!!

I met with Gayle, and in most cases her husband two times a week for counseling. At one session we dealt mainly with issues involved with the alter personalities. At the other session we dealt with issues pertaining to the evil spirits. These later sessions were team sessions and were usually attended by several strong Christians both pastors and lay. There were several pastors and lay church leaders from the local Southern Baptist, Nazarene, Mennonite, and Christian & Missionary Alliance Churches who worked with me in these sessions to provide prayer support, safety for Gayle when a spirit was manifesting, quoting of Scripture, singing songs about Jesus' blood, etc. Without these men and women the progress would have been slowed.

As we met it was quite common for evil spirits to take control of Gayle's body and attempt to challenge us in many ways. But the reality of the matter was that God is still sovereign and in control, and therefore we were safe. When they would threaten physical harm to us we would plead to them the blood of Jesus in our lives and command them to stop and be still. When they would try to state that their god was stronger than ours we would remind them that the Bible states the one who is in us is greater than the one who is in the world (1 John 4:4b). When they would try to say that in the end they would prevail, we quickly would remind them that in the end they would spend eternity in the Lake of Fire. Although we did not try to hold conversations with them, when spoken to, we would command them in the name of Jesus to be silent and then state Scriptural truth.

They were defeated at the cross of Calvary, and it was just a matter of time before Gayle was delivered altogether from them.

Oh the evil that abounds with Satan but oh the blessedness and ultimate victory that abounds with Jesus.

The poem at the beginning of this chapter was written by one of Gayle's alter personalities. There are other poems. I would like to share a few of them with you. Remember the term "us" refers to all of Gayle's alter personalities (known as her "alter family").

What Being Multiple Means to Us

A history of misdiagnosis: neurotic, schizophrenic, and psychotic

A mixture of feelings and concerns

A lack of knowledge of who we really are

A handful of different tastes, our taste buds aren't the same

A difficult time in dressing, our tastes aren't the same

A difficult time in telling you what it is we want to do

A time when we can tell you no but yes is hard to do

A difficult time in making choices again we are not you

A lot of pain and heartache that we all must share with the others

A Loss of life and childhood that belonged to some and not the others

A lack of trust belongs to us for those in the inside hurt us as much as the outside

A difficult time of understanding what purpose it is to bear this life

A loss of sleep and appetite because of the nightmares that we keep

A lot of time being tired because seldom does everybody sleep

A vision of the others who are usually within our distance

A lot of misunderstanding on the outside because only one is in their vision

A lot of misunderstanding how others on the outside can judge us so

A badge of crazy that we wear is not a badge of courage

A doubting of our own reality is part of the badge of crazy

A lack of misunderstanding from those on the outside puts more pressure on

A lot of little voices asking for a chance

A lot of adult voices praying for their chance

A list of contradictions often is the case

A fear of the secrets that the others keep

A fear of the unknown always keeps us from our sleep

A usual feeling of being alone

A feeling of pain and agony that our hearts do bear

A lack of understanding that is usually there

A lot of misinterpretation because there are so many here

A lot of misinterpretation because the ages cover an amount of years

This last poem was written by one of the alters to Eve, the alter who performed the duties of high priestess at ceremonies. Eve was greatly under demonic influence but listen to the advice the other alter gives:

Eve

The demons have kept you hidden

This we know for sure

For their own purposes

Of which they say there is no cure

They have you tied to Kala

Which we do believe

She carries much of your heartache

And it isn't hers to receive

They say she is to fulfill her duties

Where you took over and she left off

Those of a priestess as they say

Often they remind us where it's hidden in a cough

We know that in your mind

You do not need to think

Where the darkness is your memories
They're hidden in your blink

We know that you have not chosen
This life that is your own
We know that you have not chosen
The life we have been shown

Eve, we need you to bring yourself to life
Where you can see and hear and smell
Where you can be responsive
And climb out of your shell

Eve, with you comes a freedom
So reach out and take the light
A chance for your life & the others
A chance for a life that's within your right

The road may not be easy
Very difficult it may be
It may be dangerous & scary
But with your eyes we hope you see

There's a light at the end of the tunnel
A shadow you see there
That shadow is a hand
Reaching out to help with the sorrow that you bear

His name we call Jesus
Our Lord of faith, hope and life
The one who shed His blood for us
And even gave His life

At times we all question
If the hand is really there
And yet we readily reach out
To have Him help with the pain that we bear

Eve you are important to us
So please reach out your hand
Then we can help carry you
Like in the "Footprints in the Sand"

The team sessions, which dealt with the demonic issues involved, became quite intense and sometimes lasted for up to ten hours. Usually these sessions were held on a Friday evening beginning around 6:30pm and continued until 4:30, or later, in the morning. Needless to say these sessions required dedicated Christians who were willing to enter into direct confrontation with the forces of evil because of their faith in the name, shed blood, power and safety of the Lord Jesus Christ.

It was not uncommon for Gayle to come into these sessions with an evil spirit manifesting. We encountered her entering sessions with her wrists and torso cut with razor blades and bleeding. Sometimes there were pentagrams as large as 2 1/2 inches in diameter freshly cut on her forearms with razor blades. We also found razor blades hidden in her clothing. Additionally we had to pull pins out of her ankles and wrists which were placed there by the evil spirits in hopes that when we would hold her down we would push the pins deeper into her body.

On the team was a Registered nurse. When Gayle would come into the office several of the men would gain control of her and hold her down on the floor for her own safety. That being accomplished the women then begin searching her for pins and razor blades which would be used by manifesting evil spirits against her or the team. The nurse then would bandage the cuts before any work was begun.

Unfortunately Gayle moved and was unable to continue with counseling until integration of the alter personalities and therefore healing of her broken, shattered heart was complete and the evil spirits were gone.

My prayer is that I have shown the enormity of the problem we are facing with the continued rise in Satanism across our once great land. It's up to us as Christians. Will it be allowed to continue or will we be willing to enter the battle and see victory in and through Jesus Christ?

Chapter Eleven
A YOUTH EVANGELIST
WITH GENERATIONAL SPIRITS

One Saturday afternoon after we moved to Florida, I received a call from a pastor in the Atlanta, Georgia area who explained his church was sponsoring a weekend youth event with a young evangelist from a neighboring state. The evangelist, a friend of his, had come to him earlier in the day and explained he felt he was under spiritual attack and didn't understand why but knew something needed to be done as he was being plagued by evil spirits. The pastor wanted me to know he had prayed with the evangelist but had also recommended the evangelist give me a call the following Monday in Florida.

Early Monday morning I received a call from the evangelist. We discussed his situation and he decided to drive to Florida along with his wife the following Thursday for an appointment we scheduled on Friday. His wife, who was expecting a child shortly, wanted to be in the session so she could better understand why he was struggling so much. She would learn to her surprise that the unborn child was about to be part of the focus of the counseling sessions.

The evangelist and his wife, we'll call them Jim and Pam, were in their early 30's and had been married about six years. He held a Master of Divinity Degree and was ordained Southern Baptist. For the last five months he had been suffering bouts of depression and seeing evil spirits in his bedroom at night.

While obtaining background information Jim reported his mother had obtained an abortion while she and his father were dating. They eventually married and shortly thereafter Jim was born. He never bonded with his father who was a workaholic and would spank him extremely hard. His mother was emotionally unstable. Beginning at approximately age two he started seeing evil spirits outside his window at night and experienced nervous twitches and high anxiety. He stated that one evening he woke up in the middle of the night, at around age six, and saw an evil spirit face to face with him in his bed. The manifestations continued throughout his teen years. He would see spirits in his room at night and at times would be held down in bed by an unseen force and unable to get up. Upon reaching puberty, he would be awakened in the night being sexually attacked, again by an unseen force. Over the past several years the manifestations had seemed to subside. But now it was happening again with a vengeance.

Why the manifestations of evil? Why was he under attack? He was a Christian and was serving the Lord in full time ministry. He believed that as a Christian he was safe from spirit attack. After all, he was taught, an evil spirit surely could not indwell a Christian because the Holy Spirit was indwelling.[36]

As we began the first session that Friday Pam also attended since she too wanted to understand why the manifestations and attacks toward Jim were continuing.

It didn't take long to get some answers. After prayer I began commanding any spirits inhabiting Jim's soul to manifest themselves and answer questions given in the name of the Lord Jesus Christ.

The first spirit identified itself as a generational evil spirit associated with the sexual sins of Jim's father. It admitted it was a succubus[37] who had been

---

[36] Contrary to popular belief a born-again believer can be demonized. Most Christians today believe the "great myth" which is the belief that because I am a born-again believer, an evil spirit can not live in me because the Holy Spirit lives in me. The word *"demonized"* comes from the Greek word *"daimonizomai"* which means "to have a demon." E.g. Mark 5:15-16. It is improper to say a person is possessed. The proper terminology is demonized. The result of demonization is control not ownership since Satan and evil spirits can own nothing. The areas of control by the evil spirit are not in the person's spirit but in the person's soul (mind, emotions, will, and affections) occasionally resulting in physical manifestations. Scripture references that teach about the trichotomy of the human nature (body, soul, and spirit) plus the warfare against the soul are: 1 Thess. 5:23; Hebrews 4:12; 1 Peter 2:11; Psalm 71:13; John 3:3-6; Romans 7:22-23; 8:10-16; 1 Corinthians 5:5; 6:17-20; Galatians 5:16-25.

[37] A sexual spirit, still in spirit form, which assaults a man for its sexual gratification.

responsible for attacking Jim sexually at night, but had no right to inhabit Jim's soul other than the sins of his father. It had entered Jim at conception. I instructed Jim to take his authority in Jesus Christ, break the generational curse,[38] and command the spirit to leave him and future generations. As he commanded the spirit to leave, the unborn child in Pam's womb jumped violently. It was the most graphic demonstration of generational spirit activity I had ever witnessed. This spirit had already entered the unborn baby as part of the generational curse which Jim had now broken, and upon command it had to leave the baby too.

The next spirit also identified itself as a generational evil spirit which was associated with his parents aborting a child prior to their marriage. It admitted it was mainly responsible for Jim's depression but had no right to Jim's soul other than the generational curse. Again Jim took his authority in Jesus Christ, broke the generational curse, and commanded the spirit to leave him and future generations. This time Pam was ready and embraced her unborn child as it again jumped so violently in her womb it was noticeable to me as I sat behind my desk.

A third spirit was then identified and when commanded it admitted it was not a generational spirit, was responsible for trying to give Jim false guidance, and did have a right to Jim's soul at that time. I commanded the spirit to tell us what that right was. It stated when Jim was a teenager he had been involved in the use of a Ouija Board which had answered questions for him. Jim admitted to its usage and the fact that he had not realized the wrongness of the act or confessed the sin. After confessing to the Lord he commanded the spirit to leave and it did.

There were other spirits dealt with that day who were there because of past unconfessed sin on Jim's part. In each instance, when Jim confessed the sin and commanded the spirits to leave, they did.

The session lasted over four hours and was very exhausting to both Jim and Pam. We agreed to set up one more session the next Friday and deal with any remaining spirit activity at that time.

---

[38] The Bible teaches the sins of the parents are passed down to the third and fourth generation of those who disobey God. We are not responsible for their sins. But if a spirit has gained entry through sin which is never confessed and forsaken, then the spirit is passed on to future generations at conception. Spirits can split. Let us realize that our actions do have lasting ramifications for future generations if not confessed and forsaken.

The following Thursday Jim and Pam once again drove over 400 miles to attend another session on Friday. This session was much like the first. Additional spirits manifested with the same results.

Among the spirits which manifested that day was a generational spirit which stated it was responsible for trying to destroy Jim and Pam's marriage through disagreements. It had entered the generational line through the unconfessed arguing and anger of both his mother and father toward one another. It admitted it had no right to Jim's soul since he had not entered into this type of sin. Once again Jim took his authority in Jesus Christ, broke the generational curse, and commanded the spirit to leave both him and future generations. And again, the infant in Pam's womb reacted by jumping violently.

There were a few others that day but Jim left the session free from the spirits which had caused him so much distress for so many years. And Pam left with an infant who would be born a couple weeks later free of the generational curses due to the unconfessed sins of previous generations and the corresponding spirit activity. Today Jim continues in full time youth ministry and reports being free of any spirit manifestations since those two memorable Friday counseling sessions one chilly winter.

Chapter Twelve

YOUR KIDDING!
THE SPIRIT IS HER FATHER?

The sons of God

Went to the daughters of men

And had children by them.

Genesis 6:4

It was a beautiful late May day as I was sitting at commencement exercises at the Seminary. Before the day was over I was going to have my first Doctor of Philosophy degree conferred upon me Summa Cum Laude and needless to say I was excited. Unknowingly I was about to receive special recognition as I sat there relieved that the studying, hard work and writing a thesis were over.

As the awards ceremony continued it was time to award the trophy for Highest Academic Achievement. To my great surprise, my name was called. What a day. I was receiving an award for a study and report whose outline was closely scrutinized and nearly rejected by the seminary when I had originally submitted it for approval.

It all began a year earlier on a Tuesday evening while counseling at our church as leader of a team dealing with a victim of Satanic Ritual Abuse. An evil spirit was manifesting through the victim's facial features and vocal chords.

I commanded the evil spirit in the name of the Lord Jesus Christ the Son of the living God to tell us by what right it felt it could still inhabit the soul of this individual. The individual was now trusting Christ as her Savior. I might mention at this point that evil spirits are very legalistic. If there is any ground given up by which they still have the right to remain, they will do so. The evil spirit stated that it had the right to her because of the "right of birth" and that "she belonged to it." I and the other members of the team were puzzled as we had not heard this reason from any evil spirit in the past.

With puzzlement we took a short break during which time I made a long distance phone call to a Southern Baptist pastor friend in Texas who has had extensive experience in this area. I asked him if he had ever heard an evil spirit state the "right of birth." He quickly stated that he had. He explained that the mother of this counselee obviously had a sexual relationship with this evil spirit and that the spirit was in fact her father.[39] The spirit was claiming the right of birth as her father. He told me to go back into the counseling situation and acknowledge to the evil spirit the right of birth but that the second birth which she now possessed in Jesus Christ had canceled out the first birth and he no longer had any legal right to her.

Returning to the counseling situation I did as my friend had instructed. When I acknowledged to the spirit his right of birth he beamed. I then explained the second birth had, however, cancelled out his right of birth. He was then commanded in the name of the Lord Jesus to depart, and ultimately did that evening after much hesitation.

How could this be? Where were the Scriptural proof texts? I knew about Incubus and Succubus, but in those instances there is no sperm produced. Could an evil spirit take on a human body and have a sexual experience with a human being and produce a sperm and a child?

Apparently, I thought, the only way this woman had any right to the salvation of the cross was because her mother was a homo sapien. If her father was indeed the evil spirit then the individual I was dealing with was actually a spirit man.

---

[39] The mother of this woman had led a very promiscuous lifestyle and spent a lot of time in bars and with men she would meet and have a "one night stand" with. Apparently one evening in a bar she had left with an individual who actually was an evil spirit in human form. They had sexual intercourse and this woman was the offspring of that union . The Bible teaches we sometimes entertain angels unaware. This woman had entertained an evil spirit. She was in a place she should not have been, a bar.

After some initial research and speaking to Christian counselors who have dealt with the right of birth, I was convinced that evil spirits in human form do in fact have sexual relationships with human beings, and produce sperm capable of producing offspring. I decided to continue my research for two reasons. First I needed to know for my own satisfaction, and second I was going to use the research as the foundation for a Ph.D. thesis on the "Right of Birth."

A Few Thoughts About What The Bible Says
Concerning Sexual Relations
Between Evil Spirits & Humans

Evil Spirits and Sex with Humans

Demons who specialize in having sex with human beings, both male and female, are very common. For centuries they have been known and written about. They are known as *incubus* and *succubus*. An incubus is an evil spirit who takes on the male sexual role and has sexual intercourse with female human beings. A succubus is an evil spirit who takes on the female sexual role and has sexual intercourse with male human beings. These spirits do engage in full sexual intercourse with humans, but do not produce sperm being in spirit form, and therefore are incapable of procreating children. The victim, seeing nothing, feels weight and penetration. Russell deals with this phenomena: "Though having no body himself, the devil may **assume a body** in which he can have sexual intercourse, though neither incubus nor succubus can he engender offspring.[40]

The Genesis Account

The first step in learning what the Bible teaches about sexual relations between evil spirits and humans is to study the account in Genesis regarding the relationship between the sons of God and the daughters of men as found in Genesis 6:2.

The Bible states: *When men began to increase in number on the earth and daughters were born to them, the sons of God saw that the daughters of men were beautiful, and they married any of them they chose. Then the Lord said, "My Spirit will not contend with man forever, for he is mortal; his days will be a hundred and twenty years."*

---

[40] Jeffrey Burton Russell, <u>Lucifer: The Devil in the Middle Ages</u>, Ithaca, N.Y.; Cornell University Press, 1986, pg. 206.

*The Naphilim were on the earth in those days – and also afterward – when the sons of God went to the daughters of men **and had children by them.***

Who are the sons of God? Does this refer to pagan deities; to pagan rulers; to angels; or to the descendants of the lineage of Seth? We will look only at the proper view that the "sons of God" refers to pagan deities.

G.H. Livingston states that among pagans there are "Mythological stories which go back to the Hurrians (ca. 1500BC) which tell of nature deities who engage in illicit relations among themselves, and in some instances with humans."[41]

The sons of God are fallen angels (watcher angels) and the daughters of men are human women. This does not mean that the women were raped or abducted by the fallen angels. Actually the opposite appears to be true. The women gave themselves to the angelic beings to be their sexual partners, probably with the full consent of their families. This certainly makes the picture of human depravity so terrible that it certainly justifies God's decision to destroy the human race (vv. 7, 13).[42]

Wenham also holds to the angelic view of Genesis 6:1-4.[43]

He states that "the angel" interpretation is at once the oldest view and that of most modern commentators. It is assumed in the earliest Jewish exegesis (eg. , the books of 1 Enoch 6:2ff; Jubilees 5:1), LXX, Philo (De Gigant 2:358), Josephus (Ant. 1:31), and the Dead Sea Scrolls (1QapGen 2:1; CD 2:17-19). The New Testament (2 Peter 2:4, Jude 6,7) and the earliest Christian writers (e.g. Justin, Irenaeus, Clement of Alexandria, Tertullian, Origen) also take this line.[44]

---

[41] G.H. Livingston in Merrill C. Tenney ed., ZPEB, Grand Rapids, Michigan, Zondervan, 1977, 5:493.

[42] Many well-known scholars hold to this position. A few examples are Donald G. Barnhouse, The Invisible War, Grand Rapids, Michigan, Zondervan, 1965, 104-105; Arno C. Gaeberlein, The Conflict of the Ages, New York, N.Y., Publication Office "Our Hope," 1933; Merrill Unger, Biblical Demonology, Chicago, Ill., Scripture Press, 1955, 45-52; J. Warwick Montgomery, Principalities and Powers, Minneapolis, MN., Bethany Fellowship, 1975, pg. 50.

[43] Gordon J. Wenham, Word Biblical Commentary Vol. 1, Waco, Texas, Word Book Publishers.

[44] Ibid. pg. 139.

Elsewhere in the Old Testament (Ps. 29:1; Job 1:6) "sons of God" refers to heavenly, godlike angelic creatures. Additionally in Ugaritic literature "sons of God" refers to members of the divine pantheon, and it is likely that Genesis is using the phrase in a similar sense.

In the Genesis account the fault of the daughters of man lies presumably in their consenting to intercourse with "the sons of God." But the girls' fathers would also have been implicated, since, if there was no rape or seduction, the fathers' approval to these matches would have been required. The obvious avoidance of any terms suggesting lack of consent makes the girls and their parents culpable, and more so when the previous chapter in the Old Testament has demonstrated that mankind was breeding very successfully on its own.

Marriages between men and the gods are a well-known feature of Greek, Egyptian, Ugaritic, Hurrian, and Mesopotamian theology as well. The heroic figure of Gilgamesh was held to be descended from such a union. His parentage endowed him with incredible energy, but not immortality.

While we have great difficulty understanding this passage, evidently the original recipients of Genesis did not. What they understood by verses 1-2 of Genesis Chapter 6 unfortunately has not been passed on to us. Our understanding of Genesis as a book, which is written to a people who knew fallen spirit beings could take on human bodies to engage in illicit sexual relationships with human beings, inclines me very strongly, along with my experiences in dealing with demonized individuals and with sexual spirits, to the view of sons of God as fallen angelic beings.

Can spirit beings take on human bodies? Yes! Just consider for a moment the account in Genesis 19 where we are told that two angels came to Sodom in the evening and Lot invited them into his home for the night and to wash their feet. These angels were in human form. Once in Lot's home the Bible tells us that Lot made a feast and the angels ate the meal. The men of the city of Sodom had also seen these angels in human form. We are told they came to Lot's home and wanted them brought out that the men of Sodom could have sex with them. Lot tried to offer his daughters instead but the men of Sodom insisted. Further we are told that Lot was outside the home trying to reason with the Sodomites and was finally pulled into the house by the angels in human form.

If God's angels can take on human form there is absolutely no reason to believe that evil angels cannot take on human form. The angels who came to Sodom apparently were very appealing to the Sodomites.

The Seminary

I prepared an outline on the "Right of Birth" to submit to the seminary for approval so I could write my thesis. As the committee reviewed the outline I was questioned on several occasions and the final outcome from the committee was a questionable approval. I was told I could write the thesis but they would not guarantee it would be accepted.

I decided to write the thesis anyway and if it was not approved by the committee, at least I would have learned greatly from the experience. Needless to say I was surprised when I received an A+ on the thesis.

And now, I was walking down the aisle to receive the award for Highest Academic Achievement from a conservative Independent Baptist Seminary. Incredible!

Chapter Thirteen
ABORTION
EVIL SPIRITS
AND AN EVIL HONEYMOON

The Abortion

I was sitting at my desk one sunny Florida afternoon when I received a call from a young married woman named Angela. She told me she and her husband had been married for about four months and were struggling with their decision to have an abortion. Angela explained they were both born-again believers who were active in their church. They had tried to honor God by staying away from each other sexually until married, but had given way to their fleshly lusts. The result was finding herself pregnant from the one time event.

Because of their concern over their families and the church finding out about the pregnancy, they decided to abort the child. Now, she explained, they were ridden with guilt and needed counseling help. We scheduled a time for the couple to come to the office.

At the scheduled time I found myself sitting before a beautiful, vibrant, young couple who appeared deeply in love with one another, but they both stated there was a gap in the relationship because of the abortion. Angela said she felt resentment toward Ben because he instigated the sex prior to marriage. Now sexual activity was hindered. She also told me very emphatically that she felt evil had control of her thoughts at times, including guilt.

My first thoughts were to deal with the abortion and then see what additional problems may need to be addressed.

I began with prayer asking the Lord to take over as Wonderful Counselor and show or tell Angela whatever she needed to know, understand, or deal with relating to the abortion. With Ben looking on I asked Angela to just close her eyes and think back on the abortion. Instantly she saw a vivid mental picture in her mind of the event. During the abortion Ben was in the room with her and she saw him standing next to her. I asked her to look around the abortion room in her mind and see if she saw Jesus anywhere. After a couple moments she told me that she saw Him standing next to Ben.

It is always wise to test the spirits in accord with 1 John 4 and so I commanded this spirit she was seeing to tell her truthfully if He was the one who died on the cross for her sins and rose again. She stated He immediately answered "yes". Next question, "were you defeated at Calvary?" She stated He immediately answered "No." Last question, "will both of those answers stand as absolute truth before the throne of Almighty God?" Angela stated He immediately answered "yes.".

With Jesus identity proven I told her to just tell me what He does or says. Over the next few minutes she described how Jesus held Ben's shoulders and then bend down and gave Angela a hug. He told them both that He loved them and then he said: "this is My burden," "I'm here," "I'll be with you always," "I'll take good care of your baby," and "I forgive you." What an awesome God we serve!

Both Angela and Ben were in tears and felt so much forgiveness and peace in their souls. Truly Jesus is the Wonderful Counselor!

Evil Spirits

I felt it important to check for evil spirits since Angela had made the statement she felt evil had control of her thoughts at times. Having both Ben and Angela fill out a Pre-Counseling Questionnaire the following past sinful and occult activities came to light.

Ben masturbated regularly; was reading Harry Potter books; had played with an Ouija Board; regularly was experiencing nightmares; viewed pornography in the past; saw spirits in his room at night as a child; and stated there was ongoing dialogue going on in his mind telling him how bad and sinful he was.

Angela had out of body experiences as a teenager; indicated she had previously had conversations with spirits; was involved in magnetism (healing & therapy); had masturbated regularly as a teenager and still was involved in the practice at times; had experienced trances and read literature on Wicca; and had been held down in bed in the past by an unseen force which deeply frightened her.

I decided to set up two additional appointments with Ben and Angela to deal with any evil spirits they may be experiencing in their lives. I instructed them to complete an exercise by Neil Anderson called *The Steps to Freedom in Christ* prior to the next appointment in order to deal with any unconfessed sin, anger, and unforgiveness.

During the first appointment I worked with Ben. A total of twelve spirits were identified and dealt with. The first four spirits identified themselves as generational and I helped Ben take his authority in Jesus Christ as a born-again believer and command the spirits to leave him and future generations, while also breaking the generational curse. He saw them leave. Then there were two spirits who stated they gained entry to his soul through masturbation. He confessed the sin, commanded the spirits to leave, and saw them leave. There was one spirit which gained entry through his playing with a Ouija Board while visiting a friends house in grade school. He confessed the occult sin and commanded the spirit to leave him. He saw that spirit leave. Then there were five additional spirits who stated they gained entry to his soul while he viewed pornography. He confessed the sin, commanded the spirits to leave, and saw them leave. Ben stated he felt so free and forgiven.

The second appointment was to identify and deal with any evil spirits connected with Angela. A total of thirty six evil spirits were identified and dealt with during one incredibly long session. The first group identified themselves as generational spirits when tested. Three were from Angela's mothers side of the family and stated their job was to destroy her. Eight were from her father's side of the family, entered the generational line because of alcoholism and abuse, and stated their job was anger and to destroy her marriage. Three other spirits entered the generational line through ancestors reading occult material and their job was to lead Angela into occult activities. Four spirits entered the generational line through Angela's mother's adultery and their job was to lead her into adultery and destroy her marriage. These spirits were all dealt with through Angela's taking her authority in Jesus Christ, breaking the generational curse and commanding the spirits to leave. See saw them all leave in defeat.

Five additional evil spirits stated they were not generational and gained entry through Angela's practice of masturbation. After confessing the sin, Angela took her authority in Jesus Christ, commanded the spirits to leave, and she saw them leave screaming in defeat.

An Evil Honeymoon

Savannah, Georgia has always been advertised as "America's most haunted city," with ghostly tours through cemeteries and "haunted sites" throughout its boundaries. Even many Bed & Breakfast's claim to have "ghosts" occupying their residences and scaring visitors. It was in this setting that Ben and Angela decided to take their honeymoon as both were fascinated by "ghosts and spooky things." A bad choice which would prove to be spiritually dangerous!

Both shared with me their honeymoon experience. They had booked a room in a Bed & Breakfast which was advertised to be "haunted." When they made the reservation they asked to be put in the bedroom which was thought to be overrun with ghosts. They both said the room would get very cold and they were truly frightened at times during the nights they stayed there. To add to their "haunting experience" they took several of the night "haunted tours."

Did this have an adverse effect on their lives spiritually? Absolutely! As we continued through the session identifying spirits connected with Angela seventeen spirits were identified as having gained entry during the honeymoon. One admitted to being a fallen angel who's job was to haunt. It stated that it gained entry, along with five other spirits, while they were lying in bed at the Bed & Breakfast feeling a presence in the room and experiencing a lot of fear. There were eleven other spirits who admitted they gained entry during scary moments during the tours. The spirits admitted that Ben and Angela's interest in the spirits gave them permission to gain entry to their souls.

During the time I was working with Angela and identifying the spirits involved, Ben started experiencing physical problems as the spirits were inhabiting his soul too. Both had to renounce and confess the activities before taking their authority in Jesus Christ and dealing with the spirits.

No wonder this couple was not enjoying the joy of their salvation.

There are so many born-again believers in our churches today who are not enjoying the joy of their salvation and are unable to serve God as they should. They are being tormented by generational spirits and associated curses as well as spirits who have gained entry to their souls due to their own past sins. They don't realize the dangers connected with many of the activities in which they find themselves involved.

Incidentally, sexual sins, occult activities, and alcohol and street drugs are the prime open doors to spirit activity in our souls. Oh that our churches would recognize the seriousness of spiritual warfare among believers, teach on it, and help believers to be set free once and for all from the spirits who plague them.

Facing Evil
In Buildings

Chapter Fourteen

DEMONIZATION PROBLEMS
IN HOMES, CHURCHES, AND OTHER
BUILDINGS

In dealing with the spirit realm we need to be aware that evil spirits can inhabit buildings, homes, work places, and even churches for several reasons. First, because serious sin has taken place repeatedly in these structures, secondly there may be articles present that are "points of contact," or the building may actually have been dedicated to Satan.

Points of Contact[45]

An illustration concerning "points of contact." A Baptist pastor friend of mine, we will call him Chuck, who is also a Christian counselor once told me about a psychologist in his town whom he had befriended. One day the psychologist friend called and asked Chuck if he would be willing to sit in on a counseling session with one of his clients. He explained to Chuck that his

---

[45] There are many items we don't need in our homes or cars because they are connected with the occult. Crystals, dream catchers, 8 Balls, Ouija Boards, Dungeons and Dragon games, and even, at times, items missionaries have brought back from the mission field are among the items which are open invitations to demonic attack.

client, a middle aged woman, was a victim of Satanic ritual abuse. At first the psychologist had progressed well with her therapy, but lately he had come to a standstill and in fact appeared to be regressing. Chuck told his friend if the woman signed a consent, he would be glad to try to help.

About a week later Chuck arrived at his friend's office a half hour before the session was to begin in order to review the woman's case history. Upon entering the office he noticed that his friend had crystals hanging about the office and immediately questioned the psychologist about them. His friend replied by stating the woman they were about to see was always so nice and would bring him crystals[46] to hang in the office. Nice? Not really! The crystals were points of contact with the evil spirit realm. They were in essence an open invitation for evil spirits to be present.

Having explained about the crystals, they were removed from the office prior to the session. That day the session went well, and progress again was being made after the crystals were removed and the evil spirits had been commanded to leave in the name and by the blood of the Lord Jesus Christ.

"Mommy There's Monsters Upstairs"

A couple years ago a local physician referred a Christian family, living about 60 miles from our town, to us for counseling. The presenting problem appeared to be that their daughter Jane, age nine, although quiet and behaved at school, had been displaying inappropriate behavior at home. She would verbally lash out at all the family members, would punch both the sibling sisters and her mother, and would pick at her body causing sores. Additionally at night she had a hard time getting to bed and slept very restlessly with the covers all over the bed and floor in the morning.

Jane's father casually told me his family originally bought the house when he was twelve years old. As a young boy he could remember shortly after the family moved in that his eight-year-old sister's behavior started to change and she would insist there were "ghosts" in the house. Another sister started to suffer from severe depression shortly after moving in. Prior to the family originally buying the house it was told that a man had died violently in it.

---

[46] Crystals are extremely significant to New Agers, Wiccan's, and Occultists. They are contact points for conjuration, necromancy and other black practices.

Then Jane's father went on to explain that Jane was always uneasy when her mother was gone at night due to work and was scared of the upstairs stating, "There's monsters up there." He added that she said that most of the "monsters" were in and around the hall closet on the second floor.

Was this just another child's over active imagination? I think not! Was it just a fantasy? No! When are we going to start taking seriously what our children are trying to tell us about such things? Young children have not been desensitized to the spirit realm as we "mature" individuals have and therefore are more sensitive to what is happening around them.

I had several suggestions for Jane's father. First he should set apart the home for the Lord and evict any intrusive powers of darkness. As the spiritual head of the home he was to go through the entire home and have verbal[47] prayer (rooms, closets, basement, attic). Prayer in each area would include thanking God for the home, dedicating the particular room or area to Him, and then verbally commanding all evil spirits to leave and go where the Lord Jesus instructs them and never to return again. I cautioned him to be certain no area within the home was missed. Additionally, he was to place a small cross of olive oil over the door or some other location in each room as an outward sign to the spirit realm that the family's faith and trust was in the Lord.

Then I gave him a copy of a prayer written by Rev. David Cotner titled *Parental Prayer Taking Authority Over Wicked Spirits In Their Child's Life*[48] and instructed him to pray it verbally over Jane nightly for about a week when she went to bed.

Some time later Jane's father called and stated he went home and did as instructed and they have had no additional problems in the home. Spiritual warfare!

Following are a few additional encounters we have had with buildings and the spirits who inhabit them. Our first experience was of course the home in Missouri written about in Chapter One pages four and five.

---

[47] Verbal prayer is needed when making a statement to the spirit realm because evil spirits cannot read our minds.

[48] For a copy of the prayer see Appendix A, page 143.

"We Bought a House Full of Spirits"

While traveling through the south during our annual June speaking tour several years ago, my wife and I were approached by a couple and asked to help with a situation they found themselves in.

David and Joan were strong Christians who were very involved in their local church. They bought a beautiful home but found themselves not very comfortable and happy living under its roof. Some time later they learned a pornography kingpin in their area had owned the home. Apparently much evil activity had taken place with drugs, pornography, and other various questionable activities. The decision was made to sell the home, but when it wouldn't sell they decided to do some remodeling thinking that might help. Friends began to help with the work but didn't feel "comfortable" and quickly stopped coming.

Both David and Joan believed there were evil spirits in the home but were hesitant to discuss the matter with their pastor or Christian friends. Would they be believed? Would they be labeled in some way? After discussing the matter with us, I told them there was a good possibility that there were evil spirits inhabiting the home due to the fact that apparently many sinful activities had taken place there. We agreed to meet at the home, which was now vacant, about 9:00 one evening.

Upon entering the house we began in the attic. David, Joan and I spent a couple hours working our way through every room, hallway, and closet claiming every area as a place where Christians could live and commanding the evil spirits to leave in the name of the Lord Jesus Christ.

Several weeks later, after we had returned to our home, I received a letter from David and Joan that contained a check for $300.00. They told how things had changed after the spirits had been dealt with that night. Their friends began once again helping with the remodeling and would ask what they had done to the house, that it "felt" different. In any event the house now sold quickly. They wanted to share the proceeds because they knew what was the real cause of the problems with the home. Friends not wanting to be there, and prospective buyers saying "no" was the result of demonic presence in the home and that night Jesus changed the climate of that house.

Evil Spirits in Churches

Can evil spirits be in churches? Absolutely! In addition to the evil spirit activity in the church I was pastoring, which I discussed in chapters three and four, I have two church experiences to share.

Satanic ritual abuse victims also suffer from Dissociative Identity Disorder. This has been previously discussed, but let me remind the reader that the bottom line is there are many alternate personalities who are capable of taking control of the body. When an alter personality is in control *(referred to as "executive control")* many are fully able to see in the spirit realm and tell us where the spirits are and whether they are demonic or angelic, bad or good.

I recall one evening I was going to be team leader in a counseling session with a ritual abuse victim to be held in the sanctuary of a Southern Baptist church about 25 miles from our town. I had instructed the pastor earlier in the day to be sure he went through the entire building removing any evil spirits before the session began that evening. He stated he would.

The church was an older building that contained a balcony in the back of the sanctuary with steps leading up to it. As the session began I asked one of the alter personalities who knew Jesus to take executive control of the woman's body. Once in control I asked the alter to look around and tell us if there were any evil spirits in the sanctuary where we were having the session. She slowly scanned the room and then said, "Yes, there are several in the balcony and a couple on the stairs." The pastor immediately just hung his head and said "Unbelievable." When asked, he explained how he had gone through the entire building just as I had instructed him. However, the sanctuary was the last area dealt with and by then he was getting tired and didn't specifically command the evil spirits to leave the area of the steps and balcony.

Evil spirits are very legalistic. Since the pastor didn't specifically say they couldn't inhabit the steps and balcony that is where they stayed.

We then went to the steps and balcony, dealt with the evil spirits, the alter personality confirmed they had left, and we continued the session.

"I Hope There Aren't Any in My Church"

In a very similar counseling session in another church in our area, the alter personality in executive control of the counselee's body pointed out evil spirits in one corner of the balcony and "the third pew back at the extreme left end." The pastor was a little surprised, (although when he read the manuscript of this book he wrote in the margin "I was not!") but on the other hand he had worked with the demonic before. We dealt with the spirit activity through the power of the Lord Jesus Christ and continued the session.

One way spirits may end up in a church building is through local satanic covens. Often a coven will appoint one of its members as a church plant. The individual will attend the church and leave some point of contact, an object that was dedicated to Satan. At other times a female plant may try to infiltrate the congregation by attending church activities with the ultimate plan to destroy the ministry of the church through sexual seduction of the pastor or other activity.

The Bible warns we are in spiritual warfare!

Chapter Fifteen

CLEANSING HOMES, CHURCHES, AND OTHER BUILDINGS

One night I received a call from a ritual abuse victim whom I had been counseling. It was a Satanist holiday and she stated that she was being told, by an evil spirit still within her soul that she was to go to a white house near a cemetery to meet with people who were just like her. However, she said that she thought she should call me first for some unknown reason (thank you Lord). I encouraged her to not go under any circumstances to which she hesitantly agreed. Obviously she was being lured to a home where a ceremony was going to take place on this holiday.

Consider the enormity of the spirit activity in that home as Satan was worshipped with sexual atrocities and possibly even human sacrifice taking place. Now consider that one day that home might be sold to an unsuspecting individual who will inherit much spirit activity in the building because of past sins in the house.

Or to a lesser degree consider an individual who had sold street drugs, engaged in pornographic activities, etc. in a home before it was sold to an unsuspecting buyer. An example of this has been described in the previous Chapter.

What can be done to help insure that there is no demonic activity in the home of a Christian? First of all renounce any known sin on your part. Secondly check regularly to see there are no points of contact for evil spirits in the home. Examples might include an Ouija Board, Dungeons & Dragons game, horror and X-rated videos, pornographic magazines, dream-catchers, occultic books and reading material, etc. which might draw the powers of evil into the home. And then pray through the house. I might suggest that the husband, as the head of the house, on a regular basis go through each room and area in the home and prayerfully claim the room as a place where Christians can live in peace and harmony. Then renounce any evil spirits and command them in the name of the Lord Jesus Christ who died on the cross of Calvary for our sins and rose again (be specific) to leave and go where the Lord Jesus would send them never to return. Do this aloud since evil spirits can place thoughts into our minds but cannot read our minds. Then ask God to honor the command in the spirit realm. Having prayed, place a small amount of olive oil over the door or in a conspicuous place in the room as an outward sign to the spirit realm of whom your faith is in. Placing Scripture in each room, such as a Bible, New Testament or in the form of a plaque, should also be considered.

The same procedure should be utilized by a Christian when using a motel. Who knows what has been done in the room you are renting for the night. There may be much lingering spirit activity. So protect yourself and your loved ones. Take the Gideon Bible out of the drawer, open it to an appropriate Scripture that relates to an area of personal attack, and place it on the night stand.[49]

Churches are not exempt from spirit activity. In fact there may be more evil spirits in a church building than one might imagine. Refer to chapters 3, 4 and 10 for examples. Regularly check the church for objects of unknown origin and remove them from the building. And then either the pastor or a deacon should regularly go from room to room verbally renouncing any forces of evil which may be present and claiming the facility as a place where Christians can meet and worship God in peace. Again I would place a small amount of olive oil in the form of a cross in each room or area as an outward sign to the spirit realm.

Other buildings that may be purchased and used by Christians in their businesses should also be "cleansed" on a regular basis.

---

[49] See Appendix C for Scriptures relating to personal attacks

Facing Evil
In Foreign
Countries

Chapter Sixteen
EXPERIENCES WITH EVIL IN
HAITI

The August 2006 medical trip to Cap Haitien in northern Haiti was amazing. I spent a week as spiritual leader of a team of 20 including doctors, medical students, a physician's assistant, dentists and dental students, a pharmacist and others who helped with logistics. During the week there were over 900 Haitians ministered to in the medical, dental and eyeglass clinics. We had set up our own pharmacy which gave out free prescription medications. There were 40 souls saved as a result of direct witnessing from the team itself. Much could be written about the trip but there were two experiences I would like to share in this book since, in my opinion, along with the salvation decisions they were the spiritual highlights of the project.

But before I share the experiences with the demonic let me take a moment to tell you how the Lord blessed even before we got to Haiti. The Wednesday before we left a member of our church gave me $500.00 cash in a white envelope and told me I would need that for Haiti. Many times people have given me extra money for needs that may come up during a mission trip. However, on Friday evening, the night before we were to leave, I received an e-mail from Haiti telling me that in order to get the large amount of medications into the country the director of customs at the airport said he would need $500.00 US in a white envelope. Otherwise the medications would be confiscated. This is somewhat typical of a third world country. So the Lord had known the need and provided for it even before we were aware of the need. $500.00 in a white envelope, God is amazing!

Demonized Woman in the Dental Chair

On Tuesday, as we were working and ministering at a clinic in Cap Haitien, one of the dentists sent word to me there was a demonized woman in his dental chair. When I got to the dental clinic the doctor told me that the woman had told him through his interpreter that she was now trusting Jesus as her Savior but was still plagued by generational spirits which were a result of her grandfather being a voodoo priest.

As I spoke with the woman she stated she wanted to be freed from the spirits. When I laid my hand on her forehead and started commanding the spirits she started flopping around in the dental chair like a fish fresh out of water. Two of the dentists came over and laid their hands on the woman too and as the commanding continued the woman was freed from the generational spirits for the first time in her life. The name Jesus is powerful beyond our comprehension.

A Mute Teenager is Loosed and Free

A woman brought her daughter to see a doctor, hoping beyond hope that an American doctor could help her teenager. The 17 year old daughter was mute, had never spoken, and appeared to be mentally retarded as she was led by her mother's hand into the clinic. Her head hanging low. The doctor was unable to do anything for the girl but decided to send her for prayer. My interpreter, Marie, and I sat down with the two of them. The mother stated the immediate family were Christians and attended church regularly. They also regularly read Scripture to their daughter. In the course of the conversation it was revealed by the mother that there was voodoo in the family background. With the thought that possibly she was bound by generational spirits, I asked the mother if she would mind if I did some commanding against any evil spirits that might be in the daughter's life. The mother agreed. After prayer I started commanding any generational spirits binding this girl to leave in the name of Jesus. Marie was translating what I was saying for the mother. After a few minutes the girl began to nod as though she understood what was going on. Finally I tried to speak to the girl about accepting Jesus Christ as her Savior. She nodded she wanted to trust in Him. I told her I would lead her through a sinner's prayer and I would keep stopping while Marie translated. If what I was saying was her will then she would need to just nod. About halfway through the prayer the girl began repeating verbally what Marie was translating to her. She was speaking for the first time. Her mother was praising God and was so happy and excited. At the end of the prayer the girl kept on speaking for several minutes and Marie told me she first of all thanked the Lord for her new life in Christ and then started quoting Scriptures, apparently Scriptures she had heard through the family reading to her for years. We all praised God for His grace and the mother and her daughter walked away bouncing on their feet. Apparently the generational spirits had this girl bound up. Once the spirits released her from the bondage she was able to speak, trust Jesus, and gain a new life in Christ. God is so gracious!

Haitian Woman Freed from Evil Spirits and Healed

As team leader of a Global Health Outreach medical/dental team in the Port-au-Prince area of Haiti in March 2007, during in-country orientation I had talked to the team about demonization and the generational curses connected with voodoo. They were instructed to be sensitive to anything that may not be medical, or if the person stated their problem was caused by spirits.

A few days later during the clinic one of the doctors had a woman who was having chest pain and a headache and upon examination he said she was suffering from atrial fibrillation. She told him her problem was not physical but was mystical.

Atrial fibrillation is a type of irregular heart beat in which the upper chambers of the heart beat irregularly and very rapidly (300 to 500 beats per minute). As a result the ventricles, or lower pumping chambers, beat irregularly at a rate of 80 to 160 beats per minute. Chest pain can be due to reduced blood supply.

The doctor sent for me and as I questioned the woman she stated she was now trusting Christ as her Savior but her background was in voodoo and she had seen a traditional doctor in the past. She said her problem was because of the spirits connected with the voodoo.

When asked, she indicated she wanted to be freed from the spirits and the generational curse. We had her lay down on the examining table so we would have more control if there were spirits fully manifesting. She agreed to allow me to lay hands on her and also agreed to repeat any commands to the spirits that I might say since the spirits and the generational curse belonged to her.

When I laid my hands on her forehead and chest the spirits immediately bound her so she could not hear or repeat the commands. The spirits were then bound to inactivity through the name and blood of Jesus and she was able to hear and speak again. As the commanding and work with the spirits continued she was finally freed from the generational curse and the associated spirits.

When she rose from the examining table she stated she no longer had the chest pains or the headache. The doctor then reexamined her and stated her heart was now normal. Another member of the team, a young medical student, was in the room with me while working with the spirits and he stated had he not witnessed the account he would not have believed it.

God is so gracious and gave victory in this woman's life.

As part of the medical/dental project there were evangelistic meetings each evening during which 31 additional people were freed from the spirits and generational curses connected with voodoo as well as 10 salvation decisions.

Chapter Seventeen

A COOL BREEZE AND
AN EVIL SPIRIT
IN CAMEROON, WEST AFRICA

The day began, as every day had, with the sun shining brightly, the tropical flowers in full bloom, and the native people going about their morning chores. We were in the mountains of Cameroon, West Africa ministering among the Bafut people group in a rural area about seventy five miles north of Yaoundé, Cameroon's Capital. Although the sun was shining brightly, the monsoon rains would begin as they did daily after lunch.

I was working for two weeks as a Christian counselor for a medical, dental team of Christian doctors from across the United States & Canada. The first week I was involved primarily with counseling young mothers who had brought their babies in to see the doctors, some walking for hours through the mountains, only to find that both they and the babies were HIV positive and eventually would die of AIDS. In this region HIV was a death sentence due to lack of any type of drugs. Polygamy was legal in Cameroon and additionally the men were very promiscuous which allowed for an almost unrestrained spread of HIV/AIDS.

Shortly after arriving that morning at the counseling tent, two women and their babies were sitting in front of me. They had just been diagnosed with

HIV and it was my job to answer their questions and counsel them about trusting Christ as their Savior and obtaining eternal life before it was eternally too late. The clock was ticking for them and time was running out.

As we sat there I offered the two women some peanut butter crackers I had brought with me from the States. Having never tasted peanut butter crackers, they were thankful and ate with excitement. Then one of the young women pulled a cooked root from an elephant ear plant and offered it to me in exchange. Every part of my being said "don't eat it," but after all they had eaten what I had offered.

I ate the root and for the next three days I was confined to my bunk suffering from dehydration due to a *close personal relationship I was having with a piece of porcelain.* The dehydration was severe enough that the medical team had intravenous bags hanging above my bunk feeding my body. I had become so dehydrated the doctors could not find a vein to start the IV's but an oral surgeon who was part of the team finally did find a vein.

That event, although very uncomfortable, was well worth the discomfort. For both of the women did ultimately trust Christ as their Savior that day in the counseling tent. Two women who had been facing only a couple more years of life when they entered the tent now were looking forward to eternal life.

Returning to the counseling tent several days later I found myself being called upon to minister to a teenage girl brought in by her mother and pastor. The girl had been ill and her mother had taken her to a "traditional doctor" for help. The "traditional doctor," connected with the traditional religion, performed some type of ceremony on her which resulted in her becoming demonized.

The clinic room she had been place in was extremely small. It was just large enough to fit a small cot and two chairs. I was directed to one of those chairs next to the cot where the girl was lying. With me in this small room was her mother, the pastor, and a psychiatrist from the United States. There was also a small window allowing a faint circulation of air into the room.

The spirits became agitated as we prayed and I stated some commands in the name of the Lord Jesus. The spirits would manifest and growl and spit at us. At one point a spirit manifested, literally taking control of the girl, and ripped a small wooden cross and chain off the neck of the pastor.

As the growling and screaming picked up a crowd began to gather around the window so it had to be closed. Now the room, which had been just bearable in the heat, was so hot I started becoming faint and had to leave the session for a few minutes. One of the Cameroonian pastors saw me outside the room and had prayer with me asking the Lord to give me a cool breeze in that room that I might finish the work I had come to do with this girl.

Upon reentering the room I continued commanding and working with the spirits, but unlike before, a cool breeze blew continuously on the back of my neck. No window! No fan! No movement! Just God!

What did I experience that day? The blessings of the Lord and a young woman delivered.

The Lord is so gracious!

Dealing with Evil in Everyday Life
Or
Practical Ways to Lick the Lion

Chapter Eighteen

CHRISTIANS PROTECTING OURSELVES

We must learn to protect ourselves from demonic attacks. However, in today's society in the United States, even we as Christians often do not consider demonic attacks as a possible cause for some of the personal problems we face. As a result we do not take the action needed against the forces of evil that may come against us. With this in mind we need to become more aware of some of the ways Christians come under demonic attack.

The Physical Body

Scripture clearly teaches that evil spirits have the ability to attack the human body in many ways, especially through disease. In Matthew 9:32-33 we are told, *While they were going out, a man who was demon-possessed and could not talk was brought to Jesus. And when the demon was driven out, the man who had been mute spoke. The crowd was amazed and said, "Nothing like this has ever been seen in Israel."* And then in Luke 13 there is the story of a crippled woman who was healed on the Sabbath. And the Scriptures quote Jesus as saying in verse 16, *Then should not this woman, a daughter of Abraham, whom Satan has kept bound for eighteen long years, be set free on the Sabbath day from what bound her?* Obviously from the words of Jesus this was an attack on the human body by evil spirits.

I certainly am not going to suggest that all physical problems are demonic in source. However, I do suggest that more physical problems have demonic involvement than we as Christians care to consider. So often our mindset is that evil spirits can't do anything to Christians.

When we find ourselves ill, we need to obey what the Scriptures tell us? In James 5:14 and 15 we are instructed, *Is any one of you sick? He should call the elders of the church to pray over him and anoint him with oil in the name of the Lord. And the prayer offered in faith will make the sick person well; the Lord will raise him up. If he has sinned, he will be forgiven.* In addition to daily putting on the armor of God and praying against spirit attacks, Christians need to consider calling the elders of the church in accord with the book of James as important as calling the physician?

Not only can our physical bodies come under attack, but also our physical appetites. As we view our world today there is no doubt Satan and his forces of evil are making an all-out attack in the area of both sexual appetites and compulsive eating disorders even among the Christian community.

The Bible states we must contend for the flesh. When we allow Satan and his forces to take advantage of the flesh, we find ourselves under more pressure than we are capable of handling in our "normal" Christian experience. We must use spiritual weapons to destroy such strongholds of the enemy. In prayer we must resist all strongholds of sexual perverseness assigned to rule over us and we must command them to cease all activity and leave forever to go where the Lord Jesus Christ would send them.

There are specific prayers that can be utilized to remove demonic harassment and demonic influence and I would suggest "Spiritual Warfare Prayers" by Mark I. Bubeck, a folder published by Moody Press and available through your local Christian Bookstore.

Attacks on the Soul

The human psyche, especially the mind, is the real battlefield in most cases. We must realize that evil spirits can and do act on the thoughts, affections, emotions, desires and imaginations. When they find an active passion within our soul, they work upon and intensify the particular passions and fantasies. When an evil spirit sees me having an emotional or mental problem he would be a fool not to try to complicate it. Although my own desires start the process, Satan and his forces then take advantage of the struggle going on inside myself and intensify my thoughts. Therefore, I must be aware and ready to deal with my part of the problem as I also deal with the enemy. Sometimes an evil spirit will put a thought into our mind and then accuse us of having it ourselves. He then tells us if we were such good Christians, why would we think such a thought. Beware of the onset of attacks in our soul.

Attacks Because of Involvement in Innocent Looking Occult Practices

Beware of what we involve ourselves in. The following is but a partial list of proven involvements through which we can come under heavy demonic attack and even demonization itself.[50]

Acupuncture, Apport Magic, Astrology, Horoscopes, Astral Projection (Soul Travel), Blood Pacts, Channeling, Color Diagnosis/Therapy, Curses or Spells, Conversations with Spirits or Spirit Guides, Divining Rods, Dungeons & Dragons, Eastern Religions, Palm Reading, Crystal Ball, Halloween Participation, Healing Fanaticism, Pow-Wowing, Congering, Root Work, Numerology, Hypnotism *(for ANY reason)*, Levitation and Table or Body Lifting, "Light as a Feather - Stiff as a Board," Black Magic, White Magic, Magic Eight Ball, "Magic - The Gathering" Cards, Magnetism, Ouija Board, Predictive Dreams, Pendulum (used to tell fortunes or determine sex of an unborn child), Relations with Sexual Spirits, Satan Worship, Roy Masters, Silva Mind Control, Some Speaking in Tongues, Tarot Card Laying, Telepathy, Water Witching, Yoga, to name a few. Flee from these things and if you have had past involvement, repent and forsake.

Attacks Because of Sin

Sometimes attacks come because of unconfessed personal sin. Among the sins that do the most damage would be unforgiveness. When we choose not to forgive another we are choosing to allow someone other than the Lord Jesus Christ to be in control of our life. We choose to be a victim when our Lord's will is for us to be set free. Unforgiveness allows the forces of evil to take ground in the area of our soul and to build a stronghold from which they can operate. We are warned in Ephesians 4: 27, *"do not give the devil a foothold."*

After forgiveness we may continue to hurt. It exists and will not go away by just wishing. However, we must choose not to allow the hurt to control our lives. Turn the hurt over to God and let Him deal with it. He is faithful.

Be careful of Satan's lie that says because you have forgiven and still feel

---

[50] See appendix B page 145 for an explanation of many of these occult practices.

the hurt you have not really forgiven at all.   Other frequent sins include rebellion, pride and other fleshly sins.

Attacks due to Ancestral Sin

Many of the people we have counseled have had some amount of bondage due to ancestral sin.

In Exodus 20:5 we are told that *I, the Lord your God, am a jealous God, punishing the children for the sin of the fathers to the third and fourth generation of those who hate me.* He said the sins of the fathers are visited upon the children to the third and fourth generation. Then He goes on to say in verse 6, *"but showing love to a thousand generations of those who love me and keep my commandments.* One generation lives with the effects of the good or bad done by the previous generation. We see this every day in the physical realm. A child is born to parents who have AIDS, or have been on drugs and becomes an innocent victim of the sins of the parents.

The same holds true in the ream of the spiritual. If a parent gives up ground to evil spirits through unconfessed sin in their lives then evil spirits claim the right to harass the children of that person. The child is not guilty of the parents' sin but still suffers sins consequences, which must be dealt with.

Past generational sins must be renounced along with claiming back the ground given through these sins.

Please understand that although I am not suggesting that all problems are demonic, I am suggesting that demonic activity in our lives is a component in more problems that we have been willing to recognize and deal with in the past. Although the problems will almost always have a foundation in our human experience, the forces of evil will take advantage of those experiences and intensify them and make it seem as though they are unsolvable.   The assumption that the church has held that believers have automatic protection from the forces of evil has been proven to be wrong over and over again. Every defeat in this area has meant the enemy has won another battle in our spiritual warfare.

Spiritual warfare begins with demonstrating power through the Lord Jesus to meet the problems and needs in our own lives. Winning on the personal level is the first step to being able to help others in their spiritual warfare.

Chapter Nineteen

PROTECTING OUR CHILDREN

While conducting a spiritual warfare seminar at a church in the Midwest, the pastor gave me a hand written note a little girl had put in a prayer box. The note read: *Dear God: I am having trouble at home. Well not really at home it's like someone's living inside my brain and it tells me things I don't want to hear and stuff I don't want to do. I can't control it. I've never told my parents but I might."* This little girl was under attack but was not sure whether she could tell her parents.

Many times a small child will awake a parent in the middle of the night stating there is a "bad man in my room" or "there's someone under my bed." And all too often our response is "there's no one in your room, now go back to bed." In reality the child may have encountered an evil spirit but the parents have just ensured the child will not tell them again. What should parents do when confronted with a similar situation? A parent should say to the child "if there is a bad man in your room then I know who can take care of him for you." Then the parent should go put the child back in bed and verbally pray "dear Jesus, thank you for this little one. I now ask you to protect my child through this night, and if there are any bad men present then I command all of them in the name of my Savior Jesus and by the power of His holy blood to leave this place now.

When this approach is taken parents find the child sleeps soundly through the remainder of the night, faith in Jesus is demonstrated and taught, the spirit realm is defeated once again, and the child will not hesitate to share with the parents in the future.

Spiritual discernment appears to be at an all time low in both the Church and our western world culture. Christian parents too often are failing to develop the needed critical faculties concerning the enticements of the world toward our children. There are many forms of evil masquerading as harmless, innocent fun, and since most of the evil is popular and entertaining it is often accepted with little or no evaluation or criticism. Yet in God's Holy Word Paul instructs us in 1 Thessalonians 5:21-22 to *test everything. Hold on to the good. Avoid every kind of evil.* In John 7:24 Jesus warned the undiscerning people of His day to *stop judging by mere appearances, and make a right judgment.* Unfortunately right judgments about popular culture are rare today, even in the church.

Our children are under attack and in danger. The Bible is clear about issues such as witchcraft, demons, and the occult and tells us clearly from Genesis to Revelation that they are real, powerful, and dangerous. Throughout, the Bible insists that God's people should have nothing to do with them.

During presentations to youth groups in local churches I have anonymously surveyed 211 teenagers, as of this printing, with some shocking results:

45% say they have experienced a "presence" in their room that scared them.

60% say they have harbored bad thoughts about God.

40% find it mentally hard to read their Bible and pray.

70% report hearing "voices" in their mind talking to them.

20% frequently entertain thoughts of suicide

What's happening? Why does it appear our youth are under attack from the spirit realm? Clearly part of the problem is due to the amount of occult activity in which they find themselves involved. In this chapter we will discuss some allurements for our children and teens that have occult themes.

Harry Potter

Harry Potter is a fantasy novel series written by J.K. Rowling. The books detail Harry's mystical adventures as a wizard in training at Hogwart's School of Witchcraft & Wizardry. As of January 2001 the craze over Harry Potter had put 90 million books in print in over 43 languages in 200 countries.

It is extremely common for Harry Potter books to be read to students during class time in schools in spite of the fact that the Potter series favors morally flawed characters who lie and somehow justify it, practice occult techniques, use profanity and frequently depict violence. In some schools teachers decorate their classrooms to look like various locations in Harry's world. Others have designed learning experiences based on the books and even encouraged students to create Harry Potter games and activities. Major publishers have released study books and classroom discussion guides designed to help teachers lead students through "the origins and mysteries of Harry's world"[51] including the occult themes.

Nearly every area of occultism is thinly disguised in the series including alchemy, astrology, spells, mediumship, and other occultic practices. There are numerous books written on witchcraft and the occult for children, but none appears to be as ingeniously packaged to attract children like the Harry Potter series.

The Harry Potter books desensitize both children and adults to the forbidden and dangerous world of pagan occult magic spoken of in the Scriptures. And let us not forget the Scriptures remind us that we are in spiritual warfare and that Christians should have nothing to do with such practices.

We need to remember the warning of Jesus when He said in Matthew 18:5, 6, *and whoever welcomes a little child like this in my name welcomes me. But if anyone causes one of these little ones who believe in me to sin, it would be better for him to have a large millstone hung around his neck and to be drowned in the depths of the sea.*

Is it possible that the real Harry Potter is an evil spirit? The author, J.K. Rowling stated that in 1990, while traveling on a train, she suddenly saw Harry *"very, very clearly"* in her mind. He just came into her thoughts out of nowhere as a *"fully formed individual...Harry just strolled into my head...I really did feel he was someone who walked up and introduced himself in my mind's eye. I have no idea why he chose to come to me.'*[52]

Many who try to justify their children reading the books say that it is just

---

51 Beacham's Sourcebook: Exploring Harry Potter, Beacham Publishing, Osprey FL, Section VI

52 Quoted in Reuter's *"Harry Potter Strolled into My Head,"* July 17, 2000. Additionally, Interview on the Diane Rehm Show, WAMU, National Public Radio, October 20,1999

fantasy and there is no real occultism to the books. However, Ms. Rowling admits that approximately one-third of what she has written is based on actual occultism. Some scenes are not only based on reality, but often are also described using details taken word for word from sorcery and witchcraft.[53]

The underlying messages children are receiving as they read the Harry Potter books are that lying, stealing and cheating are not only acceptable, but can also be fun. Occult activities and performing "magick" can be exciting. Disobedience is not very serious if you don't get caught. Adults are Muggles who just get in the way most of the time. Rules are made to be broken. Being "special" means you deserve to escape punishment when you behave badly. And finally, revenge is an acceptable course of action.

In Deuteronomy 18:10-12 God instructs us to *let no one be found among you who sacrifices his son or daughter in the fire, who practices divination or sorcery, interprets omens, engages in witchcraft, or casts spells, or who is a medium or spiritist or who consults with the dead. Anyone who does these things is detestable to the Lord...* Concerning vengeance in the Harry Potter books God says in Leviticus 19:18 *Do not seek vengeance...Love your neighbor as yourself."* And in Romans 12:17-18,21 God says *Do not repay anyone evil for evil...if it is possible, as far as it depends on you...Do not be overcome with evil, but overcome evil with good.* God stands opposed to the contents of the Harry Potter books and we need to guide our children accordingly. We are instructed to overcome evil with good.

Everquest

Everquest is a computer role-playing game requiring an Internet connection and a paid monthly membership. There are various versions. At our local Wal-Mart I looked at an Everquest package titled *Everquest, The Scars of Velious*, which has an industry game rating of T (Teen). The packaging notes state there is animated blood and gore, animated violence, and suggestive themes. The back of this particular game states "Hundreds of new magical items to discover, trade and sell."

In the Everquest series there is violence that involves the use of axes and swords to kill, the casting of spells and throwing curses to kill opposing members, and a classic cyber world where nobody will stop you from killing other players. The chat feature allows the player to communicate with his team

---

[53] J.K. Rowling, interview on The Diane Rehm Show, WAMU, National Public Radio, October 20, 1999

and opponents often resulting in sexual harassment between players, cyber stalking, and profanity.

Magick and the occult are numerous. The player must acquire magic skills to have a chance of winning. For many players the "quest" is to attain more and more magical power and use it on those in the real world.

Included are generous amounts of nearly naked female characters. Young boys and men are being exposed to barely-dressed women at every turn and fighting and killing them when given a chance. Psychologists warn about mixing sex and violence, especially with impressionable young ones.

With the interactive chat going on between players, not only is there much profanity and sexual harassment, but the chat rooms can be entered by adult predators to converse with children. Children already pumped up by the sexy violence flooding the screen.

Everquest needs to be avoided for its violence, occultism, mature content, and chat room dangers.

Pokemon

The name Pokemon is derived from "**pocket monster**" and was originated by Wizards of the Coast, the same company that made the "Magic – The Gathering" and "Dungeons & Dragons." Although viewed by many as just a group of collector cards, in reality it is a fantasy role-playing game complete with rulebook.

What values, beliefs and philosophies does this game promote? What kind of values do the characters have? Although popular, should we allow our children to be involved in Pokemon.

Ash Ketchum, a boy, is one of the main characters. He is portrayed as an energetic and determined 10 year-old, a little too competitive, obsessed with catching all Pokemon, and driven to become the world's foremost Pokemon Master. Misty, Ash's companion, is portrayed as headstrong and stubborn and constantly quibbling with Ash. Brock, by far the most hormonal, has a fascination with the opposite sex which many times gets him in trouble. However, we are told as yet he's not had anything resembling a "score." Gary, a Pokemon trainer, is described as a real jerk, self-centered, vindictive, and obnoxious. Jessie & James are described as a mysterious and evil gang who are stuck up, fashion conscious, and prone to cross-dressing.

Now let's ask ourselves. Are headstrong, stubborn, quibbling, hormonal, fascination with the opposite sex, jerk, self-centered, vindictive, obnoxious, evil, stealing, stuck-up and prone to cross-dressing biblical values we want our children to portray. No! These characters do not portray biblical values and are not biblical role models. Pokemon does not measure up.

Pokemon has supernatural powers. Some Pokemon evolve or grow. This happens through energy cards that "make your Pokemon bigger and more powerful." The source of this power is the pantheistic power of the occult, not he supernatural power of God. Among the cards that make this very clear are the Abra and Kadabra cards. Abrakadabra has long been associated with occult magick. The dictionary defines it thus: 1) a word supposed to have magic powers and hence used in incantations, or amulets, etc. 2) a magic spell or formula. It is no accident that in Pokemon, Abra and Kadabra are psychic cards with magical powers. On the Abra card it states: "Using its ability to read minds, it will identify impending danger and teleport to safety." Then there are the occult symbols on the Kadabra card.

How long will it be before a grade school child tries to do what is written on the Weepingbell-Razor Leaf Pokemon card. "It spits out poisonpowder to immobilize the enemy, and then finishes the enemy with a spray of acid." This statement does not line up with what the Bible has to say about how to handle our enemies in Romans 12:14-22.

It is clear that Pokemon leads the player down the wrong path. In Romans 12:9 the Bible teaches that we are to *hate what is evil; cling to what is good.* Poisoning and paralyzing your enemy is clearly evil.

Magic – The Gathering

Magic–The Gathering is a series of collectable cards. The cover of the Revised Edition Rule Book calls it "a fantasy trading card game." There are many other major editions to the Magic game with "The Gathering" being only one. The games popularity has grown rapidly since the first edition in 1993.

Each player takes the role of the wizard of Dominia, a being that wanders the multiple planes and dimensions of existence in search of power.

When two wizards clash they duel it out by drawing upon their five sources (or colors) of magic powers (mana) to conjure creatures to fight against their foe. They also cast spells on themselves which is usually considered helpful, and against their foes or their foe's creatures, lands, and artifacts. Finally, they will employ artifacts ("magically powered objects") to channel magical energy for their use with the duel continuing until one wizard is dead.

All *Magic* cards come in one of two types, *land* cards and *spell* cards. The *spell* cards can be further divided into three subtypes; spells that summon creatures, spells that directly affect creatures and surroundings, and spells which conjure up artifacts. Both *land* and *spell* cards are used in combat. The *land* cards provide a source of power and the *spell* cards do the work.

Most *Magic* cards can be put in one of the following categories: combat and violence, magic spells, the real occult, life and death, spiritism (worship or communication with supposed spirits of the dead), necromancy (spirits of the dead are summoned), divination, and sacrifice.

According to the rules of *Magic* a sacrifice is a "cost that can not be prevented. In the context of playing the game this is the killing of a summoned being rather human, demi-human, or animal, to gain power or advantage. And in no other game does there appear to be as much sacrificing as in *Magic*.

Magic is a game rich in principles diametrically opposed to those set forth in the Bible. In fact common sense points out the dangers. We must remember the old adage "garbage in, garbage out."

Rock, Heavy Metal, Black Metal and Death Metal Music

Current themes tell us much about the dangers to our children listening to this type of secular music.

Rock music's current themes are:

Love – Sex

Drugs & Alcohol

Racism & Bigotry

Graphic Violence & Death

Rebellion and/or Aggression

Fascination with the Occult.

Heavy Metal & Black Metal themes are:

The Death of God

Sex with Corpses

Human Sacrifice

Sitting at Satan's Left Hand

Calling Jesus Christ the Deceiver

Glorifying the Name of Satan

Death Metal themes are:

Satanism

Torture

Murder

Rape

Suicide

Self-Mutilation

Anti-Christian

Not only is this type of music dangerous to our mental/emotional and spiritual well-being, but it can also be dangerous to the body. Dr. Adam Knieste, a musicologist who studies the effects of music upon people noted: "It's really a powerful drug. Music can poison you, lift your spirits, or make you sick without knowing why."[54]

David Tame states that "investigation has shown that music affects digestion, internal secretions, circulation, nutrition and respiration. Even the neural networks of the brain have been found to be sensitive to harmonic principles.[55]

And rock music can literally kill. The view that music is amoral or neutral with no power to effect is proven completely false by extensive research

---

[54] Family Weekly Magazine, January 30, 1983, p. 12, article by David Chagill.

[55] Tame, David, *The Secret Power of Music*,p. 136

performed on plant life. Rock music played to plants will kill plants. Soothing classical type music causes the plants to grow twice as fast.

What can parents do to help their children? First of all what are you as a parent listening to? One of the best ways to teach your child to avoid harmful music and lyrics is by modeling the same behavior, and teach your child to be discerning based on biblical standards.

When was the last time you looked through your child's collection of tapes and CD's, or sat down with them to listen to and discuss the lyrics of their favorite songs? You won't be able to understand the impact of the music on your child's life unless you are aware of it and what your child thinks about it. Remember that 1 Thessalonians 5:21 encourages us to examine everything carefully.

Consider reading Philippians 4:8 and then read with your child the lyrics of some of their favorite songs. Which songs fit the guidelines of this biblical principle? Which songs don't fit these guidelines? Why?

And don't forget, Country and Rap music have some dangerous lyrics too.

Teenage Fashions

As we have all noticed, some of today's teen fashions seem to encourage a step into the darkness to meet the needs of an inner struggle for acceptance and identity. There are stores in our malls and communities where over 95% of the items sport satanic and occultic symbols. Even some major department and discount stores are carrying these fashions. Many teens are searching for the hottest "evil-looking" article to help them gain acceptance with the crowd at school.

There are dangers in allowing our children to wear fashions decorated with satanic and occultic symbols. First of all the symbols represent values and a lifestyle that is contrary to the things of God. Secondly, in their desperate attempt to change their lives and overcome the pain of day-to-day living, many youth will try to experiment with these symbols to see if there really is any power to them. And those who play around with the occult often find more than they had bargained for.

Some of our youth today dress in black and often go so far as to dye their hair black, wear pale make-up accented with dark colors, and pain their fingernails black. Those who are obsessed with black may be mirroring an unhealthy inner fascination with darkness and may be subconsciously crying out for help.

A Sampling of Additional Games with Occult Themes to Avoid

Electronic Games

Nintindo

Ogre Battle 64

Aidyn Chronicles

Video

Alien Resurrection

DinoCrisis 2

Darkstone

Gameboy

Buffy the Vampire Slayer

Sega

Nightmare Creatures

Computer

Sacrifice

Summoner

Vampire: The Masquerade

Vampire: The Dark Ages

Werewolf: The Apocalypse

Werewolf: The Reckoning

Aberrant

World of Darkness

Wraith: The Oblivion

Wraith: The Sorcerer's Crusade

Changeling: The Dreaming

Trinity

Board Games

Nightmare on Elm Street

Tunnels & Trolls

Bloody Mary

Dungeons & Dragons

I Ching

Tea Leaves

Chivalry & Sorcery

Ouija Board

Runne Quest

Arduin Grimoire

Swordbearers

Collectable Card Games

Blood Wars

Dark Force

Doom Trooper

Flights of Fantasy

Guardians

Harry Potter

Heresy: Kingdom Come

Highlander

Hyborian Gates

Illuminati: New World Order

Jyhad

Kabal

Kult

Legends of the Five Rings

Magic

Middle Earth: The Wisards

On the Edge

OverPower

Pokemon

Rage: The Warewolf

Shadowfist

Spellfire: Master of Magic

Starwars

Tempest of the gods

Tower of Time

Wizard

Wyver

Thoughts to Consider

Where is Satan going to attack and what are we to do? Our Lord has been so gracious once again in answering that question for us. In the sixth chapter of the book of Ephesians, after explaining that we are in spiritual warfare, in verses 14 through 18 the Lord tells us what armor to put on. Let's consider this for a moment.

Satan will attack our truth

So we put on the Belt of Truth.

Satan will attack our righteousness

So we put on the Breastplate of the Righteousness of Christ.

Satan will attack our fears

So we stand on the Solid Rock by putting on the Shoes of the Gospel of Peace.

Satan will attack our feelings & emotions

So we put on the Shield of Faith.

Satan will attack our doubts and question our salvation

So we put on the Helmet of Salvation.

Satan will attack our intellect
So we take the Sword of the Spirit, God's Word, and go on the attack.

Satan will attack our will, which is our strength for battle
So we pray.

And so dear Christian, let's wake up and recognize the spiritual warfare we are engaged in, put on the whole armor of God, be sober and vigilant but not fearful, and

VICTORIOUSLY FIGHT THE FORCES OF EVIL

APPENDIX A

**MANY OF THESE DEFINITIONS DEAL WITH OCCULT BACK
GROUND. THEIR MEANINGS MAY MEAN SOMETHING ELSE
IN OTHER CONTEXTS.**

A

ACUPUNCTURE: Acupuncture is an occult practice. It is an ancient
Chinese treatment dating back several thousand years. The term means, "to
puncture with a needle" *(acus:* needle, and *punctura:* puncture*).* The treatment
involves the inserting of fine needles into the body at various points, which are
revolved or left in place for a certain period of time. Needles normally range
from one to ten inches in length and are made of gold, silver, platinum, or of
steel. Acupuncture is used to relieve pain, to anaesthetize a patient during
surgery, and to treat conditions ranging from arthritis to digestive problems.

Advocates of acupuncture explain that the process operates with reference to
the human nervous system. Directly under the skin is a widespread network of
nerves (autonomic nervous system) which receives and passes on impulses from
the deeper parts of the body (the organs, brain, muscles, and bones). When an
impulse comes from a diseased organ an alarm is felt at the nerve endings in the
skin, or at some other point in the body. For instance, a heart attack causes
pain to be felt in the left arm, and so on. The most important strands (or
channels) of the network of nerves run along what are called "meridians"; it is
on these that the majority of acupuncture points lie.

A needle inserted in the toe, for instance, may cure a certain type of headache,
we are told. A disease of an internal organ (kidney, prostate gland) can cause
some pain to arise in another part of the body ("referral pain"). In acupuncture
the process is reversed. A needle is put into the sensitive (referred) spot where
the pain is felt. The autonomic nervous system is stimulated, the impulse then
goes to the brain, and from there to the diseased organ which is relieved of
pain.

There are said to be literally hundreds of acupuncture points which form 12 groups that are associated with one of 12 major internal organs (e.g., liver, heart, kidneys, stomach, etc.). These 12 groups run along a hypothetical line known as a "meridian." Each meridian joins specific areas of the skin which may be reached by a needle.

The question is whether or not acupuncture should be classified as occult.

Many medical authorities contend that acupuncture is merely a part of Chinese folk medicine which seems to bear no relation to the human nervous system; it does, however, seem to have a powerful psychological effect upon the individual which could be likened to *self-hypnosis*. In an attempt to dispel the hypnosis theory, advocates of the treatment allege that in China acupuncture has been successfully used on animals. According to another medical source, acupuncture is said to have often failed in anesthesia and is not reliable. In some instances other forms of anesthesia, such as Phenobarbital and morphine, are used in conjunction with acupuncture. It should be noted also that many Chinese doctors with modern medical training share in this skepticism concerning the validity of acupuncture.

The practice of acupuncture raises serious questions as to its exact nature, however, because of its pagan religious and philosophical associations. The treatment is based upon the pagan cosmic principle of *Yin* and *Yang* from ancient China. In the Oriental pseudoscience of acupuncture there is the idea of the need of maintaining the balance of vital energy and vital source of Yin and Yang in the body. Yin and Yang, according to Chinese philosophy, constitute the male and female cosmic forces in the universe from which everything derives its existence. This ancient Oriental philosophy teaches that this cosmic duality is also expressed as good and evil, pleasure and pain, hot and cold, and so on. In the healing system of acupuncture the key to life and health is the maintenance of harmony between Yin and the Yang within the body. By inserting needles along the network of meridians that connect the 12 vital organs, the acupuncturist seeks to bring the flow of vital energy back to its normal balance.

The Chinese explain it all in terms of the Yin and the Yang principle from their ancient pagan philosophy. As one author observes, acupuncture, which began as a folk method of healing, developed its own *occult mystique,* some of which is still connected with the healing process. In addition to the Yin and Yang philosophy there is found in the practice of acupuncture a stress upon the mystique of key numbers (e.g., 5 and 12), mystical ideas and concepts (such as "cosmic harmony," the "Gate of Life," the *chi* force), and the use of pulse diagnosis. Acupuncturists who are adept at pulse diagnosis frequently are able not only to diagnose present ailments (by reading 12 pulses serving 12 organs, not simply the wrist pulse), but can also look into the past and discover previous ailments. All this has caused some occultists to surmise that acupuncture seems to have a *psychic dimension* somewhat in common with that of clairvoyants and mediums with ESP powers. Some suggest the acupuncturist has a psychic gift enabling him to discern vibrations from the pulse that would go unrecognized by others.

The Chinese doctors, moreover, are often Buddhists and the forces of darkness operate through the whole process. *Acupuncture definitely has occult associations.* In view of all this, enlightened Christians will not resort to questionable methods of healing derived from heathen sources, but will rely on the provision of healing in Christ's atonement (Isaiah 53 with Matthew 8:16-17; Mark 16:18; James 5:14-16).

AKASHIC RECORDS: In occultism said to be cosmic records in the form of scenic representations of every thought, word, or action which has taken place since the world began. These records are believed to contain the complete activities of every being, as well as every event in minute detail both past and present. This theory is often advanced as the method by which psychics and clairvoyants receive the hidden information about a person or event. Some, as Edgar Cayce and Arthur Ford, were said to have had access to these "records" to a remarkable degree. They are supposed to have availed themselves of the information in these records while in a state of trance. The advocates of the unscriptural doctrine of reincarnation also contend that consultations of these records can be made in order to discover one's alleged "past lives," and the present "debt of Karma" he is working out in his present life.

Actually, such information is derived from demonic sources. Deceiving spirits generally have considerable knowledge of the past and present, or have supernatural means of obtaining it, and they seduce the gullible by supplying them with information (both true and false) from these supposed "Akashic Records."

ALMANAC: The term *almanac* (or almanack) is derived from the Arabic, meaning "timetable or calendar of the heavens." Almanacs in one form or another date from ancient times and have occult associations. The occult nature of almanacs in general is found in their reliance upon astrology, the influence of the zodiac upon human life and agriculture, moon phase weather forecasting, the lunar superstitions concerning planting and gardening, folklore, lucky numbers and days, fortunetelling, charms, and many other superstitions.

Some scientific and factual information can be found in the pages of most almanacs, such as tables of annual eclipses, tidal information, table of weight and measures, and cooking recipes. However, Christians should refrain from using almanacs because of their occult nature which could possibly have adverse influences upon those who read them.

ALPHABETS (OCCULT): Many forms of writing are utilized in the occult. Sample forms of alphabets are shown in beginning on page 103. In addition to these samplers, you should be aware that spirit writing, writing backwards, symbolic writing and writings uniquely characteristic to a particular group may be used. Variations to any alphabet may also occur.

AMULET, CHARM, FETISH, GOOD-LUCK SYMBOL, TALISMAN: A supposed preservative against sickness, accident, witchcraft, and evil spirits or demons. Amulets consist of precious stones, gems, gold, and sometimes of parchment written over with some inscription. They have been widely used from remote antiquity. They are usually worn as earrings, or as a necklace. The English word "Amulet" does not occur in Scripture, but the word "charms"; Isaiah 3:30 (NIV) is generally understood to have the meaning of amulets. They also formed the part of the trappings which Jacob commanded his household to put away in Genesis 35:4 (rings in the ear).

APPORT MAGIC: The transference of objects through closed doors or sealed containers by means of the penetration of matter. Supernatural appearances and disappearances of material images in connection with the activities of a Spiritistic Medium.

ASTRAL OR SOUL TRAVEL: The practice of sending your soul on an out-of-body journey to distant places to discover hidden things. This is a common practice among more advanced New Age and Eastern religion practitioners and Spiritistic Mediums.

ASTROLOGY: An ancient art or pseudoscience which claims to forecast events on earth, human character, and man's fate by observation of the fixed stars and of the sun, moon, and planets.

AURA: An apparent envelope or field of colored radiation said to surround the human body and other animate objects, with the color or colors indicating different aspects of the person's physical, psychological, and spiritual conditions (see also Kirilian). The human aura, according to psychics, consists of a series of seven layers of radiation (emanations of light) surrounding the body. These emanations may be compared to the heat waves radiating from a stove, or the light rays surrounding a street lamp at night. The aura is said to reveal the physical, mental, emotional, and spiritual condition of an individual. Man, according to occult belief, consists of seven principles: physical body; astral body; vital force; instinctive mind; intellect; spiritual mind; and spirit. Each of these principles supposedly sends forth energy in the form of emanations of various colors of light (the aura), and is designated as the "health" aura, the "astral" aura, and so on.

AUSTROMANCY: Divination by studying the winds.

AUTOEROTIC ASPHYXIATION / AUTOEROTIC STIMULATION: The sinful practice of inducing cerebral anoxia, usually by means of self-applied ligatures or suffocating devices, while the individual masturbates to orgasm. Of the various types of abnormal sexual behavior probably the most bizarre and dangerous is autoerotic asphyxiation, also known as sexual hanging.

Some breath control advocates say that what they do is acceptably safe because they do not take what they do to the point of unconsciousness. But with asphyxiation it is hard to tell when a person is about to be unconscious until they actually become so. Therefore it's extremely difficult to know when the actual point of unconsciousness will occur until it is reached and the person is asphyxiated. So then why do people practice autoerotic asphyxiation? Because they report that when the asphyxiation starts to occur they get an enormous high. When an individual tries asphyxiation while they are having sex they seem to get an everlasting orgasm. It is thought that when the actions are slowed down by the asphyxiation the feeling seems to take longer.

Breath control cannot be done in a way that is not life threatening, but then Satan's job is to kill, steal, and destroy. The risk of experimenting with breath control play is enormous. At times the individual passes out and dies. Often to protect the family these instances are reported as suicide with no additional details given. Also known as scarfing and sexual hanging.

AUTOMATIC WRITING: Writing done while in a trance – ostensibly containing supernatural and prophetic messages. The pen is held in the hand but is directed by spiritual forces. The finished product is often in a hand-written style or language other than that of the one holding the pen.

AVERSE: Black of evil.

AVATAR: A Person who "descends" into human form from above as a manifestation of divinity and who reveals divine truth to people. Such a one has supposedly progressed beyond the need to be reincarnated in another body (i.e., there is no further "bad Karma" to work off).

An incarnation of the godhead in human flesh, according to Hindu teaching that occurs when mankind is spiritually confused and needs direction: Drishna, Buddha, Mohammed and Christ are all considered to be avatars.

AWARENESS: Thought to be an "exalted state of consciousness", usually achieved by meditation, in which one becomes aware of entities and spiritual energies.

AXIOMANCY: Divination by observation of the quivers of an ax or hatchet.

AYURVEDA: Five-thousand-year old Hindu life science, considered the mother of healing arts, using yoga, diet, Tantrism, and Vedantic philosophy.

B

BAAL: The chief god of the Canaanites.

BAAL-BERITH: "Lord of the Covenant"; A Canaanite god.

BAALIM: Masters or Arch demons- see Masters of Wisdom for names.

BAAL-PEOR: "Lord of the opening"; A Moabite god of uncleanness; also referred to as "Peor".

BAALZEBUB: A Hebrew name that means "Lord of the Flies"; in the Old Testament, the god of Ekron (see Beelzebub).

BAALZEPHON: In demonology, captain of the guard and sentinels of hell.

BACULUM: A witch's wand, staff or broom stick.

BAHIR: A source book of the Cabala; presents some of the basic teachings of Judaic mysticism.

BALEFIRE: Ritual coven fire.

BAPHOMET: At one time was worshipped by the Knights Templar and later by those who took part in the black mass. Today it is seen as a deity, a got-headed god with angelic wings, the breasts of a female, and an illuminated torch between his horns.

BAR-JESUS: Full of all deceit and all fraud, son of the devil, enemy of all righteousness.

BARROW: An Elven or Celtic burial mound.

BASILISK: A legendary dragon, serpent, or lizard whose breath or look was considered fatal.

BEELZEBUB: Traditionally one of the most powerful evil spirits; ranking in importance with Lucifer, Ashtaroth, Satan. Thought of as an evil spirit of decay. Often thought to rank directly under Satan himself.

BEL: The chief Babylonian deity.

BELIAL: This evil spirit is the most vicious of all the evil spirits. He is identified with death and evil. He is a spirit of destruction.

BELL: Rung to begin and end rituals.

BELOMANAY-RABDOMANCY: Divination by tossing or balancing arrows.

BELTANE: Celtic, pre-Christian spring festival, celebrated on May Day. One of the major witches' Sabbaths. A fertility festival that is one of the witches' major holidays.

BHAGAVAD GITA: Sanskrit poem relating a dialogue between Lord Krishna and Arjuna consistent of 700 2-line stanzas in 18 chapter; part of Krishna's revelation called an Upanishad, which is a succinct summary of dominant themes in Hindu theology. Hindu sacred scripture.

BILIOMANCY: Divination by books.

BIND: To cast a spell on someone or something.

BIOFEEDBACK: Technique using instruments to self-monitor normally unconscious, involuntary body processes such as brain waves, heartbeat and muscle tension. As this information is fed back to the person, he or she can then consciously and voluntarily control internal biological functions.

BIORHYTHM: An occult explanation for the rhythmical recurrence of physical and psychological tendencies, presuming the existence of a precise regularity used to chart behavior.

BLACK BRADON: A popular grimoire attributed to Honrius, an occultist of the 15th century.

BLACK MAGIC: Used for blighting or binding. Popularly, magick done for "evil" purposes.

BLACK MASS: The most diabolical ritual that is performed by the Satanist. It is a communion with Satan, involving the desecration of all sacred objects used in the Christian Lord's Suppers. It also can include the sacrifice of an unbaptized infant. A satanic religious ceremony which honors Satan and denigrates Jesus.

BLACK METAL MUSIC: See: *Heavy Metal Music.*

"BLACK POPE": A reference to Anton LaVey; former high priest of the Church of Satan.

BLACK PULLET: A grimoire that probably dates from the late 1700's.

BLACK WIDOW SPIDER: Mark of death.

"BLESSED BE": Phrase used by witches both as a greeting and as a farewell. Note: "So Moot it be" (used in Freemasonry) may be used as well.

BLIGHTING: The use of psychic energy to harm or destroy an organism.

BLOOD: Is the life force. The Satanist believes that by drinking another person's blood or the blood of an animal, it will transfer that life force to the Satanist magnifying the force several times.

BLOOD PACT - A pledge to Satan signed with blood from the person making the promise.

BLOOD SUBSCRIPTIONS: Using one's own blood to subscribe or to commit in a signed statement one's life to Satan. (Also to sign a contract with Satan.)

BLUE MAGIC: Used for emotional work, love, etc. Peace and protection.

BODHISATTVA: A being who has supposedly earned the right to enter into Nirvana or into illumination, but instead voluntarily turns back from that state in order to help humanity in attaining the same goal. Jesus Christ is thought to be a Bodhisattva.

BODYWORK: Rather than simple development of the outer musculature, this approach to fitness aims to reduce muscular tensions in search of "psychic freedom" by using complex yoga-like physical exercises and postures.

BOOK OF CHANGES: (See I Ching)

BOOK OF (THE) DEAD: An Egyptian handbook for guiding the souls of the dead through the underworld.

BOOK OF ENOCH: A work, apparently written in the 2nd century B.C., which forms the basis for much of the mythology with witchcraft.

BOOK OF MOSES: The standard magician's code of the Middle Ages; it contains a complicated ritual for induction of neophytes.

BOOK OF SHADOWS: In witchcraft, the personal book of spells, rituals, and folklore a witch compiles after being initiated into the coven. The Book of Shadows is kept secret and, traditionally, is destroyed when the witch dies.

BOOK OF TOTH/THOTH: A book containing the wisdom of the Egyptian gods; possibly the origin for the Tarot.

BOTANOMANCY: Divination by burning tree branches and leaves.

BOTANICA: Occult shop serving the magickal needs of the Afro-Catholic communities of Voudoun, Macumba, Santeria, etc. Botanicas sell herbs, spells, charms, votive candles, images of saints, etc.

BOUL: Ruler of the West.

BRAHMAN: In Hinduism, the principal and ultimate reality, which is identical with all that is.

BREEDER: A woman who bears a child to be used for ritual sacrifice. Impregnated by male members of the coven approximately 4 months prior to a required human sacrifice in accord with the Satanic Ritual Calendar (pp. 95-96), at the appointed date and ceremony the infant is aborted and immediately sacrificed to Satan as a human sacrifice. Since there was no recorded birth there is no record of anyone missing. Interestingly enough, Satan accepts an aborted fetus as a human being/sacrifice and has deceived many into believing it is just so much fetal tissue and not a human being at this stage and therefore abortion is acceptable.

BRIGID: A witch festival held on February 2nd Eve.

BRIGIT: Great Celtic Triple Goddess. She is matron of: the forge and smithcraft; poetry and inspiration; healing and medicine. Christianized as St. Brigit, her festival is Candlemas or Oimeic, Feb. 1.

BRUJERIA: A Mexican magical system that is an amalgamation of Catholicism and native Indian lore; a sort of synthetic mestizo-shamanism. A male practitioner is called a **BRUJO**, a female is a **BRUJA**. These people are apt to be urban dwellers who burn candles to both saints and demons with equal facility, they gain their magickal powers through self-initiation, sometimes with training. Though they often claim the more benign title of **CURANDERO** (a healer) their practices may run the gamut from love spells to curses.

BUDDHA: "The Enlightened One." An avatar or messenger.

C

CABALA (KABBALAH): Occult material that apparently originated in Chaldea and Mesopotamia and was incorporated into ancient Jewish works and traditions; also refers to practices of magic that are derived from those works.

CADUCEUS: The serpent-entwined herald's staff of Hermes/Mercury. As it was also the wizard's staff of the Greek physician Aesculapius, it has become the symbol of the medical profession.

CALF WORSHIP: Calves and bulls figured prominently in Egyptian mythology and the Israelites, in demanding a golden calf, may have been recalling Egyptian idols or perhaps were just adopting a well-known god-symbol. Every king after Jeroboam carried on sacrifices to the gold calves that Jeroboam made.

CANCER: An astrological sign (in the months of June and July).

CANDLEMAS: See Brigid.

CANDLES: Used in all rituals and ceremonies, the color reflecting the type ritual. Black is the color associated with the devil.

CANNIBAL: A person who eats the flesh of human beings.

CANTRIP: A spell cast by a witch. A written spell or charm that reads the same forwards or backwards.

CAPNOMANCY: Divination by observing smoke as it rises from a fire, such as from a burnt sacrifice or from incense.

CARD LAYING: A widespread means of fortune-telling; the obviously fraudulent and money making types, the suggestive and telepathic fortune-telling types, and the mediumistic types of card-laying based on extrasensory and demonic faculties.

CHARMING: Treatment by magic, a matter of sorcery.

CARTOMANCY: Divination or fortune-telling by means of cards.

CATHARI: From the term "cat" whose posterior they kiss and in whose form Satan appears to them.

CATS: Associated with the moon, night, wisdom, and healing. The Egyptian goddess of music, dance and celebration of life primarily in the Pagan/Neo-Pagan traditions.

CATOPTROMANCY: Divination by means of gazing at a mirror tilted towards the sun.

CAULDRON: A large pot used even today by practitioners. The opening in the cauldron represents the female womb. The cauldron is a very sacred object to practitioners.

CAUSIMOMANCY: Divination by observing how an object placed in fire burns or fails to burn.

CAYCE, EDGAR: The so-called sleeping prophet who, while resting, entered trance states in which he foretold future events, philosophized about such occult subjects as reincarnation, and purported to give cures for various ills.

CELEBRANT: The presiding priest at a ceremony.

CENTURIES: A French physician and occultist whose esoteric poetry many believe foretold events of modern history.

CEPHALOMANCY: Divination by using the head or skull of a donkey or goat.

CERANUOSCOPY: Observation of thunder and lightning for signs or omens.

CEROSCOPY: Melted wax is poured into cold water, and the resulting shapes are interpreted as a means of divination.

CEREBERUS: Three headed dog that guarded the entrance of hell.

CERNUNNOS: Latin "horned one." Ancient Celtic version of the Horned God, shown with stag antlers. Collective spirit of the wild animals. Equated with **FAUNUS**, the Red Man.

CHAKAM: A Hebrew word for "wise".

CHAKKIM: A Hebrew word for "wise one".

CHALDEAN ORACLES: Oracles and mystical sayings allegedly deriving from the Chaldean Magi and Zoroaster, but transcribed and translated by the Neoplatonist. Commentaries on the Oracles were written by Psellus, Pletho, Iamblicus, and Porphyry. The Oracles have much in common with Gnosticism.

CHALICE: Cup or goblet symbolized woman in ritual use; can contain sacrificial blood, wine or water. A goblet which can be made of glass or metal, but is always silver in color. Among Satanists, gold is the symbol of righteousness. A consecrated ceremonial cup, representing the Element Water, and containing the liquid sacrament of communion, usually wine.

CHAMMANIM: Images of the Sun.

CHANNELING: Process of receiving information from some level of reality other than the ordinary physical one and from beyond the "self" as it is generally understood. A "channeler", or medium, usually goes into a trance to establish contact with a spirit, ascended master, higher consciousness, or some other entity, and then receives and repeats messages from "the other side" of the physical world.

CHAKRAS: The seven energy points on the human body, according to new Agers and yogi(s). "Raising" the Kundalini up through the chakras is the aim of yoga meditation. Enlightenment (samandhi) is achieved when kundalini reaches the "crown chakra" at the top of the head.

CHANNELING (SPEAKING IN A TRANCE) - Under the control of demonic power a Spiritistic medium loses consciousness and deceptively imitates communication with the dead.

CHAPTERS: Branches of church organization.

CHARM: In magic, an incantation or object believed to have special supernatural power. The word derives from the Latin Carmen, meaning "a song". Compare with **TALISMAN**.

CHARTOM (CHARTUMMIN): A Hebrew term derived from Egyptian, meaning "men learned in sacred writings, rituals, spells".

CHEMOSH: A national idol of the Moabites and the Ammonites, has been identified with **BAAL-PEOR, BAALZEBUB**, or various Greek or Romans gods by some sources.

CHI (key): According to mysticism, the life-giving force of the cosmos, composed of opposites known as Yin and Yang, which flow in all living things and enter the human body through channels known as mediums.

CHILD SACRIFICE: Worship of Moloch included child sacrifice; other instances not specifically related to Moloch-worship are listed in the Old Testament. (Note: Moloch is a god also included in demonology and child sacrifice appears in various books on the occult as it relates to a "Black Mass".) Practiced today throughout the United States by Satanists. Infants are produced through **BREEDERS** within the coven.

CHIROMANCY: Divination from studying the lines of the head.

CHIROGNOMY: The study of the general shape or formation of the hand.

CHRESMOMANCY: Determining the future by the utterances of one in a frenzy.

CHRIST FAMILY: The Christ Family started in the 60's by using transient type people (late teens – early twenties). They (allegedly) harbor runaway kids. Their mission is to let us know that this is the end of times. They wear white sheets, army blankets and have bare feet. Men will wear diapers on their heads for bandannas. They appear to be into transportation of drugs. Vehicles by the Christ Family will have Star of David with lightning bolt through it. If the leader of the group is inside the vehicle, his arch angels will be armed with small caliber handguns and knives. If a single person of Christ Family is found; and he or she is hurt of injured, it is because the group left them behind. They believe anyone hurt is possessed.

CHRISTIAN SCIENCE: A cult founded in 1879 by Mary Baker Eddy, who wrote "Science and Health with Key to the Scriptures" which teaches death is an illusion, God is Divine Mind, and disease can be removed by right thinking.

CHRISTIAN SPIRITUALIST CHURCH: An organization that promotes mediums and spiritists.

CHRIST-CONSCIOUSNESS: The state of being aware, as many great religious leaders supposedly were, that you are Christ, or that you are God.

CHROMOTHERAPY: The belief that certain colors emit rays that seers and clairvoyants see spiritually to determine the condition of the body and soul;

therapists may request the person to hold and object of specific color to alleviate an organic disorder.

CHURCH OF SATAN: Headed by occultist Anton LeVey. It encouraged the development of the animal instincts, self-indulgence, and free sexuality; and included in its rituals a satanic "mass". Male and female participants in the ritual wore black robes with the exception of the naked woman who volunteered to be the "altar". Reports indicate the Church ceased functioning in 1975 and has now been replaced by the Temple of Set, headed by Michael Aquino. (Note: Anton LaVey was a former lion tamer and police photographer.)

CHURCH OF THE SATANIC BROTHERHOOD: Founded in 1972 by ex-members of Church of Satan.

CHURCH UNIVERSAL AND TRIUMPHANT: A spiritistic cult founded more than 30 years ago that teaches that spiritual purification is obtained by decreeing that you are God.

CINGULUM: A magickal cord worn around the waist and used for binding, measuring and counting.

CIRCLE: In every level of the occult, the circle represents wholeness. A ritual circle is used to protect conjurers as they stand outside the circle to summon demons; Satanists sometimes proudly insist that they stand within the circle as the demon is summoned for complete possession. Often a group of witches, called a coven, is termed a circle.

CLAIRAUDIENCE: Extrasensory data perceived as sound; generally considered a facet of clairvoyance. Also the ability to hear mentally without using the ears.

CLAIRVOYANCE (SECOND SIGHT): The ability to discern objects or information not present to the normal senses. Mental "seeing" of physical objects oR events at a distance by psychic means. Distinguished from telepathy, which involves ESP.

CLEROMANCY: Casting lots using pebbles or other objects, often of different colors.

COLORS: Colors are symbolic of various meanings. Black: evil, devil, sorrow, darkness; Blue: pornography, sadness, water; Green: nature, soothing, restful, cleansing; Red: blood, sex energy; White: purity, innocence, sincerity; Yellow: power, gory, wealth, perfection; Orange: adaptability, desanctification; Purple: progress, ambition, power.

COLOR DIAGNOSIS AND COLOR THERAPY: We are all aware of the fact that colors can have a helpful or an inhibiting effect on the human psyche. Colors can enliven or depress. Warm colors can warm a person's feelings. Cold colors harden one's sensitivity. There are those who have made a study of this subject.

> **Max Luscher,** a Swiss psychologist, has developed a color test which enables him to discover the way a person behaves, his tendencies, his conflicts, and his unconscious motivations. In this color test it is a question of which colors the individual prefers. It is generally believed there is a grain of truth in this diagnostic method, although we must guard against exaggeration.

> There is another scientist(?) **B.J.** (his name is not important since his work need not be used) who calls his method of diagnosis and therapeutic treatment *Psycho-Graphic*. This individual is without doubt an occultist. For his diagnosis he has painted twelve picture charts to which he has allotted the twelve signs of the zodiac. The patient chooses the chart which pleases him the most or the least. From this choice conclusions are drawn as to his character. If an individual requires more detail they must give their birth date so that a horoscope can be cast. This is proof of the occult nature of this type of color diagnosis.

Many color therapists believe that every human body and every organ in it has a certain frequency band of its own. Spiritist mediums can see the frequency band as an *aura*. In case of illness or strong changes of character, the frequency band is altered. These alterations can be detected by a rod and pendulum type apparatus. According to the diagnosis made, the altered frequency is corrected by means of colored threads and bags.

Some people are determined to be deceived by these methods:

"I went to the color therapist. He told me what was wrong with me by using a pendulum. Then he gave me a small bag containing a colored thread. I was told to wear the bag on the diseased part of my body and I would be healed."

"The color therapist gave me a large ball of cotton with some colored thread. I was told to wave this cotton ball around my body in circular and straight movements in order to increase the diminished frequency of the diseased organ."

Farmers sometimes use a tin can containing a colored thread which they bury under the cow barn to prevent the cows from calving prematurely or becoming sick.

As a means of guarding against cancer, color therapists give their patients an amulet containing a colored thread. this amulet must be worn around the neck.

These are but a few examples of this type of activity.

In connection with color therapy there is all manner of deception and superstition as well as the use of rods, pendulums, and spiritist aura. In short, many forms of occultism are combined. The shame is that modern, enlightened, twentieth-century Christians allow this deceit to serve them as if it were a great discovery! Those who do not have their focus on the Lord Jesus Christ, the Holy Son of God, and who do not remain sober and vigilant, will fall victim to the most absurd ideas.

CONCEPTOLOGY/ CONCEPT THERAPY: Claims to sum up the wisdom of the ages concerning man's health and welfare, and explains the underlying principle from which all philosophies, religions, and healing therapies spring. Concept therapy teaches the "laws of life" (4 laws of the body, 12 laws of the mind, 12 laws of the soul, and 7 universal laws). Through the knowledge and practice of these laws of life, A person is said to be able to release the cosmic power residing within and live in harmony with the universe, thereby attaining Heaven on earth – health, prosperity, success, and happiness.

Ideas are also a form of energy, according to Conceptology, and a person's imagination can be utilized, through concentration on the desired result, to "create" health and prosperity, as well as to influence or change events. Thoughts and ideas send out vibrations that attract to a person's life the concept or picture held in the mond.

CONSCIOUSNESS REVOLUTION: New Age advocates call for a "consciousness revolution" a new way of looking at and experiencing life. The primary focus of the new consciousness is oneness with God, all mankind, the earth, and with the entire universe.

CONTROL: The spirit that sends messages through a medium in trance.

CONE OF POWER: Imaging a vortex of energy directed toward a goal or person is a common ritual performed in witchcraft.

CONJURATION: Evoking or calling up the spirits to do what one commands them to do. They are confined to a triangle or circle drawn upon the floor. The triangle is a symbol of manifestation and the spirit force is to manifest itself inside the triangle or circle.

CORD: Used in magic and to cinch the waist when wearing robes, usually 9 feet long in cotton, silk, or wool. The color is symbolic of rank or of the ritual performed. (Note: there may be variations when working with self-styled groups.)

CONSCIOUSNESS: mental awareness of present "knowing". New Agers usually refer to consciousness as the awareness or perception of one's "inner self", or of inward awareness of external objects or facts.

CONSECRATING: To make, declare or set apart as sacred.

COSMIC CHRIST: In esoteric schools of thought, the Christ is considered to be a universal spirit or cosmic force. The primary goal of this impersonal spirit or force is to guide the spiritual evolution of mankind.

COSMIC CONSCIOUSNESS: A spiritual and mystical perception that all in the universe is "one". To attain cosmic consciousness is to see the universe as God and God as universe.

COSMIC ENERGY: In metaphysics, an undefined force in the universe by which all living beings have their subsistence, the presence of which ensures health and welfare.

COSMIC HUMANISM: In contrast to normative humanism that sees man as the measure of all things, cosmic humanism sees man as having virtually unlimited potential because of his inner divinity.

CONSULTER WITH FAMILIAR SPIRIT: Consulting the supposed spirits of the dead.

COVEN: A group of witches who gather together to perform ceremonies at Sabbats and Sabbaths. Traditionally, the number of members in a coven has been assumed to total thirteen. The earliest reference to this is the claim of Isobel Gowdie in 1662 that the Auldearne witches had "thirteen persons in each coven".

COVENANT OF THE GODDESS: An international, legally incorporated, ecumenical umbrella organization of Witchcraft covens providing legal corporate status for otherwise unincorporated groups.

COVENATOR: Minister of lowest rank.

COVENDOM: The area within three miles of the Coven's domain.

COVENSTEAD: Place where the coven meets.

COWMAN: One who is not a Witch. Outsider.

CREMATION: The practice of burning the dead body, historically founded on the Eastern mystical concept that unless the body is destroyed, it will be a prison for the soul and prevent future transmigrations (reincarnations).

CRÈME, BENJAMIN: A father of the New age movement and a guiding force through his channeled sessions when he is "overshadowed" by the spirit of Lord Maitreya.

CRESCENT: The shape of the waxing moon, symbolic of fertility and abundant growth.

CRITOMANCY: Observation of barley cakes for possible omens.

CROSS: Ancient pre-Christian symbol interpreted by some occultists as uniting the male phallus (vertical bar) and female vagina (horizontal bar). It is also a symbol of the four directions and a powerful weapon against evil. (Not all crosses represent Christianity – see *Occult Symbols*)

CROSS OF NERO: The early 60's peace symbol, an upside down, broken cross in a circle.

CRYONICS: The practice of freezing the body upon death for future thawing and rejuvenation once a cure is found for whatever caused its demise.

CRYSTALS: New age advocates believe that crystals contain incredible healing and energizing powers. Crystals are often touted as being able to restore the "flow of energy" in the human body.

CRYSTAL BALL READING: Determining the future by gazing into a fire.

CRYSTALLOMANCY: Gazing into a crystal ball or other object.

CULT: A religious organization founded by and built upon the teachings of a central charismatic figure whose authority is viewed as being equal to or greater than the Holy Scriptures. In Christian understanding, the teachings of a cult oppose or differ from historic biblical theology.

CURSE: Invocation of an oath associated with black magic or sorcery intended to harm or destroy opponents or property; curses often require the invocation of evil spirits.

CURSES OR SPELLS - Curses or the casting or breaking of spells. Curses may be incurred as a result of our sins or the sins of our forefathers (Deuteronomy 27 & 28). Spells are produced by occult practitioners by the release of demonic power through hypnosis, magnetism, mesmerism, or some other form of magic resulting in extrasensory influence. Spells stir up love or hate, persecute or defend against enemies, kill humans or animals, and heal or inflict diseases.

CYCLOMANCY: Divination from a turning wheel.

D

DACTYLMANCY: A dangling ring indicates words and numbers by its swings.

DAEMON: From the Greek, Diamon: A spirit, an evil spirit or demon. Also used as a term for beings at an intermediate level between God and people.

DAGON: The national god of the Philistines.

DAIMON (DAIMONIAN): A demon, signified among pagan Greeks as an inferior deity.

DAIMONIODAS: A Greek word meaning "from the devil" or "of the devil".

DAIMONIZOMAI: A Greek work that means "demonized", although unfortunately it is usually translated "demon-possessed". "Daimonizomai" can usually refer to a wide range of demonic influence.

DAPHNOMANCY: Listening to branches, particularly laurel branches, burning in a fire; the louder the crackle, the better the omen.

"DARK SIDE OF THE MOON": A popular album by a rock group Pink Floyd featuring spacey sounds and musically adventuresome elements that have inspired some New Age musicians; believed by some to facilitate mind expansion techniques.

DEATH METAL MUSIC: Themes include Satanism, torture, murder, rape, suicide, self-mutilation, anti-Christian. Some groups that play death metal music include "Mayhem," "Slayer," and "Deicide."

"DECLARATION OF INTERDEPENDENCE": A globalist document, drafted by the World Affairs Council in 1975, representing the New Age agenda by stating the world cannot survive unless mankind recognized "the necessity for collaborative regulation by international authorities".

DECREES: Oral affirmations invoking supernatural powers by the authority of the words spoken, similar to chanting a mantra.

DÉJÀ VU: The feeling of having already experienced an event or place that is being encountered for the very first time.

DEMON: A non-human spirit; generally thought by many theologians to be disembodied spirits from a pre-adamic earth, as differentiated from fallen angels.

DEMONCRACY: Worship of an evil nature.

DEMONIZATION (DEMONIZED) – Demonization occurs when an evil spirit or spirits inhabit a person's soul. Usually as a result of sin, generational curses, or severe trauma.

DEMONOLOGY: The study of demons, what they are designated to do and how they are summoned, as well as what role they play with mankind today.

DENDROMANCY: Divination utilizing oak or mistletoe.

DENTROLATRY: Worship of trees.

DERASH: A Hebrew word for "one that inquires of the dead".

DEVIL: The personification of evil called Lucifer or Satan. The word means accuser or slanderer.

DHARMA: Law, truth, or teaching; used to express the central teaching of Hindu and Buddhist religion. Dharma implies that essential truth can be stated about the way things are, and that people could comply with that norm.

DIABLERIE: Dealing with demons or the Devil; sorcery or witchcraft.

DIABOLUS: Two morsels, kill body and soul.

DIAKKA: Spirits that communicate with or materialize for mediums or spiritists.

DIANA: Greek fertility goddess, also known in other eras as Aphrodite, Ashtoreth, or Artemis, venerated by those New Agers who believe in the resacralization of the earth.

DIANETICS: Ron Hubbard's teaching on mental health.

DIRECTIONS, FOUR: In Western magic, the four directions are symbolized in ritual, representing the elements air, fire, water and earth, respectively.

DISASSOCIATION: Avoiding pain or unpleasantness by redefining reality with other mental associations, such as thinking that firewalking coals are cool moss.

DISCARNATE: The soul or personality of a living creature who has died.

DISCIPLE: Lay member.

DIVINATION: Methods of discovering the personal, human significance of present or future events. Means to obtain insights may include dreams, hunches, involuntary body actions, mediumistic possession, consulting the dead, observing the behavior of animals and birds, tossing coins, casting lots, and "reading" natural phenomena.

DIVINER'S STAFF: Refers to a staff used for divination.

DIVINING ROD - A forked object (hazel tree twig, wire, etc.) used to locate water (water witching) minerals or other objects. Evil spirits actually locate the water or other objects and move the divining rod.

DOWSING (DOWSER): (Also Water Diviner) A person skilled in locating underground sources of water by means of a divining rod. The dowser uses a Y-shaped rod that is generally made of hazel, but is sometimes made of metal or substitute woods like rowan or ash. As the dowser walks above the location of the underground water, the rod jerks in an involuntary and spontaneous manner, indicating to the dowser both the location and the depth of the supply. Unknown to the dowser he is working hand in hand with evil spirits and ultimately there is a "pay back" for this knowledge to the dowser's detriment.

DRAGON: In Revelation 20:2, Satan is identified as "the dragon".

DRAWING DOWN THE MOON: A Wiccan rite of invoking the Moon Goddess. A book by Margot Adler about Neo-Pagan religious movement, widely regarded as the best study of Neo-Paganism ever written.

DREAM CATCHERS: The dream catcher is very popular these days, especially for use in baby cribs. However, this is not an innocent ornament. It is actually a charm. A charm is "any magic word, formula, incantation, object, sign or amulet supposed to possess occult power."[56]

One witchcraft magazine, in an article titled "Amulets, Talismans & Charms," explains the dream catcher like this:

> *This charm, from the Ojibway tribe in Minnesota, is made of sinew stretched over a small hoop of ash. It is designed to bring a good night's sleep, especially for children, and is hung horizontally over a child's cradleboard or crib. Tradition says that the air is filled with both good and bad dreams waiting to come to a sleeping child. This net allows good dreams to find their way to the child through the hole in the center,*

---

[56] Frank Gaynor, Editor, *Dictionary of Mysticism*, New York: Philosophical Library, 1953, p. 35

while bad dreams are caught up in the web where they dissolve in the dawn's light. Dream nets continue to be used by some Ojibway people today as in ancient times.[57]

One paper explaining the *"Legend of the Dream Catcher"* states:

Long ago when the world was young, an old Lakota spiritual leader was on a high mountain and had a vision. In his vision, Iktomi, the great trickster and teacher of wisdom, appeared in the form of a spider. Iktomi spoke to him in a sacred language that only the spiritual leaders of the Lakota could understand... All the while the spider spoke, he continued to weave his web starting from the outside and working towards the center... If you believe in the great spirit, the web will catch your good ideas – and the bad ones will go through the hole. The Lakota elder passed on his vision to his people and now the Sioux Indians use the dream catcher as the web of their life. It is hung above their beds or in their home to sift their dreams and visions. The good in their dreams are captured in the web of life and carried with them... but the evil in their dreams escapes through the hole in the center of the web and are no longer a part of them. They believe that the dream catcher holds the destiny of their future.[58]

The spider (Iktomi) was known as a trickster. How can you be sure that he didn't trick the people with his tale of the dram catcher? How can you be sure that the good dreams are caught and the evil ones are filtered out? A trickster is known for lying, deception, and mischief.

Most Christians researchers will recognize the occultic connotations expressed in this story. The fantasy of a spider speaking, the use of visions, the "sacred language," and the idea that it is the dream catcher that holds each person's destiny rather than God.

Also to be noted is the phrase "web of life." The idea of an etheric or planetary web was developed by Alice A. Bailey, an occultist, but initially expressed by Chief Seattle around 1854 in his quote:

This we know... the earth does not belong to man, man belongs to the earth. All things are connected, like blood which connects one family. Whatever befalls the

---

[57] Selena Fox, *Amulets, Talismans & Charms: Past and Present,* Circle Network News, Summer 1987, Vol. 9, No. 2, p. 13.

[58] Paper entitled *"Legend of the Dream Catcher."*

earth befalls the children of the earth. Men do not weave the web of life – he is merely a strand in it. Whatever he does to the web, he does to himself.[59]

John Lash reveals that it is a key idea in New Age philosophy of holistics, and a major subject of study and exploration in geomancy.[60] Geomancy is a form of divination which is explicitly forbidden in the Bible. (Deuteronomy 18:10-12; II Kings 17:17; Jeremiah 14:14; Ezekiel 12:24; 13:6-7; Acts 16:16.)

Another catalog that sells lots of occultic materials states:

> **THE DREAM CATCHER WEB.** *Believe in its mystical powers, and you may sleep more peacefully! Through the center spirit hole flow your good dreams; trapped in the web are the "bad," which disappear with the morning sun.*[61] (underlining added)

You may have noticed even the descriptions of the dream catcher differ from place to place. Some people believe that the bad dreams are caught in the web and others believe that the good dreams are caught. Regardless of the discrepancies, this is not an item that any Christian would want in their home.

Christians do not need "protection" from occult sources. Jeremiah 7:8 says Behold, ye trust in lying words, that cannot profit. All we need to do is pray and ask the Lord to watch over our children and protect them and He will do it. Consider these verses: Psalm 118:8; Psalm 40:4; Psalm 56:3; Psalm 91:2; Psalm 5:11; Proverbs 3:5-6.

DREAM THERAPY: The theory that future events can be determined by dream analysis since these visions supposedly reveal the goal and desires of one's higher spiritual self.

DRUIDS: Celtic priests in pre-Christian Britain and Gaul. Skilled in astronomy and medicine, they worshiped the sun, believed in the immortality of the soul, and in reincarnation. Very powerful and very dangerous – still active today.

DRYAD: A tree spirit, generally seen as feminine.

---

[59] John Lash, *The Seeker's Handbook: The Complete Guide to Spiritual Pathfinding*, New York, Harmony Books, 1990, p. 268.

[60] Ibid

[61] Catalog from Red Rose Collection, Holiday 1992, p. 46

DUALISM: The doctrine that for every principle there is an opposing, separate, and ultimately irreconcilable counter-principle. Such opposing forces are conventionally arrayed along a good-evil dichotomy.

DUNGEONS AND DRAGONS: A fantasy role-playing game which uses demonology, witchcraft, voodoo, murder, rape, blasphemy, suicide, assassination, insanity, sex perversion, homosexuality, prostitution, Satan type rituals, gambling, barbarism, cannibalism, sadism, desecration, demon summoning, necromantics, divination and many other teachings. There have been a number of deaths nationwide where games like Dungeons & Dragons were either the decisive factor in adolescent suicide and murder, or played a major factor in the violent behavior in such tragedies. Since role-playing is used typically for behavior modification, it has become apparent nationwide (with the increased homicide and suicide rates in adolescents) that there is a great need to investigate every aspect of the youngster's environment, including their method of entertainment, in reaching a responsible conclusion for their violent actions.

E

EAR ACUPUNCTURE: A form of auricular therapy based on the concept that the ear is shaped like a fetus-in-utero and is a microcosm that contains reference points by which the body can supposedly be affected.

EARTH LOGOS: Some New Age advocates believe that the Earth Logos is a great spiritual being who is the ensouling life of planet earth. The earth is considered a physical manifestation (or body) of this spiritual intelligence.

EARTH-MOTHER: Female personification of the Lifeforce, fertility of the Earth and its inhabitants. One of the most widespread deity concepts in the world. (**PEIB**) The ancient Greeks called **HER GAIA**, and equated **HER** with both Mother Earth and Mother Nature.

EASTERN RELIGIONS - Any involvement in Hinduism, Confucianism, Buddhism, Taoism, Shintoism, Islam (Muslim).

EAST WEST: Monthly New Age magazine accentuating occult, mystical, and natural healing methods, along with metaphysical nutrition.

ECOSOPHY: Greek, "wisdom of the home." A holistic, pantheistic, metaphysical

world-view based on emergent evolution, imminent divinity, and the Gaeia Thesis.

ECTOPLASM: A white filmy substance pouring from a medium's bodily openings, supposedly denoting the presence of a disembodied spirit, or a sticky, milky-white substance out of which poltergeists and discarnate (disembodied) entities are said to materialize for the purpose of visible manifestation.

EDGAR CAYCE: A minister involved in "channeling" who provided "cures" for many sick persons. There are many books by and about him.

EIDOLEION: A worshiper of idols.

EIDOLOLATREIA: Something that is sacrificed to an idol.
EIDOLON: An idol.

EIDOLOTHUTON: Something that is sacrificed to an idol.

EIKON: An image, in Revelation 13, an image of the beast is made, which people are required to worship.

EL: A generic name for a god or gods; also used of God.

ELAEOMANCY: Divination by observation of a liquid surface.

ELAH: God, or a god; an object of worship used by pagans in reference to their various duties.

ELDER GODS: Gods that occasionally come to rescue men from the "Ancient Ones".

ELECTROMAGNETIC HEALING: The theory that an electrical force animates the body, and that its proper stabilization contributes to health and healing.

ELEMENTAL: A familiar, or one of the four classes of demons.

ELEMENTS: The early Greeks considered Earth, Air, Fire and Water to be the four elements.

ELF FIRE: Fire produced without the aid of metals, used to light a balefire.

ELIL: Literally an empty or vain, worthless thing.

ELIZEN (ELTZEN): Ruler of the spirits of the North.

ELVES: From Norse **AELFAR**. Originally the **TUATHA DE DANAAN** (Children of the Goddess Danu); early bronze-age Celts, also known as the **SIDHE**. Later mythologized and amalgamated with **FAERIES**.

EMAH: Idols that impress terror on their worshipers.

ENCHANTER: Sorcerer, magician, one who uses human voice or music to bring another person into psychic control. Lev. 19:26; Deut. 18:10-12; II Chron. 33:6; II Kings 17:17; Is. 47:9,11; Jer. 27:9; Dan. 1:20.

ENCHANTMENT: The act of influencing by charms and incantations the practice of magical arts.

ENOCH: According to Genesis, Enoch was a man who "walked with God" and was taken to heaven without suffering death; occultists attribute various special powers and abilities to him.

ENLIGHTENMENT: The realization that you are God (akin to self-actualization). A state of awareness (sometimes called "nirvana," "cosmic consciousness," or "transcendental bliss") that assumes all of existence is interwoven and man is innately god with untapped potential.

ENTROPY: Degradation of the matter and energy in the universe to an ultimate state of inert uniformity (see *Syntropy*, entropy's opposite).

EQUINOX: The time at which the sun crossed the equator. The equinox takes place on March 21 and September 22, and on these days the length of the day and night are equal.

EQUIVALENCY: A socialist concept that insists no nation should have an overabundance of resources, that commerce and substance should be distributed equivalently.

EREBUS: According to Greek mythology, a dark region through which souls traveled on their way to Hades.

ERHERD, WERNER: Founder of "est", a mind-expansion cult that teaches reality can be intuitively experienced because "being" is more important than "doing".

ESALEN INSTITUTE: A "growth" center that offers a wide variety of workshops for mind, body and spirit. It is located in Big Sur, California.

ESBAT: Coven meetings held on a regular basis usually at least once a month at the full moon. It is at these meetings "work" is performed such as healing and "magick".

ESOTERIC: Term applied to teachings that are secret and only for initiate of the group; mysterious, occult, "hidden". A word used to describe knowledge that is possessed or understood only by a few.

ESOTERIC CHRISTIANITY: A mystical form of Christianity that sees its "core truth" as identical to the "core truth" of every other religion (i.e. Man is divine). This form of Christianity is at home with Aldous Huxley's "perennial philosophy". (See: Perennial Philosophy)

ESOTERIC DOCTRINE: Occultists claim that there exists mystical teaching known to the most highly evolved adepts, parts of which can be found in various religions, but is wholly contained in no single one; this doctrine is presumably given by seers to the world in times of great need.

ESOTERIC PHILOSOPHY: The study of secret knowledge understood by and revealed to only a select few initiates, who usually attain such information by spirit guides or arcane, sacred books.

ESP (EXTRASENSORY PERCEPTION): The experience of, or response to, an external event, object, state, or influence without apparent contact through the known sense. ESP may occur without those being aware of it. Short for "extrasensory perception", the psychic ability to perceive things intuitively beyond the capability of the five natural senses; paranormal abilities such as telepathy, precognition and clairvoyance.

ESP CARDS: A pack of twenty-five cards bearing five symbols, including stars, squares, circles, crosses and waves.

EST: Acronym for **ERHARD SEMINARS TRAINING**, a process of getting "it" by intuitive acquisition after long hours of deprivation and verbal humiliation. Name has since been changed to The Forum.

ETSEB (ATSAR, OSTEB): A Hebrew word for an idol whose service is laborious or is cause of grief.

EVERQUEST: A computer role-playing game requiring an Internet connection and a paid monthly membership. There are various versions. At our local Wal-Mart I looked at an Everquest package titled *Everquest, The Scars of Velious,* which has an industry game rating of T (Teen). The packaging notes state there is animated blood and gore, animated violence, and suggestive themes. The back of this particular games states "Hundreds of new magical items to discover, trade and sell."

In the Everquest series there is violence that involves the use of axes and swords to kill, the casting of spells and throwing curses to kill opposing members, and a classic cyber world where nobody will stop you from killing other players. The chat feature allows the player to communicate with his team and opponents often resulting in sexual harassment between players, cyber stalking, and profanity.

Magick and the occult are numerous. The player must acquire magic skills to have a chance of winning. For many players the "quest" is to attain more and more magical power and use it on those in the real world.

Included are generous amounts of nearly naked female characters. Young boys and men are being exposed to barely-dressed women at every turn and fighting and killing them when given a chance. Psychologists warn about mixing sex and violence, especially with impressionable young ones.

With the interactive chat going on between players, not only is there much profanity and sexual harassment, but the chat rooms can be entered by adult predators to converse with children. Children already pumped up by the sexy violence flooding the screen.

Everquest needs to be avoided for its violence, occultism, mature content, and chat room dangers.

EVIL EYE: A superstition which credits certain people with the ability to dispense bad luck with a gaze; people hope to counteract by wearing charms or amulets.

EXORCISM: The act of removing demonic control from someone who is demonized; in witchcraft, purifying something from alien influences.

EXOTERIC CHRISTIANITY: A form of Christianity identified with historic or orthodox Christianity that New Agers would describe as being devoid of all spiritual authenticity.

EYES: The "evil eye" is feared.

F

FAIRIES: From the pre-Celtic past, fairies are also known as Goblins and are classified with Leprechauns, Brownies, and Pixies. They stand for the evil spirits that were once thought at the Vigil of Samhain and the Eve of Halloween. Fairies were believed to be able to predict death. They were also known as little people who created problems for the Celtics.

FALLEN ANGELS: Angels deceived by Lucifer into believing he was the anointed one, the true Son of God. These angels were cast out of heaven with Lucifer and are among the unknown number of evil spirits today.

FAMILIAR SPIRIT: A demonic spirit who serves a witch or medium, or an animal that it may inhabit.

FAM-TRAD: Family tradition. Psychic training and/or magickal traditions identified with Witchcraft and handed down as hereditary or family lore.

FASCINATION: The act of charming or casting a spell on someone nearby by a projection of power through the eye, etc.

FAUN: A minor Roman spirit of the wilderness. Humanoid, but with goat's horns, legs, hooves and tail. May be male or female.

FAUNUS: Brother/lover of Fauna. The "Red Man". Male collective spirit of the animal kingdom.

FELDENKRAIS: System of bodywork founded by Moshe Feldenkrais, teaching that emotional and spiritual balance is achieved through functional coordination, body awareness, and stipulated movements.

FERGUSON, MARILYN: Prominent New Age theorist and author of the movement's classic "The Aquarian Conspiracy".

FETISH: An inanimate object presumably inhabited by a spirit.

FINDHORN COMMUNITY: A legendary New Age community located in the North of Scotland. The group offers an ongoing educational program in the principles of New Age spirituality.

FINGER: Holds spiritual powers. Index finger is known as "poison, witch or cursing finger". Many believe you must not use it to touch a wound or it will never heal.

FIRE: Symbolizes Satan.

FIREWALKING: Supernatural ability to walk over hot coals without feeling pain. An ancient, idolatrous ritual in which one seeks spiritual purification by walking on super-heated coals to prove one's confidence in the god's protection.

FLORAMANCY: Determining the future by study of flowers.

FLOTATION TANKS: Cylinders containing a saline solution in which people lie, floating on the water's surface (often in darkness) to create the illusion of cosmic awareness to achieve spiritual enlightenment.

FORCE, THE: A concept presented by George Lucas in the "Star Wars" movie epics; based on the Taoist idea of a primordial essence that is both good and evil and may be used for either, depending on one's motive.

FORTUNE TELLING: The art of forecasting future events and reading human character. Foretelling the future in other peoples' lives, usually with the aid of the spirit world, or with aid of some "spirit" aide.

FREEMASONRY: See *Freemasonry*, Appendix B, page 235.

FREYA: Scandinavian Goddess of Love, Queen of Lower Regions. Freya's sacred day was Friday. Witches held weekly assemblies on Friday.

FULL MOON: Greatest magical power.

G

GAIA: A Greek name for the goddess of the earth. It also refers to a scientific hypothesis formulated by James Lovelock whereby all living matter on the earth is believed to be a single living organism. In such a scheme, humanity is considered the nervous system of the living earth.

GARDNER, GERALD: (1884-1964) Founder of modern Witchcraft, author of Witchcraft Today (1954) and other books. Gardnerian Wicca remains his legacy.

GARDNERIAN WITCHCRAFT: Traditional witchcraft system founded by Gerald Gardner in England.

GASTROMANCY: An ancient form of ventriloquism; prophetic utterances were delivered in this way.

GELOSCOPY: Divination from the tone of someone's laughter.

GENETHLIALOGY: Observation of the position and influence of the stars at a person's birth to predict their future.

GEOMANCY: Interpretation of figures or dots drawn on the ground, or perhaps on paper, according to accepted designs.

GHOSTS: Thought by some to be spirit apparitions through which the souls of dead persons are thought to manifest themselves. To others, a ghost is a demon spirit which has been unleashed by Satan to live in a certain environment. Some explain ghosts away by attributing strange happenings to natural causes.

GLOBALISM: A modern-day term referring to the need for transformation from the present nation-state divisions into a one world community.

GLORY DUST: See *Golden Glory*.

GNOME: An elemental who lives in the earth.

GNOSTICISM: Refers to the secret doctrines and practices of mysticism whereby a person may come to enlightenment or realization that he or she is of the same essence of God or the Absolute. The Greek word Gnosis means knowledge, and at the heart of Gnostic thought is the idea that revelation of the hidden gnosis frees one from the fragmentary and illusory material world and teaches him or her about the origins of the spiritual world, to which the Gnostic belongs by nature.

GOAT: Occultist believe Satan appears in the form of a goat.

GOAT'S HEAD: Sixteenth century symbol for Satan. (Note: This appears to still hold true in present practices.)

GOAT OF MENDES: A satanic symbol, the opposite of the Lamb of God (Jesus).

GOD: The New Age god is referred to as a "universal consciousness," "universal life," or "universal energy," an impersonal force that pervades the universe. A being who has "many faces." He (it) is considered a radically imminent being who is often referred to as a "universal consciousness," "universal life," or "universal energy". The New Age god is more or less an impersonal force that pervades the universe.

GOETIA: Tradition of black magic, including incantations, ceremonies, and techniques of sorcery, often providing practical instructions for contacting demonic spirits. (Note: Also known as the lesser key of Solomon.)

GOLDEN DAWN, ORDER OF THE: Ceremonial magickal lodge founded in 1887 by a trio of English Freemasons. Its prominent members included S.L. MacGregor Mathers, W.B. Yeats, Israel Regardie, Dion Forutne, A.E. Waite, and Aleister Crowley, who was eventually expelled. Its purpose was "to prosecute the Great Work: which is to obtain control of the nature and power of my own being."

GOLDEN GLORY: A demonically inspired activity thought by some to be the visible presence of God, the same glory that was seen on the face of Moses when he came down from the mountain of God. It appears as gold flakes that come through the pores of the skin on the face or hands or some other part of the body. Some say their fillings turn to gold. Others have experienced it raining down from heaven, falling on either people, their clothing, or their surroundings. The deception effects every denomination and has been experienced worldwide. This author has witnessed its manifestation with clients while counseling but when tested an evil spirit manifests.

GRAPHOLOGY: A psychic analysis of someone's handwriting. See *handwriting analysis*.

GREAT BEAST: The name for the Anti-Christ in the Book of Revelation, and the name popularly associated with the magician Aleister Crowley.

GREAT INVOCATION: A New Age prayer that has been translated into over 80 languages; to invoke the presence of the cosmic Christ, leading to the oneness of all mankind.

GREAT RITE: Ritual sex within the magick circle.

GREEN MAGIC: Used for working with vegetation, as in gardening. Fertility and prosperity.

GRIMOURES: A medieval collection of magical spells, rituals, incantations. Also any coven or circle's book of shadows recording spells, ceremonies and history of the group.

GRIS-GRIS ("Grey-grey"): Medicine power sometimes in the form of herbal pouches. Used in New Orleans Cajun-style "Voodoo."

GROTTO: A Satanic congregation.

GROUP GURU: A slang New Age term referring to the idea that the Cosmic Christ is incarnate in all of humanity. All mankind is seen as a single "guru".

GROVES: A group of covens potentially many who will form regional and national conferences.

GURU: Spiritual teacher who instructs disciples in the "way" of enlightenment. The guru's authority is to be implicitly accepted.

GYROMANCY: Use of a person spinning in a circle and then falling to the ground to determine the future.

H

HAIR: Holds character. In witch hunt times, it was believed a sorcerer's magical potency was in his hair.

HALLOWEEN - A November Eve witches' holiday; considered to be the day of the year most suitable for magic or demonic activity. (Oct. 31, also believed to be the time when the souls of the deceased revisited their former homes and once again enjoyed the company of their kinfolk.)

HAND OF DEATH: A cult which allegedly sacrifices people and has rituals that are Satanic. They are allegedly into cannibalism. Lucus and Toole allegedly were part of this group. Very little is known about this group.

HAND OF GLORY: The left hand of a person who has died. The hand is removed and a candle is positioned between the fingers. The ritual is used for protection against evil spirits.

HANDWRITING ANALYSIS: also known as graphology is a form of divination falling in a category similar to palm reading whereby such things as an individual's character, career potential, trustworthiness, emotional development, personality, and other hidden characteristics are said to be revealed through an analysis of his handwriting.

HARMONIC CONVERGENCE: The assembly of New Age mediators gathered at the same astrological time in different locations to usher in peace on earth and one-world government.

HAURSCOPY (HEIROMANCY, HUROSCOPY): Various names for observation of cuts, cracks, or markings in very old objects and drawing prophetic conclusions.

HEAD: Central powerhouse of the body believed to contain all magical powers. For this reason many human skulls are used on altars. Also, eating of the brain is believed to transfer power.

HEALING FANATICISM: Involvement in "faith healing" cults or with "faith healers" who are involved in sensationalism.

HEALING MAGIC: See Magic: Healing.

HEART: The symbol of eternity. Some groups believe that by eating the heart of another, you acquire the characteristics of the victim and obtain all of his power. The heart is symbolic of the center of life.

HEAVY METAL ROCK: "Heavy metal cultivates a macho image with black leather chains and spikes or studs attached to leather wrist bands, belts and jackets. When you think of heavy metal, you think of power. Women are sometimes portrayed in degrading situations. Heavy-Metal album covers and videos sometimes show women being dragged around by the hair, caged or being walked on a leash like dogs. The main focus of the heavy metaler is drugs, sex and rock'n'roll. The most alarming aspect of heavy metal is its preoccupation with the occult. There's some subtle and not so subtle Satanic overtones in Heavy Metal. Album covers include such things as illustrations of devil's heads, crucified figures, demonic babies, skeletons, pentagrams, black candles and the occult number 666". (Quotes by Darlyne Pettinichio, Probation Officer from Orange County, Calif., News Article, the Press Enterprise, Riverside, Ca., May 7, 1986.) The six themes of Heavy Metal Music are: the death of God; sex with corpses; human sacrifices; sitting at Satan's left hand; calling Jesus Christ the deceiver; and glorifying the name of Satan.

HECATE: Goddess of Lower Regions and Patroness of Witchcraft.

HECHICERIA: The surviving remnants of true Native Indian magical religion in Mexico. Practitioners are most often male and are called **HECHICEROS**, or **NAGUALS** (in Nahuatl), or sometimes even **BRUHO NATURALEZA**. They believe that those born to be hechiceros are called by the gods from a hereditary line. They worship the old pre-Columbian divinities with fragments of surviving rites and indigenous folk rituals.

HELLFIRE CLUBS: During the 18th and 19th centuries, these small groups in Europe reintroduced the Black Mass and other satanic practices, including sexual immorality.

HERBOLOGY: Use of plants as natural healing substances to promote health and cure minor illnesses.

HERMETIC TRADITIONS: Occult teachings that arose during the first three centuries A.D.

HEXAGRAM: A six-point talismatic star, also known as a Star of David. The Hexagram is believed among occultists to protect and control demons.

HIGHER SELF: The most "spiritual" and "knowing" part of oneself, said to lie beyond the ego, the day-to-day personality, and the personal unconscious. The Higher Self can be channeled for wisdom and guidance. Variations include the Oversoul, the Superconsciousness, the Atman, the Christ (or Krishna or Buddha) Consciousness, and the god Within.

HINDUISM: Dominant religion of the Indian subcontinent; teaches that God is impersonal and unknowable and that man's ultimate purpose, after the effect of bad deeds has been dissipated, is to re-emerge into the oneness of the inexplicable.

HIPPOMANCY: Divination from the neighing and stamping of horses.

HOLISM: A unitary philosophy that claims organic or environmental systems consist of similar parts, integrated as a whole. The theory that all reality is organically one. Everything in the universe is viewed as interrelated and interdependent.

HOLISTIC: Alternatively, but less frequently, spelled "wholistic"; derived from the Greek holos, meaning "whole" in the sense of "entire" or "unified". Holistic health practices emphasize the whole person, the impact of the environment, and the interdependence of all parts of the body, mind, and spirit in the prevention and treatment of ailments.

HOLISTIC HEALTH: Sees the person as an interrelated organism; needing to be treated as a whole person (body, mind and spirit), as opposed to merely treating a particular disease.

HOLOGRAM: A three-dimensional projection resulting from the interaction of laser beams. Scientists have discovered that the image of an entire hologram can be reproduced from any one of its many component parts. New Agers use this to illustrate the oneness of all reality.

HOMEOPATHY: A "natural" way of stimulating the body's healing ability by using the theory that "like cures like", which treats patients with the same substance that sickened them.

HOODOO: A combination of black magic and Voodoo used only to bring bad luck.

HORNED GOD: Symbol of male sexuality in paganism and witchcraft; part man, part goat.

HOROSCROPE: A chart showing a person's destiny as determined by astrology practice.

HOUSES: The 12 sections of the Zodiac which together symbolize every aspect of life. The planets move through the houses; thus, when a planet falls into the sphere of the given house, it comes under its respective influence. The astrologer plots all of these factors and more on a chart. This chart is called a horoscope.

HUBBARD, L. RON: Science fiction writer (1911-1986) and founder of the Scientology cult, which believes humanity descended from an extraterrestrial race of omnipotent gods known as Thetans; also wrote on "Dianetics".

HUMAN POTENTIAL MOVEMENT: A movement with roots in humanistic psychology that stresses man's essential goodness and unlimited potential; the answer is seen to be "within".

HUMANISM: A doctrine that supposes mankind is the ultimate essence of worth, and no divine being exists to determine the ideals and values of humanity. A system of philosophy that upholds the primacy of human beings rather than God or any abstract or metaphysical system. Humanism holds that man is the measure of all things.

HYDROMANCY: Observing any number of several aspects of water, including its color, ebb and flow, or ripples caused by pebbles dropped into a pool.

HYPERVENTILATION: Based on the Hindu theory that biocosmic power is in the breath and that by rapid breathing, one may transcend to a state of spiritual awareness.

HYPNOSIS: State resembling deep sleep or trance, but more active in that the person has some will and feeling but acts according to suggestions presented; a heightened sense of suggestibility to the imagination.

HYPNOTHERAPY: A psychological therapy which involves the use of hypnosis.

HYPNOTIC REGRESSION: The process by which one is said to recall past-life memories through hypnosis.

HYPNOTISM - Being Hypnotized by anyone (individually or in a group) for any purpose.

I

I-CHING: Chinese book of divination associated with Taoism. I-Ching consists of the *Book of Changes*, written by Chinese mystics, which gives the interpretation of marked yarrow sticks that are cast by the person desiring information about something. The *Book of Changes* contains mystic sayings, abstract principles, symbolic concepts and explanations which form the basis for divination. The yarrow sticks are tossed (some use coins or special cards) and their pattern is used as a guide in consulting the "Wisdom" of the *Book of*

Changes in order to find the answers to a person's questions, or to receive the guidance needed. The system is based upon numerous hexagrams (six-line figures) which reveal what the *Book of Changes* have to say.

ICONS: Sacred ornate frames decorated with images of Christ or Saints.

IDOLATRY: Worship of an idol.

IMMANENT DIVINITY: The theological position that Nature includes Divinity; that Divinity is a quality, not a quantity, and may be found within, not without.

IMMORTALITY: Immunity from any kind of death or decay that comes from having eternal, divine life; in Christianity, that immortality is received from God as his gracious gift as we believe on the Lord Jesus Christ and are saved.

INCANTATIONS: Repetitive use of words, phrases or sounds to produce a magical effect. Verbal spells recited by a practitioner in an effort to summon evil forces.

INCENSE: Any of various substances, such as hums, resins or herbs, producing a pleasant odor when burned and used in religious ceremonies for purifications and offerings.

INCUBI (INCUBUS): An evil spirit in male form sent for sexual purposes, usually with a human female. The victim feels weight and penetration but usually sees nothing. Throughout history there have been instances of women and men who were sexually assaulted or molested by some entity, usually invisible, believed to be either an evil spirit, the spirit form of a deceased person, or the astral body of a sorcerer or sorceress. The incubus is a male entity which assaults women for the purpose of gratifying its sexual appetite, and the succubus is its female counterpart which preys on men for this purpose.

These experiences cannot be dismissed as merely "sexual dreams," "hallucinations," or "hysterical delusions" by psychotic individuals, for such instances are generally reported by normal, rational persons, including Christians. Such bizarre assaults by demons and other spirit entities have long been investigated and reported by the church, as well as by other investigators.

Actual case histories are recorded by contemporary ministers, psychologists, and psychiatrists, including this writer. It is common knowledge that there are numerous instances reported by witches and mediums concerning their sexual relations with demon lovers. Some individuals actually prefer their spirit lovers to normal relations with mortal men and women. The spirits are usually invisible and even so the victims report that the entity has form and weight which can be felt, and that their method of sexual assault is precisely that of a human being.

INITIATE: One who has successfully passed through a ritual of initiation. Also, one who possesses secret knowledge.

INSTITUTE OF NOETIC SCIENCES: A tax-exempt, nonprofit foundation started in 1973 to broaden knowledge of the potentials of mind and consciousness by exploring exceptional abilities, health and healing, and societal transformation.

INTUITION: Ability of knowing, or the knowledge obtained, without conscious recourse to inference or reasoning.

INVERTED CROSS: Upside down cross often seen at occult sites. A mockery of the Christian Cross.

INVERTED PENTAGRAM: Five pointed star with single point downward.

INVOCATION: Calling power in general or calling an evil spirit.

I.P. MESSENGER: Minister of lowest rank.

IPSISSMUS: Highest order held in Satanism. Rarely attainable during a lifetime.

IRIDOLOGY OR IRIS DIAGNOSIS: Receiving treatment for an ailment, from a person not having formal medical training, which is based on the recognition or distinction of diseases by observation of the iris or rainbow membrane of your eye.

ISIS: Egyptian Goddess; Mother Mature; Queen of Heaven; wife of Osiris, mother or Horus. Isis was adopted by Greeks and Romans, and became the most widely-worshiped deity of the Mediterranean world.

ISOLATION TANKS: Alternately referred to as isolation tanks and flotation tanks, these sensory deprivation devices place the patient in a weightless state, sequestered from the outside world. Water laced with Epsom salts creates buoyancy for the purposes of psychic exploration or simple relaxation. The idea is to shut down the conscious mind and enter a state of "samadhi," deep contemplation. A dark, womb-like ambience reduces all sensory input so the patient can enter a natural infantile state.

J

JEAN DIXON - Reading her predictions or belief in her ability to foretell the future. See PRECOGNITION.

JESUS: (In New Age), an avatar who attained a high level of attunement to the Cosmic Christ. This enabled him to become a bodily vehicle for the Christ for a period of three years.

HIN SHIN JYTSU: A Japanese occult healing discipline involving body manipulation at specified points; similar to acupressure.

JUNG, CARL: A disciple of Sigmund Freud who entertained the various forms of occultism, including the idea that the ultimate reality of existence and the source of all truth lies in a "collective unconsciousness" into which spiritually developed beings can tap.

K

KABALA (CABALA): System of Jewish occult mysticism developed by certain rabbis, especially during the Middle Ages, relying heavily on mathematical interpretation of Scripture.

KAHUNA: A native Hawaiian shaman.

KALI: This word means black. Kali is a Hindu goddess who would accept only blood sacrifices. Such sacrifices still are being offered to the goddess today.

KARMA: The law of cause and effect which says that for every action (in this life) there is a reaction (in the next life). What we sow in this life we will reap in the next life.

KARMIC LAW OF JUSTICE: The idea that one's accumulated good and evil deeds will culminate in a fate commensurate with past spiritual accomplishments.

KASHAPH (KESHAPHIM): To practice magic or use incantations, usually with the intent to deceive, pervert, or do mischief; "KASHAPH" refers to the person and "KESHAPHIM" refers to the magical practice.

KATEIDOLOS: Full of idols.

KEMARIM: Idolatrous priests.

KEPPEN ROD: Magical wand used in various ritualistic ceremonies.

KEY OF SOLOMON: Probably the most famous grimoire ever written; some legends hold that it was written by demons and hidden under Solomon's throne. Various versions in different languages survive today.

KIRILIAN: A type of high-voltage photography that uses a pulsed, high-frequency electrical field and two electrodes, between which are placed the object to be photographed and an unexposed film plate. The image captured is purported to be an aura of energy that emanates from plants, animals, and humans an changes in accordance with the physiological or emotional shifts.

KINESIOLOGY: Study of the principles of mechanics and anatomy in relation to human movement.

KNIGHT, J.Z.: Middle-aged housewife who claims to be the "channel" for the entity known as Ramtha, an evil spirit.

KREIGER, DELORES: Originator and popularizer of the therapeutic touch theory.

KRIS: Magic knife of the Malaysians.

KRISHNA: 8th incarnation and avatar of Vishnu, the Preserver god. He has been the most celebrated and revered of all Hindu gods for over 2,000 years.

KRONE TRAINING: New Age motivational teachings, developed by Krone, that critics say are based on the occult teaching of the Armenian mystic Gurdjieff.

KUNDALINI: Psycho-spiritual power thought by yogi(s) to lie dormant at the base of the spine. Believed to be a goddess, Kundalini is referred to as "the serpent power".

L

LADY: Female leader of a coven.

LAMMAS: August witch celebration (August 1, Great Sabbat)

LAMPODEMANCY: Observing lights or torches for omens.

LAVEY, ANTON: American Satanist of Romanian-German-Gypsy parentage, who was the founder and head of the Church of Satan in San Francisco, Calif. Earlier in his career, Lavey played oboe in the San Francisco Ballet Orchestra, worked as a lion-trainer, assisted in hypnotism shows, and became a police photographer. He began holding an occult-studies group, which included filmmaker Kenneth Anger, and in 1966 he shaved his head and proclaimed himself high priest of the Church of Satan. Lavey claimed an affiliated membership of nine thousand members in the United States, France, Italy, Germany, Britain, and South America, and was an advisor on several occult feature films, including, The Mephisto Waltz and Rosemary's Baby – where he appeared on screen as the Devil. Lavey's books include the Satanic Bible (1969) and the Satanic Rituals (1972).

LAZARIS: The entity (an evil spirit) that is channeled through California businessman Jack Purcel.

LEFT-HAND PATH: Occultists who spend their time being destructive, manipulative and "evil". (**PEIB**)

LEMEGETON: A particular grimoire that contains symbols of evil spirits.

LETHE: Stream of forgetfulness in Hell.

LETTERS OF PROTECTION: Magic letters, lucky letters and letters of protection, etc., in spite of their religious exterior belong to the domain of superstition and sorcery.

LEVITATION: The act of raising an object or a person from the ground and causing them to float in the air through supernatural power. People or objects are raised up and appear to float in the air or sail through the air, as if held or thrown by an invisible hand. In actuality evil spirits are raising or moving the person or object.

LIFESPRING: Motivational training technique, founded by Mind Dynamics graduate John Hanley, that declares, "We are intelligent and well-meaning beings…there is nothing that needs to be fixed."

LIFE TRAINING: An imitation of "est" started by two Episcopal priests, involving the rapid "processing" of painful past trauma.

LIGATURE: A spell which prevents a person from doing something.

LIGHT AS A FEATHER – STIFF AS A BOARD: A "game" usually played at slumber parties and sleepovers whereby one participant lays on the floor and is levitated by the other participants with their fingers under the individual on the floor. Actually an occult form of levitation.

LINKING: A mental identification with a person or spirit; usually as part of a practice of magic.

LITHOLATRY: Worship of stones.

LITHOMANCY: Divination using precious stones, possibly colored beads; usually stones are thrown on a flat surface, and whichever reflects the most light is considered the omen. Blue means good luck, green means realization of a hope, red means happiness in love or marriage, yellow means disaster or betrayal, purple means a period of sadness, and black or grey means misfortune.

LOA: Term used in Vodoun for spirit entities. The Loa are 'fed' by tending their altars, and worshiped by being allowed to possess the bodies of devotees in trance, whereupon they take on specific attributes.

LORD MAITREYA: The New Age Christ, who is said to be the fulfillment of all the great religious leaders of the world. Maitreya was originally a savior in Buddhist thought.

LUCID DREAMING: Dreaming while being aware that one is dreaming and therefore being able to control the dream. Instead of changing the dream one becomes able to control their behavior in the dream and therefore able to alter the dream so that one can do what they've ever wanted and go anywhere they want to go. Often involved with this occult practice are out of body experiences. See *Out-of-Body Experience (OBE)*.

LUCIFER: Means "Morning Star;" the archangel who was at the throne of God. Because of pride, he had a revolt against God, and was cast out of heaven along with one third of the angel population who he deceived into believing he was actually the Son of God, the Messiah. Also as the "light bearer," considered a neutral being or force which man can use for good or evil in his attempt to gain godhood.

LUCIFERIANS: A satanic sect active during the Medieval Period, this group sacrificed to evil forces and felt that Lucifer was the son of God and was wrongly expelled. Therefore they worshiped Satan. Still active.

LUCIS TRUST: Originally incorporated as the Lucifer Publishing Company, the Lucis Trust oversees the Lucis Publishing Company, World Goodwill, and Arcane School. Lucis Trust owns all the copyrights of the Alice Bailey books.

LYCANTHROPY: The assumption of an animal form by an occultist.

M

MACLAINE, SHIRLEY: Award winning actress whose personal problems led her to investigate psychic phenomena from channeling to astral projection, resulting in a series of best-selling books.

MACROBIOTICS: Metaphysical dietary system of eating and healing using whole grains, vegetables and fish, and avoiding meat and processed foods.

MACUMBA: A religion similar to Vodoun, Macumba was started by African slaves in an attempt to continue their ancestral tribal religion after being captured by the Portuguese. Now heavily over laden with Catholic symbolism. A low criminal form of spiritism (African), a mixture of black magic, designed to prosecute enemies, and protect from enemies.

MAFU: A discarnate being who speaks through medium Penny Torres.

MAGE: A general term for anyone doing magic, especially of the active kinds often used as a synonym for "magus".

MAGIC: The technique of harnessing the secret powers of nature and seeking to influence the events for one's own purposes.

MAGIC, BLACK: Magic performed with evil intent. The "Black Magician" or sorcerer calls upon the supernatural powers of darkness – devils, demons and veil spirits – and performs ceremonies invoking bestial or malevolent forces intended to harm another person.

MAGIC: BLACK, WHITE, NEUTRAL, HEALING - Divinely forbidden arts of bringing about results beyond human power (counterfeits of divine healing or miracles) by recourse to superhuman spirit agencies (Satan and demons).

MAGIC, CEREMONIAL: Magic that employs ritual, symbols and ceremony. Ceremonial magic stimulates the senses by including its ritual ceremonial costumes, dramatic invocations to the gods or spirits, potent incense, and mystic sacraments.

MAGIC, CIRCLE: Circle inscribed on the floor of a temple for magical ceremonial purposes. Believed to hold magical powers within and protect those involved in the ceremony from evil.

MAGIC DEATH OR DEATH MAGIC: Using a magic charm or spell or item to pass the sickness of the living over onto the dying.

MAGIC – THE GATHERING: See *Magic – The Gathering* page 81.

MAGICAL HYPNOSIS: The occult form of hypnosis which can produce extremely harmful results.

MAGICK: Magic that employs ritual symbols and ceremony, including ceremonial costumes, dramatic invocations to the gods, potent incense and mystic statements. Denotes black magic usually.

MAGISTELLUS: An elemental servant or familiar.

MAGISTER: Male leader of a coven.

MAGNETICISM: An occult form of healing which supposedly uses magnetic forces. Also known as Mesmerism.

MAGUS: A male witch.

MAIDEN: Title sometimes conferred upon a Lady's daughter.

MAITREYA: The name has its roots in a legendary Buddha figure. Some New Age advocates believe that the "second coming of Christ" occurred in 1977 in the person of Maitreya.

MAITREYA, LORD: The supreme member of a spiritual hierarchy who has supposedly incarnated in the body of an Asian new age messiah and who claims that sharing is the only way to achieve peace on earth.

MANDRAKE: A Eurasian plant, Mandragora officinarum; thought to resemble the human body. The plant was once believed to have magical powers.

MANDALA: A design, usually concentric, that focuses attention to a single point.

MANTEUMAI: A Greek word that means divine, prophesy, or give an oracle.

MANTRA: A "holy" word, phrase, or verse in Hindu or Buddhist meditation techniques. A mantra is usually provided to an initiate by a guru who is supposed to hold specific insights regarding the needs of his pupils. The vibrations of the mantra are said to lead the mediator into union with the divine source within.

MARE: An evil spirit which sits on the chest and causes a feeling of suffocation.

MARGARITOMANCY: Divination using pearls which were supposed to bounce upward beneath an inverted pot if a guilty person approached.

MASKIN: Seven subterranean evil spirits.

MASKITH: An image usually painted or carved.

MASLOW, ABRAHAM: Founder of the Association of Humanistic Psychology, he also coined the New Age terms "peak-experience", "synergy" (mutual cooperation), "self actualization", and "humanistic psychology"; is considered the founding father of the Human Potential Movement.

MASS: Ceremony.

MASSEKAH: A statue or image made from a mold.

MASTER: Top leader.

MASTERS OF WISDOM: The arch evil spirits of Satan. In the Bible they are **Master Meon** (Numbers 32:38), **Master Peor** (Numbers 25:3, Deuteronomy 4:3), **Master Perzim** (II Samuel 5:20), **Master Shalisha** (II Kings 4:42), **Master Tamar** (Judges 20:33), **Master Zebub** (II Kings 1:2) and **Master Zephon** (Exodus 14:2).

MATERIALIZATION: Physical manifestation of a spirit being.

MASTEBAH: Something that sits upright, like a statue or pillar.

MAYA: A Hindu teaching that the only reality is the deity Brahman, the Supreme Absolute, and that all else in the material world is an extension of Brahman's thoughts and therefore illusory or transitory.

MAY EVE: Festival Roodman.

MEDITATION: The mystical process of stilling the mind and senses so that sensory stimulation is limited and awareness of internal essence becomes acute. An altered state of consciousness obtained via breathing techniques, chanting words or phrases (mantra), or use of Yoga or other Eastern Religious techniques.

MEDIUMS: In spiritualism, one who acts as an intermediary between the world of spirits and discarnate entities and the everyday world or normal reality. Spirits are summoned during a séance and their influence may be perceived through materializations, through Ouija board communications, through an agreed code of rappings and knocks, or through automatic writing or automatic painting and drawing. If an evil entity takes over the body of the medium during a séance, that being is known as the control. A psychic person whose body is used as a vehicle for communicating with spirits.

MENDES, GOAT OF: Form in which the devil is said to manifest during the witches' Sabbath.

MENTALISM: An ancient performing art in which the practitioner uses mental acuity, principles of stage magic/or suggestion to present the illusion of mind reading, psychokinesis, precognition, and clairvoyance or mind control. These are the techniques of fortunetellers, mind readers, sorcery, wizardry, and witchcraft. The Bible strongly warns people not to consult practitioners of mentalism for the truth, but to inqauire of God (ISa. 8:19). Those who practice these arts receive their power from demons and are being deceived. The Bible condemns and forbids these practices several times (Deut. 18:9-14; Isaiah 44:25; Jeremiah 27:9; 2 Kings 21:6, 23:24). King Saul died because "he consulted a medium for guidance" rather than God (1 Chr. 10:13-14.)[62i]

MENTAL TELEPATHY: The use of mental images to receive and transmit messages.

MENTOR: Senior brother and sister.

MERIDIAN: In acupuncture, a presumed pathway in the body similar to the circulatory system, through which the universal life-energy flows.

MERODACH: Regarded for a time as a supreme deity of the Babylonians; sometimes associated with Bel (Bel-Marduk). (Marduk is in the Dungeons & Dragons Manuals.)

MESMER, ANTON: Nineteenth-century German physician who experimented with mind control techniques resembling hypnotism, first known as "Mesmerism". Magnetism was introduced by Mesmer.

---

[62] Scott, Bryan, booklet Criss Angel "MindFreak", Titusville, FL, Center for Christian Counseling, 2006.

MESMERISM: Similar to hypnotism, used largely by occultists. Similar to the "gifts of spirit" for Christians, it is "a gift of Satan to occultists". Magnetism was introduced by Mesmer.

METAGNOMY: Divination by viewing events while in a hypnotic state.

METAPHYSICS: System of principles relating to the transcendent or supernatural. The science relating to the transcendent, to the mysteries of occult knowledge, and to speculation about the psychic, strange, and unknown.

METAPSYCHOLOGY: Quarterly New Age journal emphasizing trance-channeled information.

METEMPSYCHOSIS: Ancient Greek word which essentially means the same thing as reincarnation.

METEOROMANCY: Observing meteors or similar phenomena for omens.

METOPOSCOPY: The reading of character from the lines on a person's forehead.

MIDSUMMER: Festival of Beltane (May 1st).

MIGHTY ONES: Ancient gods revered by witches.

MIND SCIENCE: A religious philosophy based on the ideas of Ernest Holmes, who denied orthodox Christian doctrines in favor of promoting the possibility of "Christ-realization" by all men.

MINOR LUMINARY: Lieutenants to leaders.

MIRRORMANTIC: Division through the use of such objects as crystal balls, mirrors, rock crystals, or bodies of still water.

MISSAL: Book with rituals and teachings.

MOJO: Magickal power from the lower chakras, especially equated with Love and Power in Voodoo spells.

MOKSHA: The final state of "deliverance" from the burdensome cycle of reincarnation.

MOLYBDOMANCY: Divination by observing the hissing of molten lead.

MONISM: Literally means "one". In a spiritual framework it refers to the classical occult philosophy that "All Is One"; all reality may be reduced to a single, unifying principle partaking of the same essence and reality. Monism also relates to the belief in Pantheism that there is no ultimate distinction between the Creator and the creation.

MOON MANCY: The observance of the full moon when planting, casting spells, getting married, and so on.

MULTIPLE TRANSMUTATION OF ALTER PERSONALITIES: An occult practice of removing alter personalities formed during extreme ritual abuse from an individual's soul and placing them into the broken soul of another individual with hopes that neither soul will ever find healing.

MUMMIFICATION: The ancient Egyptian means of preserving the physical body after death to facilitate its journey into the next life.

MYOMANCY: Drawing prophetic conclusions from rats and mice, particularly their cries or destruction they cause.

MYSTICISM: Belief that God is totally different than anything the human mind can think and must be approached by a mind without content. Spiritual union or direct communion with Ultimate Reality can be obtained through subjective experience such as intuition or a unifying vision. Mysticism denies the utterly transcendent reality of God.

MYTH: Metaphor, particularly one with a ploy and a cast of characters.

MYTHOLOGY: A gestalt composed of myth and theology that forms the religious world-view of people.

N

NATAL ANNIVERSARY: The idea that the positions of the planets and other heavenly bodies, as they were located at one's birth affect that individual on recurring birthdates.

NATURALISM: View that asserts that nothing beyond nature is real. Human beings are therefore to be understood strictly in terms of heredity and environment.

NATUROPATHY: Non-intrusive form of medical care using herbs instead of drugs, generally practiced by chiropractors and osteopaths.

NECROLATRY: Worship of the dead.

NECROMANCY: A practice in which the "spirits of the dead" are summoned to provide omens relating to future events or to discover secrets of the past.

NECRONOMICON: Communication with the supposed spirits of the dead, usually with the use of bones or some part of the corpse.

NECROPHILIA: Sexual intercourse with the dead. This sometimes arises with psychopathic murderers who believe their victims to still be alive. Necrophilia seems to be a feature of the more debased forms of black magic.

NEO-AMERICAN CHURCH: Their symbol appears to be a three-eyed frog. The Neo-American church recruits children into their activities and also hinders the finding of missing children. The Neo-American church people usually drive vans with gun racks located behind the driver's seat. They will show up with Rainbow tribe and also associate themselves with other groups.

NEOPAGAN: Follower of some Western religious tradition other than Judaism or Christianity. Neo-pagan groups have a close affinity for nature, occult and initiatory traditions, and may be patrons of ancient Greek or Egyptian religions, Druidism, witchcraft, ceremonial magic or even Satanism.

NEOPHYTE: One who is about to go through the initiation into a coven.

NETWORK: An informal, decentralized organization created by like-minded individuals who are interested in addressing specific problems and offering possible solutions. All of this takes place outside of conventional institutions.

NETWORKING: The New Age concept of linkage of ideas, practices, and metaphysical efforts; combines the endeavors of various aspects of the movement worldwide through written and verbal communication, as well as telepathic communiqués.

NEUROLINGUISTICS: A behavioristic form of motivational training and therapy, it supposes that observing body languages enables a counselor to help a client overcome his phobias, learning disabilities, and insecurities.

NEW AGE JOURNAL: Bimonthly New Age magazine emphasizing human potential aspects of the movement.

NEW AGE MOVEMENT: A spiritual, political and social phenomenon networking many occult/metaphysical organizations and groups intending to transform individuals by means of "mystical enlightenment" so that a new age of unprecedented peace, prosperity and harmony can be introduced on earth.

NEW AGE MUSIC: A contemporary music genre, usually instrumental and often acoustic, based on classical and jazz styles; generally played in a free-form or unstructured style for the purpose of altering the listener's consciousness and perception of reality.

NEW THOUGHT: A late 1800's philosophy of mental healing promoted by Warren Felt Evans, who influenced May Baker Eddy, the founder of Christian Science, and Charles and Myrtle Fillmore, who founded Unity.

NIRVANA: Literally, a "blowing out" or a "cooling" of the fires of existence; the main word used in Buddhism for final release from the cycle of birth and death into bliss.

NOSTRODAMUS: Sixteenth-century occult mystic who wrote ten volumes of prophecy called "Centuries", supposedly predicting the world's future in minute detail; his own description of "receiving" these so-called prophecies is clearly divination; lived 1503-1555.

NECROLATRY: Worship of the dead.

NECROMANCY: A practice in which the "spirits of the dead" are summoned to provide omens relating to future events or to discover secrets of the past.

NECRONOMICON: Communication with the supposed spirits of the dead, usually with the use of bones or some part of a corpse.

NECROPHILIA: Sexual intercourse with the dead. This sometimes arises with psychopathic murders who believe their victims to still be alive. Necrophilia seems to be a feature of the more debased forms of black magic.

NEOPAGAN: Follower of some Western religious tradition other then Judaism or Christianity. Neo-pagan groups have a close affinity for nature, occult and initiatory traditions, and may be patrons of ancient Greek or Egyptian religions, Druidism, witchcraft magic or even Satanism.

NEOPHYT: One who is about to go through the initiation into a coven.

NETWORK: An informal, decentralized organization created by like-minded individuals who are interested in addressing specific problems and offering possible solutions. All of this takes place outside of conventional institutions. NETWORKING – The New Age concept of linkage of ideas, practices, and metaphysical efforts; combines the endeavors of various aspects of the movement worldwide through written and verbal communication, as well as telepathic communiqués.

NEUROLINGUISTICS: A behavioristic form of motivational training and therapy, it supposes that observing body languages enables a counselor to help a client overcome his phobias, learning disabilities, and insecurities.

NEW AGE JOURNAL: Bimonthly New Age magazine emphasizing human potential aspects of the movement.

NEW AGE MOVEMENT: A spiritual, political and social phenomenon networking many occult/metaphysical organizations and groups intending to transform individuals by means of "mystical enlightenment" so that a new age of unprecedented peace, prosperity and harmony can be introduced on earth.

NEW AGE MUSIC: A contemporary music genre, usually instrumental and often acoustic, based on classical and jazz styles; generally played in a free-form or unstructured style for the purpose of altering the listener's consciousness and perception of reality.

NEW THOUGHT: A late 1800's philosophy of mental healing promoted by Warren Felt Evans, who influenced May Baker Eddy, the founder of Christian Science, and Charles and Myrtle Fillmore, who founded Unity.

NIRVANA: Literally, a "blowing out" or a "cooling" of the fires of existence; the main word used in Buddhism for final release from the cycle of birth and death into bliss.

NOSTRODAMUS: Sixteenth-century occult mystic who wrote ten volumes of prophecy called "Centuries", supposedly predicting the world's future in minute detail; his own description of "receiving" these co-called prophecies is clearly divination; lived 1503-1555.

NOVEMBER EVE: This is All Hallow's Eve, also called Sambain, which is Scottish Gaelic meaning All Hallow's Eve, occuring on Oct. 31.

NUDITY: Believed essential to raising forces through which magic works.

NUMBERS OF SIGNIFICANCE –

   ONE - equate with primal chaos

   THREE - triple repetitions, effective in incantations

   FIVE - symbolizes justice

   SEVEN - in occult rites, possesses mystic implications

   THIRTEEN - number of members in a coven, members being associated with thirteen   lunar moons

4 x 4 - in Talmudic computations the Devil's own
number

7 + 9 - multiples of these possessed thaomaturgic
potency; odd numbers lucky; triple repetitions is characteristic
of magical rituals

666 - sign of the beast, Devil's calling numbers

O

OBJECT LINK: An object that is supposedly impregnated with the magnetism of a proposed victim or subject or a spell.

OCCULT: A term, which means hidden, secret or mysterious.

OCCULTISM: Belief in secret supernatural forces and beings.

OCULOMANCY: Divination by observing a person's eyes.

OFFICER: Third leader in a coven, after Magister and Lady.

OLINOMANCY: Looking for omens form wines.

OMEN: A prophetic sign.

ONEIROMANCY: Interpretation of dreams.

ONE WORLDERS: Those who advocate the abolition of nations, working to hand over power to a single-world government; off shoots of the United World Federalists found in the 1930s.

ONOMANCY: Finds meaning and omens in the names of persons and things; onomancy is seldom used today, except for interpreting a person's proper name.

ONOMANTICS: Onomancy applied to personal names.

ONYOMANCY: Interpretation of various characteristics from a person's fingernails as one aspect of Palmistry.

OOMANTIA (OOSCOPY): Ancient practice of divination by eggs.

OPIOMANCY: Divination from serpents.

O.P. MESSENGER: Student ministers.

ORANGE MAGIC: Used for pride and courage. Heroism and attraction.

ORDO TEMPLI ORIENTIS (O.T.O.): Initials for Ordo Templi Orientis, a sect whose members practiced sexual magic. The order was founded by Karl Kellner. The famous Aleister Crowley was a member who helped to revive O.T.O. in the middle 1920s.

ORIENS: Rules over all the spirits of the east.

ORISHAS: Yoruban term used in Santeria for African nature spirits of deities called "Loa" in Vodoun and Voodoo.

ORNISCOPY (ORNITHAMANCY): Observation of the flight of birds for omens.

OSIRIS: Egyptian "green man", God of Vegetation who dies and rules in the underworld as Lord of the Dead. Husband to Isis and father of Horus, his reincarnation.

OUIJA BOARD: Board with letters and numbers with which spirits can communicate.

OUT-OF-BODY EXPERIENCE (OBE): Leaving the physical body while conscious, at rest, asleep, or near death. Departing one's physical body and observing both one's self and the world from outside of one's body. The experience is quite common. Some people experience OBE while under the influence of an anesthetic or while semi-conscious due to trauma. Some have an OBE while under the influence of drugs. Surveys show that about 15% to 20% of the population have had an OBE at some time during their life. This occult activity has reported been used by spy agencies so that an individual can leave the body and sit in on secret meetings, etc.

OVER SHADOW: The term used when an invisible entity takes over the mind, emotions, will, or the body of a spirit medium.

OVOMANCY: A type of divination from eggs.

OWL: In many cultures the bird is associated with death and evil powers.

P

PACT: A vow of secrecy given by a witch who joins a coven.

PACT WITH SATAN: Selling one's soul to the devil; promising to serve him.

PAGAN: The term is used derogatorily to describe a heathen or "unbeliever", but has now assumed a new currency among practitioners of witchcraft and magic. The so-caled New Pagans are dedicated to reviving the old religion and reestablishing the worship of Nature and the lunar goddess.

PAGANISM: A practicing pagan.

PALMISTRY: A form of divination which attempts to analyze an individual's character, or predict his future, by studying the lines and other features of his hands. The size, shape, and proportions of the hands and fingers, the length of the lines and their characteristics, and the areas called "mounts" all influence the reader's interpretation. The palmist gives particular attention to 4 lines and 7 mounts in the hand, and makes use of astrology, believing that the planetary influences upon a person's life are also written in the palms. Each of the mounts is named for a heavenly body (e.g., Jupiter, Mars, Venus, etc.), while the nature of such mount is supposed to reveal character traits (e.g., ambition, pride, meekness, sexuality, etc.). The four principle lines in the hand are said to represent the head, life, heart, and fortune. The head line is supposed to indicate intelligence, the heart line reveals affection, the fortune line indicates success or failure in life, and the life line forecasts a person's physical well-being and length of life.

As the practice is under the influence and control of the powers of darkness it is not surprising that those who have become involved in palmistry, or who have had their palms read, generally suffer some form of occult oppression as a result.

PALO MAYOMBE: A Cuban sect of Santeria followed by many Latin American drug gangs; sort of a "magickal mafia", leaders engage in human sacrifice and other terror tactics to keep followers in line and enemies at bay.

PAN: "In ancient Greek mythology, the son of Hermes and Dryope. Pan was the god of flocks and shepherds, but also had a more far-reaching role as lord of nature and all forms of wildlife. He was depicted as half-man, half-goat, and played a pipe with seven reeds. Regarded as high god."

PANTHEISM: Belief that God and the world are ultimately identical; "All is God". Everything that exists constitutes a unity, and this all-inclusive unity is divine. God is the force and law of the universe but not a Being with personality.

PANTHEON: A temple dedicated to all the gods.

PARANORMAL: Faculties and phenomena in psychical research that are beyond the "normal" in terms of cause and effect as presently understood.

PARAPSYCHOLOGY: The study of occult phenomena such as telepathy, clairvoyance, precognition and psychokinesis.

PAST LIFE THERAPY: Therapy that assumes the reality of reincarnation and which involves being "taken back" into past lives by a channeler or spirit guide, to discover the supposed roots of present trauma or trouble, such information should be considered to have been given by demons.

PEACE SYMBOL: The early 60's peace symbol is now commonly thought of as the "Cross of Nero" by heavy metal heads and occultists.

PEALE, NORMAN VINCENT: Pastor and author who pioneered the positive thinking concept and from whose premises certain New Agers have drawn inspiration.

PEGAMANCY: Divination by observing spring water bubbling fountains.

PENDUMLUM: Heavy object on a string, used for dawning or fortune telling.

PENTACLE (PENTAGRAM): A five-pointed star used as a magic symbol in rituals, also knows as the Pentagram.

PENTAGRAM: A pentacle surrounded by a circle. It represents the four elements. When the star is inverted with two points up, it stands for black arts. When turned with a single point up, it symbolizes white magic. Pentagrams are also worn for "protection" and identification among the craft.

PERCIPIENT: Person who receives telepathic messages.

PERENNIAL PHILOSOPHY: A term coined by Aldous Huxley that sees all religious truth or experience as one and the same. This philosophy proposes that even though the externals of the various religions may differ, the essence or core truth is the same in each.

PESSOMANCY: Divination by pebbles.

PHILOSOPHER'S STONE: A psychic substance used in Alchemy.

PHRENOLOGY::: Divination from interpreting head formations or bumps on the head.

PHYLLORHODOMANCY: A means of divination that comes from Ancient Greece; a person slaps rose petals against his hand, and the success of a venture is judged by the loudness of the sound.

PHYSIOGNAMY: Analysis of a person's character through observation of a person's features or physical characteristics.

THE PLAN: A New Age reference to a "conspiracy" that would replace present religious, political, and economic systems with an intuitive thrust for planetary harmony under New Age concepts.

PLANETARY CITIZENS: A New Age activist group committed to engendering a "planetary consciousness" among both New Agers and the general Public.

PLANETIZATION: New Age advocates believe that the various threats facing the human race require a global solution. This solution is "planetization". The word refers to the unifying of the world into a corporate brotherhood.

POLARITY THERAPY: Bionergetic healing therapy teaching that illness results from blockage of energy at certain places in the body, a hindrance that can supposedly be removed by strategic laying-on of hands.

POLTERGEIST: "Rattling Ghost", a ghost that tends to throw or break objects or generally cause mischief.

POLYTHEISM: The belief that there are many deities.

POSITIVE IMAGING: A form of psychological reinforcement that seeks to replace negative mental images with carefully constructed positive ones, out of which a new reality can be created; basically mind over matter.

POWER OBJECT: An object with "witch power" placed in a subject or victim's vicinity to complete a spell.

PRANA: The power whereby everything in the universe supposedly exists, known as chi in Taoism and vital breath in Hinduism; the force of life, which is said to emanate from the impersonal energy of Brahman (god).

PRECOGNITION: The supernatural ability to have knowledge of, or to see, events which are yet in the future and predict their occurrence, such as Jeane Dixon's predictions of President Kennedy's assassination as well as that of Gandhi, Eisenhower's election, and Russia's launching of the first satellite. Although many have been deluded into believing that this is a manifestation of the Biblical gift of prophecy, a careful examination of the origin of this woman's psychic powers indicate that their source is not from heaven.

PREDICTIVE DREAMS/VISIONS: Dreams or visions which reveal the future or hidden knowledge (counterfeit biblical prophesy).

PREMONITION: A foreboding of the future.

PROGNOSTICATION: To foretell from signs or symptoms; prophesying without the Holy Spirit; soothsaying. Is. 47:12-15; Josh. 13:22.

PROPHECIES: Ability to foretell the future.

PROPHETS: Senior brothers and sisters.

PROVISIONAL MASTER: Lieutenants leaders.

PSI: The twenty-third letter of the Greek alphabet; a general New Age term for ESP, psychokinesis, telepathy, clairvoyance, precognition, and other paranormal phenomena that are non-physical in nature.

PSYCHIC: Pertaining to phenomena which are supernatural, or perhaps actually demonic; or a person who has this power.

PSYCHIC BIRTH: A quickening of spiritual or cosmic consciousness and power. This new consciousness is one that recognized oneness with God and the universe. Psychic birth is an occult counterpart to the Christian new birth.

PSYCHIC ENERGY: Extrasensory energy that enables people to do miracles.

PSYCHIC HEALER: A person who cures mental or physical illness from the cosmic energy emanating through the healer's hands.

PSYCHIC SURGERY: Surgery by a medium having no ordinary medical knowledge, while in a trance.

PSYCHOANALYSIS: Tracing mental and physical ills back to hurtful childhood experiences; based on Sigmund Freud's theories.

PSYCHOGRAPHY: A form of mysterious writing, usually of a divinatory type.

PSYCHOKINESIS: Power of the mind to influence matter or move objects. Popularly known as PK (see also Telekinesis).

PSYCHOMETRY: The gaining of impressions from a physical object, usually having to do with the owner or the object's history.

PSYCHOTECHNOLOGIES: Refers to the various approaches or systems aimed at deliberately altering ones consciousness.

PUNK ROCK: Punk rock began in England as a revolt against the economic, educational and political system. Shabby clothes, spiked hair, Mohawk haircuts, shaved heads, and outlandish make-up represented the British youth rebellion against the status-quo. When punk rock came to America the issues faded, but the anti-establishment statement was the same. Whatever society cherishes - religion, law, tradition

punkers denigrate. Punkers want to do anything they want, to be angry and alienated. Kids who follow punk rock groups view themselves as society's victims. Punkers' ultimate goal is to live recklessly and to be young and fast. The punk rock dance, called the slam dance, involves slamming into someone else, kicking them and punching them. Many seem bent on self-destruction, and it's not unusual for them to wound themselves with razor blades, knives, cigarettes or cigarette lighters. (Quotes by Darlyne Pettinicchio, probation officer from Orange County, Calif. Director of the Back in Control Center, news article, The Press Enterprise Riverside, Calif., Ma, 1986). Note: While punk is not typically occult, one should remember that adolescents involved in this type of negative, violent activity sometimes become involved with occult groups.

PURPLE MAGIC: Used for wealth and good fortune. Prosperity, domination and command.

PYRAMID POWER: The belief that pyramid shapes are antennae that pick up frequencies of universal energy that bring healing, sound sleep, nutrition, and superior sexual experience.

PYROLATRY: Worship of fire.

PYROMANCY: Divination by fire, usually involving powered substances thrown in.

R

RAMTHA: The entity (demon) channeled through J.Z. Knight and who is followed closely by actress Linda Evans.

READINGS: Information or revelations gotten during a séance.

REBIRTH: In the occult, technically from reincarnation in that the individual who does it is not reborn as the same self.

RED MAGIC: Used for physical work, as in healing of people and animals. Passion and sex.

REFLEXOLOGY: A belief that the sole of the foot contains reflex points that correspond to all internal organs and bodily functions, and that manipulation of these points relieves pain and disease.

REIKI: An occult form of healing. See *Reiki* Appendix D, page 249.

REINCARNATION: The belief that the soul after death passes on to another body. Any belief that after death your soul will experience rebirth into a new body (human or animal).

REMOTE INFLUENCE: The practice (sometimes by Christians who should know better) is the attempt to influence the subconscious minds of others while they are asleep or in another room and is an unwarranted telepathic invasion of the God-given privacy of the subconscious mind of another individual.

The psychic dangers or adverse effects in such an unscriptural practice are the same as in other forms of telepathy. Such intrusion is a trespass upon the prerogatives of God. The excuse that such remote suggestions are intended to influence someone for "good" overlooks the occult nature of the practice.

REMOTE VIEWING/HEALING: Discerning telepathically or transmitting healing across distances without the psychic's being in direct physical contact with person, object, or circumstance.

REPERCUSSION: Injuries received by a projected form that appear on someone's physical body.

RESPONDER: At rituals he states the natures of Lucifer and Christ.

RETROCGNITION: The process of knowing past information which is usually attained through some paranormal methods.

RHABDOMANCY: Divination by means of a rod or stick; the forerunner of the divining rod.

RHAPSODOMANCY: Opening a book, usually poetry, and reading words or passages at random, looking for omens.

RIGHT BRAIN LEARNING: The right hemisphere of the brain is believed to be the center of intuitive and creative thought (as opposed to the rational nature of the left hemisphere). New Ager's have seized on this as a justification to bring "right brain leaning techniques" into the classroom. These techniques include meditation, yoga, and guided imagery.

RIGHT HAND PATH: In mystical and occultism, the esoteric path associated with spiritual illumination and positive aspiration. It is the path of light as distinct from the so-called left-hand path of darkness which equates with evil, bestiality, and black magic. Occultists who spend their time being constructive, manipulative and "good".

RITES OF PASSAGE: Ritual commemoration of life's transitions. Such passages include: being born- becoming an incarnate being; onset of puberty- becoming sexually fertile; marriage- becoming bonded to a partner; giving birth- becoming a mother or father; menopause- becoming a wise crone; death- going to the underworld to await rebirth.

RITUAL: A magical ceremony used in both white and black magic.

RITUAL ABUSE: Victimizing someone (usually sexually) in a satanic ritual. For those who do not believe Satanism is prevalent in the United States, a reading of the *Illinois State Law #87-1167 Ritualized Abuse of a Child* on p. 103 will change that opinion. Please remember this law was not written in the Salem witch hunt days but in 1993.

ROBERTS, JANE: Best selling author and channel for the spirit Seth (a demon); there are numerous "Seth" books.

ROCK MUSIC – The Six themes of Rock Music are: love-sex; drugs & alcohol; racism & bigotry; graphic violence & death; rebellion   and/or aggression; fascination with the occult. See *Rock Music* page 89.

ROLFING: A deep, forceful massage technique that is said to restructure the body so it more properly aligns with gravity and the energies of earth.

ROSE CROSS – A golden cross with a rose at its center, the emblem of the esoteric order of the Rosicrucians.

ROSICRUCIANS - A brotherhood order (headquartered in California) teaching a system of metaphysical and scientific philosophy aimed at awakening the latent powers of man.

RUNES: From the German "raunen" meaning a secret or mystery; occult symbols that are known in many areas of Northern Europe. (Note: Runes are used for Magick. We are seeing them in the United States in certain incidents which involve ritualistic crime). Stones inscribed with letters of the ancient Scandinavian alphabet, believed to have been used by the Vikings for predictive purposes and revived today for fortune telling.

RYERSON, KEVIN: Channeler consulted by actress Shirley MacLaine.

S

SABBAT: One of the eight annual festivals of the seasonal round celebrated by nearly all Pagans, including Witches. The solstices and equinoxes are known as Quarters, and the others are Cross-Quarters, also known as Grand Sabbats by Witches. Several are also celebrated by both Christians and Satanist: Ostara spring Equinox, Mar 21 (Easter), Beltane- May1 (May Day), Litha- summer solstice, June 21 (St. John's), Lughnasad- August 2 (Lammas), Mabon-autumn equinox, Sept. 21 (Harvest), Samhain- Nov 1 (All Saint's Day), Yule- winter solstice, Dec. 21 (Christmas), Oimeic- Feb 2 (Imboic, Brigit, Candlemas).

SACRAL: Pertaining to sacred rites or observances.

SACRAMENTAL: Consecrated.

SACRAMENTARIAN: A person who regards the sacraments as merely visible symbols.

SACRIFICE: An offering made to a deity, often upon an altar. Scarifies are performed ritually to placate a god and to offer blood, which is symbolic of the life-force and invariably associated with fertility. Some magicians believed that the ritual slaughter of a sacrificial animal releases life energy, which can be tapped magically and used to attune the magician to the god invoked in ritual.

SACRIFIST: Presiding priest.

SACRILEGE: Misuse, theft, desecration or profanation of anything consecrated.

SACROSANCT: Sacred and inviolable.

SADISTIC: One who will deliberately torture or hurt any living creature.

SALAMANDER: An elemental who lives in fire.

SAMANDHI (SATORI): Ultimate or highest state of God-consciousness or enlightenment in classical Hindu yoga. Satori is the equivalent in Zen Buddhism: a state of existential intuitive enlightenment.

SAMHAIN: (pronounced "so-ahn") The Great Sabbat, or cross-quarter festival, occurring midway between autumn Equinox and Winter Solstice. Traditionally celebrated on Nov. 1.

SAMSARA: The continual cycle of rebirth.

SANAT KIMARA: To the initiated of the occult, this is the king of the world, this is Lucifer who is the "light" of the world.

SANCTUM: Main ritual room.

SANTERIA: a mingling of African tribal religions and Catholicism established by African slaves brought to the Americas and Caribbean.

SATAN: The angelic being created by God. He was an archangel who rebelled and was cast out of heaven.

SATANIC: Refers to anything that pertains to Satan, which is evil.

SATANIC BIBLE: A diabolically inspired work written by Anton LeVey. It consists of three parts: Book of Lucifer, Book of Belial, and Book of Leviathan. Chapter titles include such demonic and perverted subjects as: Satanic Sex; An invocation for the Conjuration of Lust; The Black Mass; The Practice of Satanic Magic; Satanic Ritual; Invocation to Satan; Invocation for the Conjuration of Destruction, and How to Sell Your Soul. The book advocates indulging in the seven deadly sins forbidden by Scriptures (pride, envy, greed, anger, gluttony, sloth, and lust), as they will give physical, emotional, and mental gratification, and will release one from prudish guilt-feelings about sin.

The Satanic Bible teaches there is no God but that man himself is god and his own redeemer. Christ is blasphemed as weak and impotent, and the king of slaves and weaklings. There is no heaven or hell; therefore, man should make the most of life here and now by indulging in sensuous pleasures instead of practicing abstinence or temperance. The Satanist is encouraged to indulge in all his natural appetites and desires in order to eliminate his frustrations. The righteous and good die young because the denial of natural appetites leads to deterioration of the mind and body.

SATANIC RITUAL CALENDAR: See *Satanic Ritual Calendar* page 96.

SATANIC WORSHIP: Worshipping Satan, attending a satanic church, being part of a coven.

SATANIC MASS: In Satanism, a blasphemous ritual that parodies the Catholic Mass, invokes the powers of darkness and sometimes employs the use of a naked woman as an altar.

SATANISM: The worship of Satan. It claims to be a religion of the flesh, world, and the carnal – all ruled over by Satan. Satanism advocates, for example, sexual freedom, interpreting this to mean indulging one's sexual lusts in any way desired (homosexual, heterosexual, self-gratification, bi-sexual, the practice of sadism, masochism, or any other lewd perversion), and with as many others as desired, as long as the parties consent.

SATANIC RITUAL CALENDAR – A yearly calendar used in Satanism. See page 96 for the calendar itself.

SATANIC WORSHIP/SATANIC BIBLE - Worshipping Satan, attending a Satanic Church, being part of a coven, or reading Anton LeVey's Satanic Bible.

SCARFING: See Auto Erotic Stimulation.

SCIENTOLOGY: A healing movement founded by Dr. Ronald Hubbard and discussed in his book <u>Dianetics</u> which employs an E-meter in the healing process.

SCIOMANCY: Various forms of divination involving direct communication with spirits.

SCREENING (raddiesthesia): A small box used to screen out harmful "earth" rays; a mediumistic field which can be clairvoyantly perceived through the mediumistic powers of dowsers and pendulum practitioners and the like.

SCRYING: Divination by gazing, as in crystal, mirror, water, etc.

SEAL: A demon's summoning diagram or signature.

SEAL OF SOLOMON: Two interlocking triangles that form a hexagram. This seal is said to offer the greatest protection for the practioner.

SEANCE or SPIRITUALISM - Any gathering of people where an attempt is made to contact a dead person or a spirit to receive communication from the spirit world. See Spiritism.

SECOND COMING OF CHRIST: Understood by some as the coming of the Cosmic Christ in all humanity, related to the New Age concept of the "Mass incarnation". The Second Coming is supposedly now occurring in the hearts and minds of people all over the earth. Others associate it specifically with the appearance of Maitreya as the avatar of this age.

SEEING: The ability to hold the item of another and see events or know facts about that person.

SEER: One who can see the hidden; a diviner.

SELF ACTUALIZATION: The state of fulfilling one's potential so fully that one realizes one's self-deity.

SELF-HYPNOSIS: For relaxation, consciousness expansion, incarnation regression, and a variety of other New Age intents, some consider self-hypnosis the best tool for entering altered states of the mind. Movement catalogues offer subliminal devices to induce self-hypnosis, including audio cassettes that coach the subject into alpha states. For some, self-hypnosis is the pathway to rapidly releasing latent psychic powers. Practitioners are told to accept intuitively whatever images enter their minds under hypnosis. They are also warned to expect rebirthing stages and the possible intervention of entities seeking to use them as channels.

SELF IDOLATRY: Worship of self.

SELF REALIZATION: The act of acknowledging that one's self (ego) is identifiable with God and that one's highest inner nature is though to be pure and devoid of all evil.

SEMEL: A likeness or image.

SENSITIVE: A person who frequently demonstrates extrasensory gifts such as clairvoyance, telepathy, or precognition.

SENSITIVITY TRAINING: A problem solving technique which involves discussing a person's life, job, and marriage in a group setting, as well as touching one another's bodies when the lights have been turned off.

SEPHIROTH: The occult satanic tree of life: one side negative, one positive, one side masculine, one feminine, one side severe, one merciful; the tree as ten steps one must pass through in order to achieve priesthood in satanic religion.

SERPENT: Serpent w/horns is symbolic of the demons.

SERVERS: Ritual assistants.

SERVITOR: A familiar.

SET: Egyptian name for Satan, in 1975 Michael Aquino established the temple of set church religion in the United States.

SETH: Spirit entity channeled by Jane Roberts, with numerous books printed on his "messages".

SEXUAL HANGING: See autoerotic asphyxiation.

SHADE: The supposed spirit of a dead person.

SHADOWS, BOOK OF: The personal book used and kept by the high priest within the coven or group. All of his rituals and spells are kept in this book. When the high priest dies, the book is destroyed. The book is also used by pagans and by dabbler Satanists as a diary of personal activities.

SHAMBALLA: Legendary kingdom of spiritually developed adepts (similar to the occult concept of Atlantis), proposed by locale and an aspect of astral existence.

SHAKTI: The Female Principle in Hinduism.

SHAMAN: A medicine man or witch doctor.

SHAMAYIM: A Hebrew phrase that means "viewers of the heavens".

SHAMBALLAH: A palace where Lucifer and the masters are believed to reside. Initiated occultist believe Shamballah to be lost in the Gobi dessert or a hidden valley in Tibet.

SHARE INTERNATIONAL: Publication of Tara Center, expounding the teachings of Lord Maitreya and various New Age doctrines.

SHEBISIM: A "sun-pendant".

SHIGGUTS: An abomination or a detestable thing.

SHRINE: Ritual table.

SIDEROMANCY: Divining by observing the forms made by burning straws with a hot iron.

SIGIL: A "symbolic signature" inscribed on a talisman.

SIGIL OF BAPHOMET: A symbol of the Church of Satan-two concentric circles with a pentagram within the smaller one. Within the five-pointed star there is a picture of the Goat of Mendes.

SIGNS: The signs of the Zodiac. Everyone is born under one of these 12 signs or constellations: **Aquarius** Jan. 20 - Feb. 18; **Pisces** Feb. 19 - Mar. 20; **Aries** Mar. 21 – Apr. 19; **Taurus** Apr. 20 – May 20; **Gemini** May 21- June 20; **Cancer** June 21 – July 22; **Leo** July 23 – Aug. 22; **Virgo** Aug. 23 – Sept. 22; **Libra** Sept. 23 – Oct. 22; **Scorpio** Oct. 23 – Nov. 21; **Sagittarius** Nov. 22 – Dec. 21; **Capricorn** Dec. 22 – Jan. 19.

SILVA MIND CONTROL: "Mind expansion" techniques developed by Jose Silva to control one's future and fortune through self-hypnosis and the alteration of reality by mental supposition.

SILVER: The perfect metal to be used in occult objects and jewelry.

SKULL: Human or animal used in rites.

SKYCLAD: Nude.

SOCIETY FOR PSYCHICAL RESEARCH: Organization developed to para-psychological research and the scholarly collection of related information concerning the paranormal.

SOLAR LOGOS: Believed by some to be a mighty spiritual being who is the ensouling life of the solar system. The material solar system is simply a physical manifestation (or body) of this living intelligence.

SOLOMON: The king of Israel who is said, by some involved in the occult, to have written several grimoires, one such called "The Lesser Keys of Solomon". Practitioners also use the Seals of Solomon.

SOLSTICE: Either of two times of the year when the sun has no apparent northward or southward motion. Summer solstice is approximately June 22 and Winter Solstice is approximately December 22.

SO MOTE IT BE: Words said at the end of an occult ceremony and in Freemasonry to end a prayer. Similar to "amen" in traditional religious services.

SOOTHSAYER: A medium.

SOOTH SAYING: The act of foretelling events; prophesying by a spirit other than the Holy Spirit. Joshua 13:22; Micah 5:12-15; Acts 16:16-18.

SORCERER: A wizard, witch or magician; a practitioner of black magic.

SORCERY: Magic, usually of the black variety.

SORILEGE: Casting lots hoping to find a good omen.

SOUL FORCE - Any attempt by faithful church members to bring backsliders back to the church by means of mental powers at a distance (remote mental suggestion).

SOUL TIE - A spiritual union created by placing yourself in subjection to another person's authority or through sexual intercourse.

SOUL TRANSFER: Based on the premise that some soul types incarnate through a process of soul transfer. Commonly called 'Walk-ins', 'Crawl-ins', or 'Wanderers'. These are souls that agree to transfer into another soul's physical vehicle or body at a given point in the subject's life. The Apostle Paul had something to say about soul travel: "We are of good courage, I say, and are willing rather to be absent from the body, and to be at home with the Lord" (2 Cor. 5:8). The Bible is clear on the subject of soul travel. When your soul leaves the body it is destined for one of two places depending upon your salvation, Heaven or Hell. It is clear that the Christian is not to practice in soul travel.[63]

SPELL: An incantation designed to bring about magic.

SPIRAL DANCE: A Wiccan greeting dance celebrating spiral symbolism. Also a book by Starhawk.

SPIRIT GUIDE: A spiritual entity who provides information or "guidance", often through a medium or channeler. The spirit provides guidance only after the channeler relinquishes his perceptual and cognitive capacities into its control.

SPIRIT PHOTOGRAPHY: A photograph taken during a séance which, when developed reveals the face of the dead.

SPIRIT SPEAKS: Bimonthly New Age publication featuring occult phenomena.

SPIRITISM / SPIRITUALISM: A spiritual activity grounded in the persuasion that people can by means of certain Spiritistic Mediums make contact with the deceased (where contact actually occurs with demon spirits and not deported impersonations) and so acquire revelations from the beyond.)

SPIRITISTIC HEALING: See *Magic: Healing*.

SPIRITISTIC MEDIUM: A person under the direct influence or control of evil spirits who possesses occult powers.

SPIRITISTIC VISIONS / DREAMS - Visions leading to sensationalism which promote errant doctrines.

SPIRITUALIST or SPIRITIST: A person who believes in the ability to contact departed souls through a medium.

---

[63] Scott, Bryan, booklet <u>Criss Angel "MindFreak"</u>, Titusville, FL, Center for Christian Counseling, 2006.

SPIRITUAL HIERARCHY OF MASTERS: New Age advocates believe these spiritual "masters" are highly evolved men who, having already perfected themselves, are now guiding the rest of humanity to this same end.

SPIRITS: Discarnate entities, often thought to be the spirits of ancestors, who are believed to influence the world of the living. In reality, fallen angels and demons are the "evil" spirits who are summoned during incantations.

SPIRITISM: Worship of or communication with the supposed spirits of the dead. These spirits are in reality evil spirits in disguise.

SPIRITUALISM: An ancient occult practice which teaches that the spirits of the deceased are alive to communicate with people here on Earth through "mediums" who act as intermediaries between the material world and the spirit world.

SPONDOMANCY: Finding omens in soot or cinders.

SPONTANEOUS PAST-LIFE RECALL: The process by which one is said to remember his/her past life without artificially induced means (i.e. hypnosis).

STAR GAZING / ASTROLOGY: The divination of the supposed influence of the stars upon human affairs and terrestrial events by their positions and aspects. Is. 47:12-15; Jer. 10:2.

STARS: Spiritual wisdom and development.

ST. JOHN"S EYE: The midsummer witch celebration; June 23.

STICHOMANCY: A form of Rhapsodomancy. See *Rhapsodomancy*

STOLISOMANCY: Observing oddities in a person's dress for omens.

STOLICTES: The neophyte grade of the Hermetic Order of the Golden Dawn.

SUBJECT: Person used for experiments in ESP studies.

SUCCUBUS (SUCCUBI): A female demonic force who copulates (sexual intercourse) with human males. See *Incubus*

SUFISM: Persian mystical religion based on Islam.

SUPERCONCIOUSNESS: That aspect of one's soul beyond the rational world of material reality that can achieve God-realization.

SUPERIORS: Junior mothers and fathers.

SUPERSTITION: Trust in magic or chance; a belief resulting from fear of the unknown.

SWEDENBORG, EMANUEL: 18th century son of a Lutheran minister, expounded supposed symbolic meaning of Scripture and developed such mediumistic abilities as astral projection and automatic writing and founded his own cult religion.

SYCOMANCY: Divination by writing possible responses to questions on tree leaves, and observing which one dries the fastest; a modern equivalent is to put responses on pieces of paper, roll them up, and place them in a strainer above a steaming pot to see which opens first.

SYLPH: An elemental who lives in air.

SYNCRETISM: Fusion of different forms of belief or practice; the claim that all religions are one and share the same core teachings.

SYNCHRONICITY: Meaningful coincides interpreted as having some higher, connecting purpose that could be accounted for by PSI phenomena.

SYNERGY: Quality of "whole making"; the New Age belief in the cooperation of natural systems to put things together in ever more meaningful patterns.

SYNTHESIS (in astrology): The interpretation of a complete astrological chart.

SYNTROPY: Belief that living matter has an inherent drive to perfect itself in increasingly complex patterns of association, communication, cooperation and awareness. The opposite of *Entropy*.

T

TABLE TILTING: The levitation or shifting of a table to help determine communication with the dead.

T'AI CHI: Chinese martial art of slow physical movements used with meditation to develop self-discipline and spiritual awareness; part of body work.

TALISMAN: A power object, usually an amulet or trinket.

TANTRA: Series of Hindu and Buddhist scriptures concerned with special yogic practices for swift attainment of enlightenment; also the practices, techniques, and traditions of these teachings.

TAOISM ("Dowism"): A Chinese religious philosophy founded in the sixth century B.C. by Lao-Tse, who taught that the "tao" or way of virtues is an eternal, all pervasive harmonizing force in the universe.

TARA CENTER: Non profit organization founded in 1980 by Benjamin Crème, dedicated to the p rinciple of internationally shared resources and the reappearance of the "Christ" in the person of Lord Iitreya.

TAROT CARDS: A set of 78 cards with illustrations into which are incorporated a vast amount of arcane symbolism. Considered by many to contain the sum total of all occult knowledge. The ancestor of our modern playing cards, the Tarot is today used primarily for divination (cartomancy). Playing cards with specially inscribed figures and emblems (such as the moon, sun, devil, and Egyptian god Isis) that are said to reveal the cosmic purpose of the universe and the future of each individual's life; a form of divination or fortune telling. Fortune telling by the manipulation and placing of cards which have certain meanings (e.g. the seven of hearts is a card of love.)

TASSEOGRAPHY: (See Tea Leaf Reading)

TAU MEGA THERION: A reference to the anti-Christ, literally means "the Great Beast". Appellation used by Aleister Crowley.

TEACUP READINGS: Interpreting the future by the arrangement of tea leaves in the bottom of a cup.

TEA-LEAF READING: An imprecise method of divination suggesting that the patterns formed by tea leaves left in the bottom of a cup reveal hidden truths about the subject in question.

TELEKINESIS: Movement of objects by occult power. A phenomenon that occurs when an object (table lifting or tumbler moving) is set in motion or a musical instrument is played without a visible or tangible cause.

TELEPATHY: The ability to communicate directly from mind to mind. Telepathy includes either the power to transmit thoughts to another person (words, symbols, images, ideas, sensations, or emotions), or the power of thought-reading or telepathic reception from another mind, and sometimes both.

TELEPORTATION: Instantaneous movement of a person or object form one place to another without going through normal space-time.

TEMPLE OF SET: A satanic organization founded by Dr. Michael Aquino. ("Set" is the Egyptian god of death)

TEPHRAMANCY: Divination by looking for messages in ashes, often burned tree bark.

THAUMATURGY: The use of magick to effect changes in the reality outside of the magician. The scientific and technical aspects of such workings. Also known as Sorcery.

THEOCENTRICITY: Belief that God is central to the propositions of man and omnipotent in his control of history's destiny.

THEOSOPHY: Literally, "Wisdom of God"; a religion incorporating some Christian concepts along with reincarnation, karma, and spiritistic practices.

THEOSOPHICAL SOCIETY: A highly developed system of occultism based on mystery religions and Hindu philosophy, founded on the writings of Helena Petrovna Lavatsky, a nineteenth-century Russian mystic; forerunner of much New Age thought.

THERAPEUTIC TOUCH: A form of spiritualistic healing asserting that properly passing hands over a patient's body, his "energy" can be properly distributed to bring health.

THEURGY: The use of magick to effect changes in the magician's own internal reality. Magick used for self-actualization or personal apotheosis. Focus is on prayers, invocations, medications.

THE WAY: Bringing about social change with three million people by 1990. They allegedly claim they will be in the White House. The Way appears to try to infiltrate law enforcement. They have a military group.

THIRD EYE: An occult concept assuming that a spiritually intuitive center of consciousness exists in the center of the forehead, the so-called seventh charka of enlightenment in yoga; hence the red dot in the forehead of Hindu women.

THOUGHT ADJUSTERS: In the cult Urantia, spirit guides that are "undiluted parts of Deity" and communicate with one's higher self.

THURIBLE: Also known as the witch's censer, the thurible holds incense that is used in ritual observances.

TIBETAN BOOK OF THE DEAD: Scriptures of Tibetan Buddhism based on esoteric experiences concerning the nature of the soul and the stages to be encountered during death.

TIROMANCY: A form of divination using cheese.

TOTEM: A species of plant or animal regarded as having an ancestral or affinitive relationship to a specific tribe, family, or individual.

TRANSCENDENTAL MEDITATION (TM): The Novice receives a Mantra, a special sound which he must keep secret. During meditation (which lasts for twenty minutes, twice each day), one must simply repeat the mantra mentally while ignoring all other thoughts. Regular meditation is supposed to let the mind descend to the deepest level of consciousness. The medit ator experiences full relaxation, renewed energy and creativity, and a sense of well being. TM is a religious system. The use of Mantras comes directly from the Hindu Yoga tradition and the "deepest level of consciousness" of which Maharishi speaks and seems to be identical with the ground of being, i.e. Brahman. For these reasons Maharishi can be considered a Guru. Those followers who discount his religious role are misguided at best.

TRANSMISSION: A method of spiritual communication forming an extradimensional entity that relays its messages through thought-to-thought transference or other mediumistic conveyances.

TRANSVECTION: Levitation, or the projection of a wraith form.

TRINITY (OCCULT STYLE): The triangle is the symbol of manifestation. It is here that the spirit will appear. A magician will do well to study the symbolism of the triangle and of the number three. Among other things, the triangle, represents the trinity, the triple nature of our world (mental, psychic, and physical), and the electromagnetic dynamism of the universe.

TRUMPET SPEAKING: Musical notes supposedly made by spirits through a special trumpet during a séance.

TRANCE: An altered state of consciousness, induced or spontaneous, that gives access to many ordinarily inhibited capacities of the mind-body system. Trance states are generally self-induced.

TRANCE CHANNELING: The phenomenon of a spirit's speaking through the mouth of a medium, or channeler, and often subjecting the channel to oblivion so that the channeler's neurosensory and psychomotor functions are completely possessed (through often mimicked by charlatans and fake channelers).

TRANSMIGRATION: The movement of the soul from one body to another. Transmigration is commonly used as broadly referring to reincarnations of many different types of life form, such as mineral, vegetative, and animal, as well as human.

TRANSPERSONAL PSYCHOLOGY: Technique for psychologically exploring the spiritual aspects of human nature; developed by Abraham Maslow.

TRANSFORMATION: New Age advocates promote both personal and planetary transformation. Personal transformation involves the changes wrought in one's life by increasing self-realization. As more and more people are personally transformed, the planet too will be transformed into a global brotherhood.

TRANSFERENCE: Evil spirits apparently leave the body or being of one individual, and enter into another. This sometimes happens at the choice of the individuals, at other times at the choice of the spirit. It frequently happens when a Christian is seeking deliverance for another person, and the spirit enters the would-be deliverer.

TISKELE OR TRISKELION: The tiskele is a symbol which appears in many logos today. Although the name may not be recognized by most people, they would recognize the symbol. "The triskelion (Greek for three legs) is a symbol of the sun intended to express motion. A similar device, with four legs, called a triskelion is a modification of the swastika." (Thomas Albert Stafford, Christian Symbolism iln the Evangelical Churches, Nashville, Tennessee, Abingdon Press, 1942. p. 75) The triskele is actually a Celtic version of the Yin-Yang symbol of life, and a modification of the swastika, so what we know about the yin/yang and the swastika applies to this symbol as well.

TRUMPET MEDIUM: A psychic or sensitive who brings forth "spirit voices" through a trumpet at séances.

U

UFO: Unidentified flying object; flying saucer. Frequently associated with the spirit world.

UMANDA (also see MACUMBA): Common in Brazil. Traces back to Africa plus Indian magic of the Americas, plus spiritistic elements, and some Catholic components. Headed by Cult Father, and Cult Mother. Mediums are sambas.

UNDINE: An elemental who lives in water.

UNITY: A cult that denies biblical doctrines of sin and salvation, yet uses Christian terminology to promote a unity of non-Christian/beliefs while claiming a reverence for Jesus as a great teacher; based on the teachings of Charles and Myrtle Fillmore, late 19th century spiritualists, who adapted the teachings of Christian Science and concluded that Jesus was merely a great teacher who acquired a "Christ-Consciousness" that we all can attain.

UNITY IN DIVERSITY COUNCIL: A New Age "metanetwork" of over 100 networks and groups rallying for global cooperation and interdependence.

UNIFIED FIELD THEORY: A concept of physics suggesting that an underlying principle guides all physical phenomena and is embodied in a single force that ensures stability and peace in the universe.

URANTIA FOUNDATION: Promotes psychic revelations and a cosmological view of the universe based on the 2,097-page "Urantia Book", supposedly dictated by extraterrestrial beings.

UROBOROS: A serpent depicted as eating his own tail; the symbol being used to show the unity of the sacrificer and the one sacrificed.

UPANISHADS: Philosophical literature by Indo-Aryans regarding the nature of ultimate truth and reality. The final section of the Vedas.

V

VAMPIRE: According to legend, one who rises from the grave by night to consume the blood of persons.

VAUDERIE (VAULDERIE): The witches' Sabbat.

VEDAS: The oldest Hindu scriptures, including a collection of hymns, and prose text on sacrificial rites and ceremonies, advice for the elderly retired, and the monistic philosophical speculations of the Upanishads. The main ideas are called Vedanta Hinduism.

VENFICA: A witch who uses poisons and philters.

VIBRATIONS: A magical aura or atmosphere.

VINNANA: In Buddhism, it is the "unconscious disposition" of the deceased which is reborn. It is not to be confused with the conscious self, soul, mind, etc.

VISUALIZATION: Attempts to manipulate reality through the mind.

VISUALIZATION HEALING: A form of New Age consciousness which intimates that the natural healing process of the body can be accelerated and activated by right thinking.

VOODOO: An ancient religion combining Catholicism and Sorcery. Those involved are extremely superstitious. Members use spells, sorcery, potions, and fetishes to control the actions of others or the outcome of events.

VOW: An earnest promise or pledge that binds one to perform a specific act or behave in a certain manner.

W

WALPURGIS NIGHT: The eve of May Day, believed in medieval Europe to be the occasion of a witch's sabbath. An episode or situation having the quality of nightmarish wildness associated with this sabbat (April 30).

WAND: Made of ash, willow or hazel, usually 21 inches long, plain or decorated priapic wand has an 8 or 9 inch phallus on one end.

WARLOCK: Originally meaning "one who breaks faith". It is more often used by non-witches to refer to a male witch. Actually designates a traitor.

WATCHER: A familiar acting as a guardian.

WATER WITCHING: See Dowsing.

WATER WITCHING or WATER DIVINING or WATER SMELLING: Locating water using a Divining Rod or other occult methods.

WAXING MOON: Changing Moon.

WEREWOLF: According to legend, a person who has been turned or turns himself into a wolf-like creature.

WHITE MAGIC: Used for blessing, or anything! Popularly, magick done for "good" purposes.

WICCA: An Old English word from which we get the word "witch". This is the paganistic end of the witchcraft spectrum. See *Wicca* Appendix E, page 251.

WINDHAM HILL: New Age music label started by two college dropouts who wanted to record and distribute solo instrumental music; thought to be the largest New Age music distributor.

WITCH: One who practices magic. Can produce magic alone or can be a member of a coven.

WITCH"S CORD OR GIRDLE: Also known as the cingulum, the witch's cord is used for ritualistic purposes.

WITCHCRAFT: The practice of sorcery or magic. The practice of the old religion which focuses on the goddess in her many forms: Hectate, Aphrodite, Astarte, Diana. Women play important roles in witchcraft.

WITCH'S SABBATH: Meeting of a witches' coven held in order to perform magical rites and ceremonies. A large number of witches and warlocks who would gather around a bonfire or cauldron, light black candles, and perform sacrifices. The Sabbath would culminate in a sexual orgy.

WITNESS: Student minister.

WIZARD: One skilled in magic, sorcerer; male witch .

WIZARDRY: The art of practices of a wizard; sorcery.

WRAITH: A projected astral body or mobile form of witch power.

WORLD GOODWILL: A New Age political lobby that aims to unfold "the Plan" as spelled out in the writings of Alice Bailey.

WORLD HEALING MEDITATION: A December 31, 1986 gathering of New Agers to mediate for peace under the inspirational tutelage of John Price.

WORLD VIEW: A common consensus about the nature of reality; a set of presuppositions or premises held consciously or unconsciously about the makeup of the cosmos.

X

XYLOMANCY: Divination using pieces of wood, either by interpreting their shape or noting the order in which they burn in a fire.

Y

YAHWEH (sect): Allegedly black Hebrew Israelite. Originally headquartered in Miami and have an alleged branch in Tampa. It appears that their philosophy is a black supremacy philosophy. Their mode of dress is Biblical garb. (They have been identified in other areas of the United States).

YANG: The male force.

YANTRA: The visual equivalent of a mantra, supposing that a meditative state can be induced by staring at a colorful diagram of concentric or geometric design.

YELLOW MAGIC: Used for mental work, meditation, etc. Intellect.

YIN YANG: Chinese names referring to the active and passive principles of the universe. Yin refers to the female or (inactive) negative force; Yang to the male or active force. These two polar forces continually interplay with each other. The words are used to describe the constant flow of motion and change in the universe (i.e. the "Tao"). Known as "chi" force.

YIN: The female force.

YOGA: Literally, "yoking" or "joining"; any system or spiritual discipline by which the practitioner or Yogi seeks to condition the self at all levels-physical, psychical, and spiritual. The goal of the Indian religious tradition is a state of well-being, the loss of self-identity, and absorption into union with the Absolute, or Ultimate Being. The rising popularity of *Hatha-Yoga* in the Western world warrants a discussion of the practice of Yoga as a dangerous form of occultism. See *Yoga* Appendix F, page 261.

YOGI: Master of one or more methods of Yoga who teaches it to others.

YULE: A midwinter witch festival, occult Holiday, Winter Solstice, December 22, the shortest day of the year.

Z

ZEN: Two-branched type of Buddhism thought best known for its emphasis on an experience of enlightenment that occurs from breaking down the commitment and attachment to the logical and rational ordering of experience.

ZODIAC: Imaginary belt in the heavens that encompasses the apparent paths of the principal planets for Pluto. Divided into twelve constellations or signs based on the assumed dates that the sun enters each of these "houses" or symbols, the Zodiac is used for predictions in Astrology.

ZOMBIE: In actuality, one who has been deliberately poisoned with puffer fish venom and thought to be dead when body functions slow and become unrecognizable. Often they are buried by the family after which the perpetrator removes the body and revives the individual in a disorientated state by forcing ingestion of jumson weed combined with hypnosis.

ZONE THERAPY: The philosophical basis for such practices as reflexology and iridology, which supposes that certain zones of the body can give "a picture" or   "connect" with symptoms of disease in other, unrelated portions of the body.

ZOOLATRY: Worship of animals.

APPENDIX B

Freemasonry

Freemasonry is an open indictment against the Christian Church in America because it is so widely accepted among those who believe in Jesus Christ as their Savior. Although they profess faith in Christ, these people turn from Jesus, the Light of the world, to seek more so-called "light" as they approach the "Worshipful Master in the east," Freemasonry's representative for the rising sun.

Freemasonry is an indictment against the Christian Church because it indicates the Church's gross lack of spiritual insight and discernment. In 1 Corinthians 2:15 Paul said that "the spiritual man makes judgments about all things." Yet, the Church has not apprehended the true nature of Freemasonry's idolatrous system. The Church largely embraces Masonry as a social and ethical institution advocating high moral standards for its adherents. Many look upon Masonry as synonymous with Christianity. As we will discover in this booklet, Freemasonry is in no way equivalent to Christianity, and neither are its morals or ethics.

It is our prayer that no individual Mason will be offended by this work. Our effort here is not directed to the individual Mason, rather to the Masonic system itself.

We are approaching this subject with questions and answers. Each question is deliberately designed to teach some aspect of the Masonic philosophy, ritual and ceremony.

The History of Freemasonry

Freemasonry is an oath-bound fraternity which began in England, not in Palestine, Egypt, Greece, or Rome as some have suggested. The first lodge whose records survive starts its documentation in 1701; however, Scotland had lodges in the 16th century. The stonemasons of England and Scotland had developed certain organizations such as the lodge, which seems to have taken its basic form in the 14th and 15th centuries. These organizations or lodges arose to meet the needs of the craft whose members were often itinerant masons. They assembled for fellowship and mutual help. The lodge organization aided in the enforcement of the codes of discipline within the craft and helped to preserve secrecy about the trade's practices. There gradually evolved a secret ritual, as well as a system of signals for mutual recognition of its members. Legends later grew up concerning the supposed ancient origin of the society, the most common version perhaps being that which traces their beginnings to Hiram, the master-mason and builder of Solomon's Temple (1 Kings 5-6). This inaccurate legend claims that Hiram was murdered because he refused to reveal the mason's secrets.

The first annual meeting of the Grand Lodge was held in London in 1717. Benjamin Franklin was a member of the first unchartered lodge in America which was located in Philadelphia. The first chartered lodge in this country was located in Boston, Massachusetts in 1733, and was called the "First Lodge." Several early Americans were Freemasons, including George Washington, Alexander Hamilton, Paul Revere, Admiral John Paul Jones, and nine of the signers of the Declaration of Independence. At least thirteen United States Presidents have been Freemasons, and many contemporary political leaders are members of the organization, including cabinet members, Supreme Court justices, senators, representatives, state governors, and congressmen. It is reported that in the United States there are over 15,000 lodges and 49 Grand Lodges with 4,000,000 members. Britain has some 750,000 Freemasons, and over a million more are found throughout the rest of the world.

Three basic degrees are offered in Freemasonry: Entered Apprentice, Fellow-Craft, and Master Mason. There are also a variety of higher degrees for those who can attain them. Various bodies have different names, such as Craft Rite, Knights Templar, Scottish Rite, Shrine Temple, and so on. There are also women's orders, such as Order of the Eastern Star, White Shrine, and Daughters of the Nile.

According to the Highest Masonic Authority,

What is Freemasonry?

According to Freemasonry's highest Masonic authority, Prince Adept Albert Pike, "Masonry is a search for Light. That search leads us directly back, as you see, to the Kabalah (Jewish Book of Magic). In that ancient and little understood medley of absurdity and philosophy, the Initiate will find the source of many doctrines; and many in time come to understand the Hermetic philosophers, the Alchemist, all the Anti-papal Thinkers of the Middle Ages, and Emanuel Swedenborg." (*Morals and Dogma of the Ancient and Accepted Scottish Rite of Masonry*, p. 741)

Does Freemasonry Foster or Emphasize a Specific Religion? Is it not Actually a Religious Institution?

Dr. Albert G. Mackey claims, "The truth is, Masonry is undoubtedly a religious institution" (*Textbook of Masonic Jurisprudence,* p. 95). Again, Dr. Mackey explains "As Masons we are taught never to commence any great or important undertaking without first invoking the blessing and protection of deity, and this is because Masonry is a religious institution." (*Manual of the Lodge,* p. 40)

What Kind of Religion is Freemasonry?

Dr. Mackey reveals, "The religion then of Masonry is pure theism on which its different members engraft their peculiar opinions, but they are not permitted to introduce them into the lodge or to connect their truth or falsehood with the truth of Masonry." (*Lexicon of Freemasonry,* p. 404)

Dr. J.D. Buck MD, 32nd degree, says, "Masonry is not only a universal science, but a world wide religion, and owes allegiance to no one creed, and can adopt no such sectarian dogma as such, without ceasing thereby to be Masonic…that "Masonry is the universal religion only because and only so long as it embraces all religions." (*Mystic Masonry,* pp. 113-114)

Robert Morris proudly proclaims, "So broad is the religion of Masonry, and so carefully are all sectarian tenets excluded from the system, that the Christian, the Jew, and the Mohammedan, in all their numberless sects and divisions, may, and do harmoniously combine in its moral and intellectual work with the Buddhist, the Parsee, the Confucian, and the worshipper of Deity under any form." (*Webb's Monitor of Freemasonry,* p. 280)

Does Freemasonry have a Priest?

Robert Morris defines "chaplain" in this way: "The Master of the Lodge is its priest, and director of its religious ceremonies. His duty is to select the Scriptures, prayers, etc., and he should be present at the burial of the dead." (*Webb's Monitor of Freemasonry,* p. 231)

Is Freemasonry a Christian Institution?

Dr. Albert G. Mackey clearly states, "Freemasonry is not Christianity, nor a substitute for it." (*Encyclopedia of Freemasonry,* p. 162)

What is a Masonic Lodge?

According to Albert Pike, "Every Masonic Lodge is a temple of religion; and its teachings are institutions in religion." (*Morals & Dogma*, p. 213)

Is Freemasonry Based on the Bible?

We find this statement on the subject: "Masonry has nothing whatsoever to do with the Bible, that it is not founded on the Bible, for if it were it would not be Masonry, it would be something else." (*Digest of Masonic Law*, pp. 207-209)

Again according to Albert Pike, "The Bible is an indispensable part of the furniture of a Christian Lodge, only because it is the sacred book of the Christian religion. The Hebrew Pentateuch in a Hebrew Lodge, and the Koran in the Mohammedan one, belong on the altar; and one of these, and the square and Compass, properly understood, are the great lights by which a Mason must walk." (*Morals and Dogma*, p.11)

Which of These Furnishings
Does Freemasonry Esteem the Least?

The Bible! Because according to Mr. Pike's answer to the previous question, the Bible only appears with the Square and Compass in so-called Christian lodges, while the Square and Compass must appear in every Lodge.

Is the Name of God and His Son Jesus Reverenced Among Masons?

In the <u>Masonic Handbook</u>, p. 184, we discover, "Whether you swear or take God's name in vain don't matter so much. Of course the name of the Lord Jesus Christ, as you know, don't amount to anything, but Mah-hah-bone – O, horror! You must never, on any account, speak that awful name aloud. That would be a most heinous crime – unmasonic – unpardonable."

Does Freemasonry Equate Jesus Christ with the
Sun-god of Hinduism, Krishna?

J.D. Buck makes this declaration, "It has been shown that every act in the drama of the life of Jesus, and every quality assigned to Christ, is to be found in the life of Krishna." (*Mystic Masonry*, pp. 119, 138)

Is a Christian Allowed to Witness in a Masonic Lodge Concerning Christ's Redemptive Work?

Dr. Albert G. Mackey admonishes, "A Christian Mason is not permitted to introduce his own peculiar opinions with regards to Christ's meditorial office into the lodge." (*Lexicon of Freemasonry*, p. 404)

Does Freemasonry Offer Its Candidates Regeneration, or the New-birth, without Jesus Christ?

Daniel Sickles explains, "The Rite of Induction signifies the end of a profane and vicious life, the palingenesia (new-birth) of corrupt human nature the death of vice and all bad passions and the introduction to the new life of purity and virtue." (*Ahiman Rezon*, p. 54)

Does Freemasonry Promise Life After Death Without Jesus Christ?

Daniel Sickles claims, "If we with suitable true devotion maintain our Masonic profession, our faith will become a beam of light and bring us to those blessed mansions where we shall be eternally happy with God, the Great Architect of the Universe." (*Ahiman Rezon*, p. 79)

How Does a Mason Obtain Freedom From Sin?

According to Albert G. Mackey, an Acacian is a term signifying a Mason who by living in strict obedience to the obligations and precepts of the fraternity is free from sin." (*Lexicon of Freemasonry*, p. 16)

Does Freemasonry Mutilate the Scriptures to Suit Its own Purposes?

Yes! On page 31 of the <u>Royal Arch Degree Charge at Opening</u>, an edited version of the following verse of Scripture is read: "Now we command you, brethren, **in the name of the Lord Jesus Christ** that ye withdraw yourselves from every brother that walketh disorderly, and not after the tradition which ye received from us." (2 Thess. 3:6)

> *(The portion in bold in the verse above is omitted by Freemasonry and for a very obvious reason: the name of Jesus is not permitted in the Lodge.)*

Are Ministers Forbidden to Pray in the Name of the Lord Jesus Christ in a Masonic Lodge?

In the <u>Masonic Handbook</u>, p. 74, we find: "When a brother reveals any of our great secrets; whenever, for instance, he tells anything about Boaz, or Tubalcain, or Jachin, or that awful Mah-hah-bone, or even whenever a minister prays in the name of Christ in any of our assemblies, you must always hold yourself in readiness, if called upon, to cut his throat from ear to ear, pull out his tongue by the roots, and bury his body at the bottom of some lake or pond."

Has such a Horrible Thing ever been Done Among Masons?

We will continue the preceding quotation as follows: "Of course, all this (the cutting of the throat and burying in some lake or pond) must be done in secret, as it was the case of that notorious man Morgan, for both law and civilization are opposed to such barbarous crimes, but then, you know you must live up to your obligation, and so long as you have sworn to do it, by being very strict and obedient in the matter, you'll be free from sin." (*Masonic Handbook*, p. 74)

NOTE: Captain William Morgan, a Mason of some thirty years, took it upon himself to expose what he knew of Masonry. He wrote his manuscript Freemasonry Exposed, and was allegedly murdered, in the opinion of all who have carefully examined the evidence. The Masonic Handbook at least intimates that this was the case.

Are Masons Truthful?

In the Masonic Handbook we read: "If your wife, or child, or a friend, should ask you anything about your initiation – as, for instance, if your clothes were taken off, if you were blindfolded, if you had a rope around your neck, etc., you must conceal…hence, of course, you must deliberately lie about it. It is part of your obligation, nevertheless. But you know if you live in strict obedience to your obligation, you'll be free from sin." (p. 74)

Again we find, "You must conceal all the crimes of your brother Masons, except murder and treason, and these only at your own option, and should you be summoned as a witness against a brother Mason be always sure to shield him. Prevaricate, don't tell the whole truth in this case, keep his secrets, forget the most important points. It may be perjury to do this, it is true, but you're keeping your obligations, and remember if you live up to your obligation strictly, you'll be free from sin." (*Masonic Handbook*, p. 183)

Are Masons Ethical?

The Masonic Handbook clearly states, "Whenever you see any of our signs made by a brother Mason, and especially the grand hailing sign of distress, you must always be sure to obey them, even at the risk of your life. If you're on a jury, and the defendant is a Mason, and makes the Grand Hailing sign, you must obey it; you must disagree with your brother jurors, if necessary, but you must be sure not to bring the Mason guilty, for that would bring disgrace upon our order. It may be perjury, to be sure, to do this, but then your fulfilling your obligation, and you know if you live up to your obligations you'll be free from sin." (p. 183)

Are Masons Honest?

Again the Masonic Handbook reveals, "If you cheat, wrong, or defraud any other society or individual, it is entirely your own business. If you cheat the Government even, Masonry cannot and will not touch you, but be careful not to cheat, wrong, or defraud a brother Mason or a lodge, whoever else you may defraud; live up to your obligation, and you'll be free from sin." (p. 184)

Do Masons have the Well Being of all Men at Heart, or only Their Fellow Masons?

The Masonic Handbook further explains, "Whether you quarrel with or strike other men is none of our business, but your obligations enjoin you not to strike a brother Master Mason. It may be wicked and sinful, to be sure, to strike any man, or to quarrel with anybody, but our rules make no provision except for the protection of Masons only, and if you live in strict obedience to your obligation, you'll be free from sin." (p. 184)

Are Masons Taught that Moral Chastity be Practiced Among all Peoples, or Among the Families of Master Masons only?

The "Chastity Covenant" of the Master Mason states, "Furthermore, that I will not violate the chastity of a Master Mason's wife, mother, sister, or daughter, knowing them to be such. This gives you full permission, my dear sir, to do as you please outside of the Masonic order, but you must always respect the female relatives of Masons." (*Masonic Handbook,* p. 184)

Why Are Masons Taught Temperance?

The drinking of alcoholic beverages is synonymous with the activities of the "Mystic Shrine;" yet, Masons are taught temperance. Why?

Daniel Sickles explains, "The chief aim and the essence of these virtues is to keep safely the secrets of Masonry. Temperance is enjoined, not for its own sake, but for the reason that when a Mason is intoxicated, he might unwittingly reveal the secrets of Masonry." (*Ahiman Rezon,* p. 96)

Is Masonry Kind and Benevolent?

Mr. Edmond Ronayne, Past Master of Keystone Lodge No. 639, Chicago, Ill., claims, "All my experience in and out of Masonic Lodges, has gone to establish the fact in my mind that Freemasonry in all its departments is the most corrupt and wicked, and contains the greatest amount of falsehood of any other institution on the face of the globe. . . It is positively and absolutely selfish in every single element of its pagan composition, and can truthfully lay no more claim to charity, benevolence or goodness of any other name or description than could say of the heathen organizations which Christian civilization has long since banished from the world." (*Master's Carpet*, p. 38)

(Author's Note on Morals and Ethics)

We question the morals and ethics of this supposedly benevolent and highly moral fraternity, because according to its own claims, it is only moral or ethical in respect to its own members. This is due to the fact that Masons are not subject to the law of God, but to their own law, the universal law of nature. Temperance is taught in Masonry, but not for the physical or spiritual well being of the adherent, but to keep safely the secrets of Masonry.

Oaths and Obligations

In Pierson's <u>Traditions of Freemasonry</u> we read: "A solemn method of confirming an oath i.e. in the 'Mysteries,' was by placing a drawn sword across the throat of the person to whom it was administered, and invoking heaven, earth and sea to witness the ratification. Among the Druids it was a necessary duty of the bards to unsheath the sword against those who had forfeited their obligation by divulging any of the secrets of the order." (p. 35)

First or Entered Apprentice Degree

"I do most solemnly and sincerely promise and swear, without the least equivocation, mental reservation, or self evasion of mind in me whatever; binding myself under no less penalty than to have my throat cut across, my tongue torn out by the roots, and my body buried in the rough sands of the sea at low watermark, where the tide ebbs and flows twice in twenty-four hours; so help me God, and keep me steadfast in the due performance of the same."

Second or Fellow Craft Degree:

"I do most solemnly and sincerely promise and swear without the least hesitation, mental reservation, or self evasion of mind in me whatever; binding myself under no less penalty than to have my left breast torn open and my heart and vitals taken from thence and thrown over my left shoulder and carried into the valley of Jehosaphat, there to become a prey to wild beasts of the field, and vulture of the air, if ever I should prove willfully guilty of violating any part of this my solemn oath or obligation of a Fellow Craft Mason so help me God, and keep me steadfast in the due performance of the same."

Third or Master's Degree:

I do solemnly promise and swear, with a fixed and steady purpose of mind in me to keep and perform the same, binding myself under no less penalty than to have my body severed in two in the midst, and divided to the north and south, and my bowels burnt to ashes in the center, and the ashes scattered before the four winds of heaven, that there might not the least track or trace of remembrance remain among men, or Masons, of so vile and perjured a wretch as I should be, were I ever to prove willfully guilty of violating any part of this my solemn oath or obligation of a Master Mason. So help me God, and keep me steadfast in the due performance of the same."

(Author's Note on Oath Taking)

In each of the first degrees the candidate is brought from the preparation room with a rope or "cable tow" around his neck. In the second degree the cable tow is around his right shoulder, and in the third degree the cable tow is around his waist. The symbolism of this rope cable tow is very simple: the candidate is bound with the rope until he is bound with the oath. Once he is bound by an invisible rope of fear, the little blue rope is no longer needed.

We question just what kind of god would listen to such horrible and barbarous oaths as those sworn by Masonic candidates? Surely it is not the God of the Bible. The oaths would be much more suitable as oaths to Satan, the god of this world.

Does the God of the Bible take these oaths seriously? God considers spoken vows so important that the Bible advises against taking oaths (Ecclesiastes 5:2-6, Matthew 5:33-37, James 5:12). Although the God of the Bible would never require keeping such horrendous oaths as those imposed by Freemasonry on its followers, these oaths made to other gods are a serious indication of the idolatry inherent in the Masonic religion.

Does Freemasonry Believe in the Personal God of the Scriptures?

No! In J.D. Buck's <u>Mystic Masonry</u>, p. 216, we read concerning the personality of God: "The only personal God Freemasonry accepts is 'humanity in toto.' God (the Great Architect of the Universe) personifies himself, that is expresses that potency of himself which personality is, through man. Humanity therefore is the only personal god that there is."

To What Other Deities might Freemasonry's Great Architect be Compared?

Freemasonry's Prince Adept Albert Pike says, "It is but an old term revived. Our adversaries numerous and formidable as they are, will say and will have a right to say that our Creative Principle is identical with the Generative Principle of the Indian and Egyptian, and may fitly be symbolized as it was symbolized anciently by the linga (penis)." (Blavatsky's *Isis Unveiled*, vol. 2, p. 377)

Martin L. Wagner observes, "From what we have learned in our study of freemasonry, it is this creative or generative principle that it worships as its specific god, and if this is true, then according to the testimony of Mr. Pike, the greatest of Masons, Masonry has abandoned the worship of Jehovah, and is simply wallowing in the styes of Paganism." (*Interpretation of Freemasonry*, p. 74)

(Author's Note on the god of Freemasonry)

Freemasonry like all other religions has its own revelation, the revelation of visible nature. Freemasonry's deity is not the God of the Bible, but a generative or creative principle synonymous with the Creative Principle of the Indian and Egyptian.

What is the Sin of Freemasonry?

The great sin of Freemasonry is idolatry! *"Although they claimed to be wise, they became fools and exchanged the glory of the immortal God for images made to look like mortal man and birds and animals and reptiles...They exchanged the truth of God for a lie, and worshipped and served created things rather than the Creator – who is forever praised, Amen."* Romans 1:22,23,25

Conclusion

We feel that sufficient evidence has been presented to convince any person of a sincere spirit that the god of Freemasonry is not the great God of the Universe who created the heavens and the earth, but the god of this world, Satan. It offers a lost sinner a way to heaven without the God of the Bible, the Lord Jesus Christ, or the Church.

So very little of Freemasonry has been questioned by its adherents, yet so very much has been revealed by its literature. It is obvious that no professing Christian should ever be a part of Freemasonry.

Illinois State Law #87-1167 Ritualized Abuse of a Child

The State of Illinois, Public Act #87-1167, Effective January 1, 1993. Be it Enacted by the Legislature of the State of Illinois RITUALIZED ABUSE OF A CHILD-EXCLUSIONS-PENALTIES-DEFINITION.

(a) A person is guilty of a felony when he commits any of the following acts with, upon, or in the presence of   a child as part of a ceremony, rite, or similar observance.

(1) **Actually** or in simulation, tortures, mutilates, or **sacrifices** any warm-blooded animal or **human being**;

(2) Forces injection, ingestion, or other application of any narcotic drug, hallucinogen or anesthetic for the purpose of dulling sensitivity, cognition, recollection of, or resistance to any criminal activity:

(3) Forces ingestion or external application of human or animal urine, feces, flesh, blood, bones, body secretions, non-prescribed drugs or chemical compounds;

(4) **Involves a child** in a mock, unauthorized or **unlawful marriage**

ceremony with another person or **representation of any force or deity, followed by sexual contact with the child;**

(5) Places a living child into a coffin or open grave containing a human corpse or remains;

(6) Threatens death or serious harm to a child, his or her parents, family, pets, or friends which instills a well-founded fear in the child that the threat will be carried out, or;

(7) Unlawfully dissects, mutilates or incinerates a human corpse.

(Bold print added by author)

Reiki

In the *Encyclopedia of Alternative Health Care*, author Kristin Olsen says Reiki is "an energy healing system based on ancient Tibetan knowledge discovered by a Japanese theologian." Many people have commented on the ecumenical aspect of Reiki. Supposedly it was founded by Dr. Mikao Usui, a Japanese Christian minister in Kyoto, Japan, in the mid-1800's. When one of his students challenged his belief that Jesus Christ healed people with His hands, Dr Usui began a quest for proof that this type of healing actually did exist.

When he was unable to find the answers he looked for in the Bible, Usui set out to learn the ancient language of Sanskrit and then began to read the sutras, the ancient books of esoteric Hindu religious teachings. After completing years of study and meditation, Usui came upon what to him was a healing knowledge he termed "Reiki." This name comes from the Japanese words *rei*, meaning "boundless and universal," and *ki*, meaning "vital life energy force that flows through all living beings."

We are told that after Usui discovered this healing in the sutras, he undertook a three week fast atop a mountain in Japan. On the last day of his meditative quest, he reported that a ball of light containing the symbols of what later would become Reiki hit him on the forehead. This new power proved itself to Usui when he stubbed his toe as he came down the mountain after the fast. His toe, so he claimed, was immediately healed with his new energy healing system.

Today Reiki is an energy technique that is passed from Reiki masters to initiates. According to Olsen, these Reiki masters themselves don't understand how it works. They can only describe it as a linking with the cosmic radiant energy, an opening of chakras, or an attunement with universal life energy.

Olsen is struck by the similarities between the empowerment rituals of Tibetan Buddhism and the Reiki initiation ceremony. She describes it as a modern secular adaptation of ancient sacred knowledge used in healing and self-healing.

How Reiki Works

The Reiki treatments consist of a series of usually three or four sessions lasting about one hour each. The practitioner's hands are held at twelve basic positions for five minutes each. Although there are many possible hand positions, a practitioner allows his or her own intuition to guide the placing. Over problem areas the holding time is doubled. During a Reiki session the practitioner supposedly draws energy and focuses it through his hands, thus providing a link between himself and the patient. Some Reiki teachers have described this connection as "lighting up."

Proponents say this technique can be applied to the practitioner himself, to other people, to plants, or to animals. Reiki practitioners say they can even heal long distance! They do not claim to diagnose or to possess medical skills. But with practice they claim to be able to detect energy responses from the body that often give clues to the site of the organic problem and its seriousness.

What are the spiritual aspects?

Reiki practitioners staunchly deny that what they do has anything to do with religion or God. The Reiki master is not a guru, they insist. However, it is difficult not to notice the channeling of universal energy which is the very basis of the Hindu prana and other energy manipulating techniques. There are definite spiritual aspects to this practice.

Evidence of Reiki healing relies on stories and testimonies. Often these are full of unexpected effects and cures.

As with so many other questionable practices, Reiki is couched in medical disclaimers. A Reiki teacher named Michael O'Leary is quoted in the *Encyclopedia of Alternative Health Care* as saying this energy work can help the terminally ill, but "not so much to cure the cancer, because sometimes there is just not enough wholeness to expand to sustain physical life."

Needless to say, this questionable therapy is one that needs to be avoided.

Wicca

Wicca is an occult religion based on witchcraft. And although witchcraft can be traced back several centuries before the coming of Christ, for the purpose of this information booklet, we will concentrate on Wicca's modern revival in 1949.[64]

As the basic functional unit is a coven (except in the case of a solitary), Wiccans pool their financial resources in order to purchase that which is necessary for the running of the coven such as robes, cakes, wine, etc.

Gerald B. Gardner is generally credited with the modern revival of Wicca in England in the 1950's, although he was neither the first to practice nor the founder of Witchcraft. In 1949 Gardner published his *High Magic's Aid*, a novel about "The Craft" under the pen name of "Scire,"[65] which was later followed by several others.

Throughout his life, Gardner was fascinated with many different aspects of the Occult. He had been a follower in varying degrees of such people and philosophies as Aleister Crowley, Ordo Templi Orientis, the Hermetic Order of the Golden Dawn and Rosicrucianism.[66]

The Craft and The Old Religion are sometimes used to refer to the magical aspects of Wicca or to its revival of ancient non-Christian traditions. Historians have credited Doreen Valiente, a follower of Gardner who he initiated into the Craft in 1953, with "increasing the emphasis on the Goddess[67]

---

[64] **The Encyclopedia of Witches and Witchcraft**, Rosemary Ellen Guiley, pp. 368-374.

[65] **Drawing Down the Moon**, Margot Adler, p. 61

[66] **The Encyclopedia of Witches and Witchcraft,** Rosemary Ellen Guiley, p. 375

[67] Ibid

While followers of Witchcraft had been in the United States since it's inception, Witchcraft's greatest growth took place during the 1960's and 1970's, during a general revival of interest in the Occult.[68] Historians of Wicca generally credit Raymond and Rosemary Buckland with Wicca's successful spread into American society. The came to the U.S. in 1962, having been followers of Gardner.[69]

In 1973, one of the most prolific publishers of Occult material, Llewellyn Press, *"sponsored a meeting of Witches in Minneapolis."* This gathering was attended by Witches from seventy-three different Craft traditions and attempted to write a statement of principles. The attempt failed to satisfy all participants and was followed in 1974 by the Council of American Witches which did finally complete the Principles of Wiccan Belief. Later, in 1975, thirteen covens would *"ratify the Covenant of the Goddess."*[70]

Most modern followers prefer the term Wicca to Witchcraft. *"As a religion Witchcraft often is called 'Wicca,' an Old English term for 'witch,' in order to counter the negative stereotype of Witches as ugly, evil, and Devil-worshippers"*[71]

Because of the autonomous nature of Wicca, several key groups, known as traditions, have sprung into existence over the past few decades. Some of these prominent traditions include the Gardnerian tradition which originated in England, by Gerald Gardner in the 1950's and is one of the most modern Wiccan traditions; the Alexandrian tradition which originated in England in the 1960's by Alexander Sanders and whose rituals are said to be modified Gardenarian; the Dianic tradition which is the WitchCult in Western Europe, has been pegged as the "feminist" movement of the Craft, focuses mainly on the goddess, and is tracked back to Margaret Murray in 1921; the Celtic Wicca which is a mix using Celtic/Druidic pantheon, stressing on the elements (earth, air, fire, water) and the ancient ones; and finally the Seax-Wica tradition founded in 1973 by Raymond Buckland, who authored this tradition without breaking his original Gardnerian oath.[72]

---

[68] Ibid

[69] **Encyclopedia of Occultism and Parapsychology**, Leslie Shepard, Vol. 1, p. 133

[70] **Drawing Down the Moon**, pp. 99-103

[71] **Harper's Encyclopedia of Mystical and Paranormal Experience**, p. 647

[72] **Encyclopedia of Witches and Witchcraft**, pp. 377-379

Basic Beliefs

Wicca is a nature-based belief system. The natural world (i.e. trees, grass, rocks, mountains, etc.) is seen as a part of God. Christianity, on the other hand, teaches that these things were created by God, and not to be worshipped.

Wiccans believe in a dual male/female divinity. The god and goddess are seen as separate but equal deities, each with unique talents and virtues. Some traditions see all of the gods and goddesses of the world as "faces" of the two true deities. Others worship a god and goddess whose nature changes with the seasons.

They believe that the natural world, the creatures of the world (including humans) and the divine are inseparable. Harm done to any of the aspects reflects on the others, causing pain and suffering needlessly in the spiritual and physical realms. As a result, many Wiccans are ardent environmentalists.

One other group that is Wiccan in its overall philosophy is the School of Wicca founded by Gavin and Yvonne Frost. By some estimates this group *"may have created a hundred covens through its activities"*.[73]

---

[73] **Drawing Down the Moon**, p. 125

Organizational Structure

Each individual coven is autonomous and therefore have their own organizational structure. Generally the high priestess is considered the leader of the Coven.

Doctrine

The theology of Wicca varies from tradition to tradition and even more from coven to coven. The following are a few of the doctrines that most Wiccan covens will believe and practice.

1. **Autonomy.** *"There is no central authority or liturgy; various traditions have their own rituals, philosophy and beliefs, Some have added elements from Eastern, Native American Indian, aboriginal and shamanic systems; others have injected politics into their traditions. New ritual, songs, chants, and poetry are continually created."*[74]

2. **Experience vs. Dogma.** Because of the autonomy of each Coven and even to a large degree of each individual member of Wicca, the experience of the individual is of greater importance than any set of dogmatic doctrines. *"Generally speaking Witches are very open-minded people, especially where religion is concerned. They have no hard and fast 'Commandments,' no catechisms".*[75] Adler adds, *"By creating our own divinities we create mental steps for ourselves, up which we can mount toward realizing ourselves as divine. The lack of dogma in the Craft, the fact that one can worship the goddess without believing in her, that one can accept the goddess as 'Muse' and the Craft as a form of ancient knowledge to be tested by experience; these are precisely the things that have caused the Craft to survive, to revive, and to be re-created in this century."*[76]

3. **Rituals.** The individual or Coven experiences are gained through self-designed rituals. *"We are talking about the rituals that people create to get in touch with those powerful parts of themselves that cannot be experienced on a verbal*

---

[74] **Encyclopedia of Witches and Witchcraft**, p. 376

[75] ibid

[76] **Drawing Down the Moon**, p. 173

level. Rituals are also created to acknowledge on this deeper level the movement of the seasons and the natural world, and to celebrate life and its processes."[77]

They celebrate 8 Sabbats (seasonal festivals) in the year, four Greater and four Lesser. The Greater Sabbats include Imbolc, Beltane, Lughnasa and Samhain while the Lesser Sabbats comprise the Summer and Winter Solstices and the Spring and Autumn Equinoxes. In addition 13 Esbats are convened each lunar month (every 28 days), usually around the time of the full moon, for the purpose of conducting coven ritual/s and business. Additional rituals include the conferring of the three degrees of Wicca, Wiccanings (the blessing of a new-born child), Handfastings (the marrying of a couple for 1 year and 1 day) and Requiems (celebrations for the dead).[78]

Wiccan rituals may also include the performance of simple candle-burning (usually but not always practiced by an individual witch) and workings such as the "Drawing Down of the Moon" during which the coven High Priest/ess invokes the goddess. Cord magic rituals may also be performed and along with candle-burning may be classed as spell-casting. New rituals and new ways of performing old rituals are continually being devised. The number of rituals and their nature is limited only by the imagination of the Wiccan.

4. **Magic:** Many of the rituals involve divination or magic. *"In his book of shadows, Gardner lists eight ways to raise magical power (singly or in combination): (1) meditation or concentration; (2) chants, spells, and invocations; (3) trance and astral projection; (4) incense, wine and drugs; (5) dancing; (6) blood control by binding parts of the body with cords; (7) scourging (not enough to draw blood); (8) ritual sex."[79]*

5. **Ethics?** The Wiccan Rede perhaps best describes the Wiccan ethic in one sentence: *"An it harm none (if it harms noone) do what you will."[80]* Sometimes witches perform "black" magick on certain individuals or groups. Two famous British Wiccans, Janet and Stewart Farrar try to justify such actions with the comment that *"...if somebody is known to be*

---

[77] **Drawing Down the Moon**, pp. 197-198

[78] **Farrar and Farrar**, 1984

[79] **Harper's Encyclopedia of Paranormal Experience**, p. 649

[80] **Farrar and Farrar**, 1984

evil acting and harming others, witches are fully justified in stopping him.'[81] One more recent addition is a strong feminist ethic which has given it political overtones as well illustrated in the newspaper article which states: *"…Women want to be active in their spirituality, not simply the receivers of someone else's – usually a man's-expression of spirituality…'[82]*

6. **The Rule of Three:** The Rule of Three states: *"Any energy that you send out will return to you three-fold."* This includes magical energy, as well as emotional and spiritual energy. Wiccans interpret this rule to mean that any good works, bad works, arguments, etc. will return to them three times as powerfully as they left.

7. **Goddess Worship:** Worship of the goddess sometimes manifests itself as the worship of *"the Mother Goddess in her three aspects of Maiden, Mother, and Crone."* Sometimes it is the worship of *"what we potentially are.'[83]* In many covens the high priestess is seen as the personification of the *"mother goddess who is the principal deity of witchlore.'[84]*

8. **Feminism:** Even though not all feminists are Wiccans, many find the philosophy of Wicca compatable. *"Women who have come to the goddess outside the channels of Neo-Paganism and the Craft are beginning to find rituals and concepts that allow for the same idea. They are finding the goddess within themselves and within all women. And, as might be expected, those feminists who have found joy in rituals, and who have discovered that the concept of 'goddess' feels right inside, are often drawn into the Craft.'[85]*

9. **Evil:** Wiccan groups do not accept the existence of evil. They explain: *"Wicca can be defined as a pagan mystery religion with a polarized deity and no personification of evil."* In the *Principles of Wiccan Beliefs* is stated, *"We do not accept the concept of 'absolute evil' nor do we worship any entity known as 'Satan' or 'The Devil' as defined by the Christian tradition.'[86]*

10. **The Horned God:** Some Wiccan covens not only worship a mother goddess, but also a masculine deity. *"Many Craft traditions worship a god,*

---

[81] Ibid, p. 141

[82] **Rowe and Cavender,** 1991, p. 266

[83] **Drawing Down the Moon**, pp. 10-11, 202

[84] **Man, Myth and Magic**, Vol 14, p. 1866

[85] **Drawing Down the Moon**, p. 205

[86] Ibid, pp. 100, 103

related to the ancient horned lord of animals, the god of the hunt, the god of death and lord of the forests.'[87]

11. **Seasonal Festivals:** The worship of nature or natural order is of paramount importance. *'Wicca is basically a fertility cult and its great festivals are geared to the seasons.'*[88]

Key dates on the Wiccan calendar correspond with some of the key dates on the Satanic calendar. For example:

Wicca – February 2 – Candlemas

Satanism – February 2 – Candlemas (Sabbat Festival), blood/sexual sacrifices, animal or human, female 7-17

Wicca – March 21 – spring equinox

Satanism – March 21 – spring equinox, orgies – oral, anal, vaginal, any age male or female

Wicca – April 30 – Beltane

Satanism - April 30 – Beltane, blood sacrifices – animal and/or human, any age

Wicca – June 22 – summer solstice

Satanism – June 21 – feast day, orgies – oral, anal, vaginal animal and/or human sacrifice, any age – male, female, or animal

Wicca – August 1 – August Eve

Satanism – August 1 – Lammas Day, animal and/or human blood sacrifices, any age male or female

Wicca – September 21 – autumn equinox

Satanism – September 20 – Midnight Host, blood sacrifice and dismemberment, hands planted, female infant to age 21

---

[87] Ibid, p. 11

[88] **Man, Myth and Magic**, Vol. 14, p.1866

September 21 – fall equinox, orgies – oral, anal, vaginal, any age male or female or animal

Wicca – October 31 – Halloween

Satanism – October 29 – November 1 – All Hallows Eve – blood and sexual sacrifice, sexual climax association with the demons, any age male or female

Wicca – December 21 – winter solstace

Satanism – December 22 – Feast Day (Sabbat Festival), orgies – oral, anal, vaginal, any age male or female or animal

What Does God Have to Say

Since followers of Wicca do not believe the Bible to be the Word of God, it is extremely difficult to show them the error of Wicca from a biblical point of view. However, from the Christian perspective, Wicca's teachings have been condemned for centuries.

1. Witchcraft and magic (enchantments) are condemned. Leviticus 19:26, 31; Deuteronomy 18:10-11; 2 Chronicles 33:6.
2. Worship of other gods (or of goddesses) is condemned. Exodus 20:3; 1 Kings 11:4-5.
3. Esteeming nature above God is condemned. Romans 1:21-25.
4. Satan and his influence of evil are real. Zechariah 3:2; Mathew 4:1-11; Luke 6:45.

And if time would permit a more detailed discussion these Scriptures are but the tip of the iceberg.

Beware Christians! Prospective members may be drawn from the public or from the friends and/or acquaintances of Wiccans if they are deemed suitable. A prime recruiting focus is on High School age individuals. Our children are being lured into Wicca. Late in 2001 we worked with a teen-age boy here in Florida who was a member of a Southern Baptist Church, attended youth meetings faithfully on Wednesday evenings, and professed Christ as Savior. However, he got involved in a local Wiccan Coven. He cast spells and was involved in astral projection among other occult practices. He had a curse placed upon him and this was causing much distress.

Unfortunately he was unwilling to renounce his activities within the coven, confess his sins, nullify the curse, and deal with the associated spirit activity. He is still suffering. Let's teach our youth to avoid such activities.

Yoga

The rising popularity of *Hatha-Yoga* in the Western world warrants a discussion of the practice of Yoga as a dangerous form of occultism.

Yoga is a system of physical exercises and mental discipline which is a vital part of Hindu religious philosophy aimed at the *union* of the human soul with the Universal Soul. The term *yoga* is from the Sanskrit meaning "union." This goal is supposed to be achieved through deep meditation and concentration, controlled breathing exercises, and certain physical postures. There are various types of yoga, each one a stage in the attainment of liberation from the cycle of reincarnation through union with the Universal Soul of God. The types of yoga are: Karma-yoga; Bhakti-yoga; Jnana-yoga; Raja-yoga, and Hatha-yoga already noted.

Raja-yoga constitutes what is generally thought of as yoga (in the West especially) and seems to have arisen about the second century B.C. Its origin is attributed to a Hindu sage named Patanjali. The primary source book for the system is entitled *Yogasutras*.

The final goal of yoga is deliverance from the endless cycle of rebirths (reincarnation) and the burden of Karma. The body is thought to be the prison of the soul, and man's bondage and adversity stem from this union of body and soul. Liberation of the soul from its prison comes through right knowledge of this fact. Through the yoga system of self-discipline and mental concentration the soul can be liberated from its bondage and will at death be absorbed by the Brahma or World Soul. Although for the present he is still in his body, he is able to rid himself of nature's control over him.

In Raja-yoga there are eight stages, the highest being *Samadhi*, which is the attainment of super-consciousness or trance. At this stage the yogin is said to achieve union with the Universal Soul and now has an awareness of true reality and knowledge. In this state the yogin may remain in a state of "hibernation," maintaining the same posture for weeks. Some have actually been buried for long periods while in this state of trance. Through yoga other occult powers of telepathy, clairvoyance, and astral projection of the soul are often achieved.

Along with the Eastern religions yoga has also penetrated the Western world. The most popular form of yoga most adapted to our Western culture is known as *Hatha-Yoga,* which is primarily a system of physical exercises and mental concentration concerned with health and longevity. However, yogis stress the fact that Hatha-yoga is not an end in itself, but preparation for the higher principles of Hindu philosophy. The unscriptural Hindu concept that the soul is imprisoned in the body and must be liberated is at the very center of Hatha-yoga. It is in direct conflict with the teaching of the Bible which asserts that the body is the Temple of the Holy Spirit and that the Christian is to glorify God in his body (1 Corinthians 6:19-20; cf. Romans 12:1-2).

In Hatha-yoga it is the *mind and soul* which are aimed at, according to one author and advocate of yoga. The physical exercises and mental disciplines are designed to overcome the body of flesh, for the *ultimate goal* is preparation of the soul for union with the Universal Soul. Whether or not one is aware of this purpose does not change the fact that in Hatha-yoga, like its other forms, *an individual is involving himself in Hinduism and opening himself to the influence and control of satanic forces.* There are instances of individuals becoming demonized by evil spirits through their practice of Hatha-yoga merely as a means of physical exercise.

There are thousands of classes in Hatha-yoga conducted daily all over America and Europe, not including those on television. Impressive numbers of these participants, moreover, are not involved in mere physical exercises, but are seeking self-knowledge, self-realization, and a spiritual experience through such occult meditation. A sincere approach to yoga ultimately leads into a study of Hindu philosophy, deep trance, the pagan chanting of Sanskirt phrases, and other mystical aspects of the occult. Participation in any form of the occult invariably results in some form of oppression by the powers of darkness which are operating behind the yoga system to ensnare the unwary.

How a Born-Again Believer Can Become Demonized

By: Rev. David Cotner

Missionary Church, Senior Pastor, Retired

The Question is Often Asked
"Can a Born-Again Believer be Demonized?"

Contrary to popular belief a born-again believer can be demonized. Most Christians today believe the "great myth" which is the belief that because I am a born-again believer, an evil spirit can not live in me because the Holy Spirit lives in me.

The word "*demonized*" comes from the Greek word "*daimonizomai*" which means "to have a demon." E.g. Mark 5:15-16. It is improper to say a person is possessed. The proper terminology is demonized. The result of demonization is control, not ownership, since Satan and evil spirits can own nothing.

There are two reasons for this: first of all they are created beings and not God the Creator and owner of everything (Psalm 24:1-2; 115:15-16; Ezekiel 28:13-15), and secondly, Christ has purchased us for God (Revelation 5:9).

The areas of control by the evil spirit are not in the person's spirit but in the person's soul (mind, emotions, will, and affections) occasionally resulting in physical manifestations.

Scripture references that teach about the trichotomy of the human nature (body, soul, and spirit) plus the warfare against the soul are: 1 Thessalonians 5:23; Hebrews 4:12; 1 Peter 2:11; Psalm 71:13; John 3:3-6; Romans 7:22-23; 8:10-16; 1 Corinthians 5:5; 6:17-20; Galatians 5:16-25.

The Biblical Evidence that a
Born-Again Believer can be Demonized

A DISCLAIMER

The Scriptures do not conclusively prove a born-again believer <u>can</u> be demonized. Neither do the Scriptures conclusively prove a born-again believer can <u>not</u> be demonized. However the Scriptures do conclusively prove that <u>people</u> can be demonized.

THE OLD TESTAMENT

1 Samuel 15:1-35 esp. 23; 16:14; 18:10

The demon was sent by God to torment Saul because of his disobedience to God (see also Matthew 18:34-35) and caused great changes in Saul's nature and controlled his physical behavior.

THE GOSPELS

Matthew 8:28-32 – Two violent men in the country of the Gadarenes.

Matthew 9:32-33 – The man who could not speak.

Mark 1:23-27 – The man in the Synagogue in Capernaum.

Luke 8:1-3 – Women who had been healed of evil spirits and followed Jesus.

Many other examples are found in the four Gospels.

THE BOOK OF ACTS

Acts 5:1-4 – The word *"filled"* in vs. 3 is the same word Paul uses in Ephesians 5:18 for a believer to "be filled or controlled with the Spirit." Satan and an evil spirit had taken control of Anannias' heart and produced the greed and lie.

THE EPISTLES

1 Corinthians 5:1,5 – This believer in the Corinthian church was living in an open, unrepentant incestuous relationship. Paul's only option was to turn the man over to satan for discipline. He would be killed but at least his spirit would be saved.

1 Corinthians 10:14-22 – Paul clearly warns the believers not to *"share"* in demons. The word for *"share"* in Greek is the word *"fellowship"* or *"fellow participant."*

Paul's point is that just as we have fellowship with Jesus during the eating of the bread and drinking of the cup during communion, so we have fellowship with demons during idol worship. Paul clearly states in vs. 21 that it is possible for a believer to *"drink the cup of demons"* and *"partake of the table of demons."* This verse is not teaching about the Lord Jesus and a demon <u>dwelling</u> together in the believer at the same time, only that a believer can not have <u>fellowship</u> with the Lord Jesus at the same time he is having <u>fellowship</u> with a demon. Note also that unconfessed sin breaks our fellowship with God.

Ephesians 4:26-27 – Paul warns the Ephesian believers not to give the devil a *"place"* KJV, NIV is *"foothold"*, NASB is *"opportunity."* The common sense of the word in Greek is *"place"* or *"location."* It can also have the transferred sense of *"opportunity."* Unchecked anger gives the devil an opportunity to control a place in the believer's life.

1 Peter 5:8 – In Greek the word *"devour"* means *"drink down, swallow, digest."* The Septuagint uses this word to translate the word *"swallow"* where the great fish *"swallowed"* Jonah.

Satan would like nothing better than to *"devour"* believers and destroy them. He does not have the power to do that, but he does have the power to control believer's lives to the point where their relationship with God is seriously hindered, they are in bondage to sin, and their lives are ineffective in service to Christ.

How Can an <u>Evil</u> Spirit Live in the
Same Body with the <u>Holy</u> Spirit?

TWO BIBLICAL ANSWERS

1. In the same way that the Holy Spirit can live in the same body with our sin and our sinful nature, (Romans 7:15-25) the Holy Spirit can live in the same body with a demon "squatter."

2. Our bodies are temples of the Holy Spirit. 1 Corinthians 3:16-17; 1 Corinthians 6:19-20; 2 Corinthians 6:16-18. The Old Testament temple was a "type" of the New Testament temple which is our body (John 2:19-20). In the Old Testament the temple could be defiled yet the presence of God was still there. 2 Kings 23:4-8).

The Experiential Evidence that a Born-Again
Believer can be Demonized

The experiences of many spiritual warfare counselors attest to this. One recommended book for reading would be Dr. Roger Boehm's – <u>In the Face of Evil, A Wake-Up Call for Christians</u> available through the Center for Christian Counseling. Other books available on the subject include:

C Fred Dickason – <u>Demon Possession & The Christian</u> p. 208-209

Neil T. Anderson – <u>The Bondage Breaker</u> p. 171-172

Timothy Warner – <u>Spiritual Warfare</u> p. 104-105

Mark I. Bubeck – <u>The Satanic Revival</u> (<u>The Rise of Fallen Angels</u>) p. 148

How can a Born-Again Believer
Become Demonized?

THROUGH PERSiSTENT, UNREPENTANT SINNING Hebrews 12:1. Following are the major categories of sin which are known to be entry points for the control of evil spirits:

1. **All forms of lying** (John 8:44). Includes deceiving and exaggerating as well as believing lies and deception.
2. **Unbelief** (Hebrews 3:12,19). Includes all doubting and lack of faith and trust in God and His Word.
3. **Pride** (Proverbs 16:18; 1 Peter 5:5).

4. **Anger** (Ephesians 4:26-27). Includes bitterness (Hebrews 12:15) and unforgiveness (Ephesians 4:31-32) which grows out of anger.
5. **Rebellion** (1 Samuel 15:23). Includes lack of submission to authority both in and outside the church (Hebrews 13:17; Romans 13:1-5).
6. **Sexual sins** (Romans 13:12-14; 1 Corinthians 6:9-20). Includes all forms of sexual activity outside of marriage.
7.

THROUGH CULT AND OCCULT INVOLVEMENT

All cults and occult activity is a satanic counterfeit of Christ, Biblical Christianity, the true works and ways of God and the Kingdom of God, 2 Corinthians 2:11; 11:14.

Brief List of Cults:

Hare Krishna, Scientology, Christian Science, Mormons, Unification Chuirch, The Way International, Bahai, Hinduism, Islam, Jehovah's Witnesses, Masonic Lodge, Theosophy.

Brief List of Occult Activity:

Ouija Board, Crystal Ball, Satanism, 8 Ball, Witchcraft, Séance, Palm Reading, Rod & Pendulum, Astrology, Telepathy, Satanic Ritual Abuse, Levitation, Light as a Feather & Stiff as a Board, Acupuncture, Magic or Lucky Charms, Blood Pacts, Dungeons & Dragons, Satanic Video Games, Psychic Hotline, Handwriting Analysis, Crystals, Tarot Cards, Black & White Magic, Wicca, Fortune Telling, Halloween & Related Activities, Spirit Guides, Astral Projection, Water Witching (divination) Wearing Magnets, Psychic Healings, ESP, Magic Cards & Game, Pokemon, Harry Potter, Magic Spells & Curses, Kabala, Native American Objects.

DEMONIC TRANSFERANCE

From your ancestors (Exodus 20:5-6; Lamentations 5:7) or from a demonized person through sexual activity outside the marriage bond or through sexual, physical, verbal, or emotional abuse (1 Corinthians 6:16).

SEEKING FOR SPIRITUAL GIFTS AND EMOTIONAL EXPERIENCES

Matthew 12:38-45; Acts 8:14-23; 1 Corinthians 12:1-3

Believers are most commonly demonized when they seek to speak in tongues, search for an emotional spiritual "high" and accept the indiscriminate laying on of hands. The proper way to "lay hands" on a person is by the elders of the church in obedience to James 5:14.

Speaking in tongues are very easy for a demon to counterfeit as are emotional "highs" 2 Corinthians 11:14. Laying on of hands is the prescribed means by which Satanists transfer power to each other.

It is always dangerous to seek for a gift or a spiritual experience that God may not wish to give you. In doing so you open yourself up to a demonic substitute. If you speak or pray in tongues be sure to test the spirit of the tongue, 1 John 4:1-2 (Any appropriate Biblical test questions may be used).

MISUSE OF BIBLE DOCTRINE

Ephesians 1:3; Colossians 2:9-10; 2 Timothy 3:16-17.

Examples:

In Ephesians 1:3 we are told that God has given to us every spiritual blessing in Christ, and in Colossians 2:9-10 we are told that we are complete in Christ. Therefore seeking for spiritual blessings and benefits outside of Christ Himself is dangerous. We may receive something, but it will not be from God.

Another example is when a believer is told to seek for the *baptism of the Spirit."* The truth is that at the moment of salvation a person is baptized in the Spirit. I.e. the person is "placed into" the Spirit, the Spirit is "placed into" them, and they are "placed into" the church. (*To dip, submerge, or place into"* is the meaning of *'baptism"* in Greek). John 3:6-8; Romans 6:1-10; Galatians 3:26-28; 1 Corinthians 12:13. To seek the *"baptism of the Spirit"* after salvation is to open up one's-self to receiving a false & evil spirit.

Another example is when we pray for God to, "come and be with us" or we pray for, "more of Jesus" or, "more of the Holy Spirit." The truth is that Jesus is always with us (Hebrews 13:5) and God is omnipresent (Jeremiah 23:24). The truth is that when we receive Christ at the moment of salvation, God gives us all of Jesus and all of the Holy Spirit. However, they do not have all of us as far as their control of every area of our life. The process of being *"filled with the Spirit"* (Ephesians 5:18) is to allow Jesus through the Holy Spirit to *"fill"* (control) all of our life. Asking for "more" of God whom you already have in His fullness is dangerous for you are then open to receiving a demonic counterfeit. Asking God to "come" when He is already here is dangerous for you are then again open to receiving a false and evil spirit in your presence.

10 Signs of Possible Demonization
in the Born-Again Believer

1. Inability to gain victory over "besetting sins." Sexual sins, anger, rage, unforgiveness, resentment, unbelief, etc.
2. Inability to stop negative, abnormal and destructive behavior.
3. A persistent sense that, "Something is wrong but I don't know what. I've tried everything but I don't get any better."
4. A history of early childhood abuse or trauma.
5. A generational family history of identical problems.
6. Past or present involvements in cults, the occult, or sex outside of marriage.
7. Persistent unbelief and doubts over Biblical and spiritual issues.
8. A persistent problem concentrating during Bible reading, prayer, and worship services. Sometimes even being unable to read the Bible or memorize Scripture.
9. Chronic physical problems with no medical cause.
10. Paranormal or supernatural experiences. Such as hearing voices in your mind, seeing "shapes" in your room or house, hearing unexplainable sounds in the house, frequent nightmares, feeling an evil presence near you or touching you.

The Victory of the Born-Again Believer
Over Demonization

For the believer who is demonized victory is guaranteed.

Satan and his evil spirits have all been defeated by the Lord Jesus Christ through His death and resurrection. Genesis 3:15; 1 Corinthians 15:24-27; Colossians 1:15-23; 2:13-15; Hebrews 2:14-18; 1 Peter 3:22; 1 John 3:8; Revelation 19:11-16; 20:1-15.

The Believer is in complete victory over Satan and his hosts because we share in Christ's authority over them. Psalm 108:12-13; Matthew 12:28-29; 18:18; 28:18-20; Luke 10: 17-19; 2 Corinthians 10:4; Ephesians 1:17-2:6; Colossians 1:12-14; James 4:7; 1 John 4:4.

Highly recommended for every believer as a tool for spiritual growth, regardless of suspecting demonization, is Neil T. Anderson's "Seven Steps to Freedom in Christ." Each of the "7 Steps to Freedom" involves the four necessary elements for any believer to become free from bondage to evil spirits:

1. Examination for sin. 1 Corinthians 11:28
2. Confession of sin. 1 John 1:9
3. Repentance from sin. 2 Corinthians 7:8-10
4. Renouncing all evil spirits. James 4:7

When renouncing and evicting evil spirits from your life:

1. Identify the evil spirit and it's area of control ("place"). Ephesians 4:27
2. Remember your position & authority in Christ. Ephesians 1:17-2:6
3. Speak the name of the Lord Jesus Christ. Philippians 2:9-11
4. Speak the blood of the Lord Jesus Christ. Revelation 12:11
5. Speak the truth of the Word of God. John 8:32
6. Command the evil spirits, in the Name of the Lord Jesus Christ and by the power of His holy blood, to leave and go where the Lord Jesus Christ sends them, never to return.

In addition a highly successful way for a born-again believer to deal with demonization issues is by meeting with a qualified Christian counselor who uses the Christ-Centered Counseling method where the Lord Jesus Christ is the primary Counselor.

Bibliography

Bibliography

Anderson, Neil T., The Bondage Breaker, Eugene, OR, Harvest House, 1990.

Victory Over the Darkness, Ventura, CA, Regal, 1990.

Walking Through The Darkness, San Bernardino, CA., Here's Life Pub., 1991

The Seduction Of Our Children, Eigene, OR., Harvest House, 1991.

Released From Bondage, San Bernardino, CA., Here's Life Pub., 1991.

Living Free In Christ, Ventura, CA., Regal, 1993.

Setting Your Church Free, Ventura, CA., Regal, 1994.

Arnold, Clinton, 3 Crucial Questions about Spiritual Warfare, Grand Rapids, MI., Baker   Book House, 1997.

Barnhouse, Donald G., The Invisible War, Grand Rapids, MI, Zondervan, 1965.

Boehm, Roger, Evil Defined from a Christian Perspective, Titusville, FL, Lulu Publishing, 2006.

In the Face of Evil – A Wakeup Call for Christians, Titusville, FL, Lulu Publishing, 2006.

Bubeck, Mark, The Adversary, Chicago, IL., Moody Press, 1975.

Overcoming the Adversary, Chicago, IL, Moody Press, 1984.

The Rise Of Fallen Angels, Chicago, IL., Moody Press, 1995.

Raising Lambs Among Wolves, Chicago, IL., Moody Press, 1997.

Dickason, Fred, Angels Elect & Evil, Chicago, Illinois, Moody, 1975.

Demon Possession And The Christian, A New Perspective, Chicago, IL., Moody Press, 1987.

Friesen, James G. PhD, Uncovering the Mystery of MPD, San Bernardino, CA., Here's Life Publishers, Inc., 1992.

Gaeberlein, Arno C., The Conflict of the Ages, New York, N.Y., Publication Office "Our Hope," 1933.

Montgomery, J. Warwick, Principalities and Powers, Minneapolis, MN., Bethany Fellowship, 1975.

Russell, Jeffrey Burton, Lucifer: The Devil in the Middle Ages, Ithaca, NY, Cornell University Press, 1986.

Russell, Jeffrey Burton, The Devil: Perceptions of Evil from Antiquity to Primitive Christianity, Ithaca, NY, Cornell University Press, 1987.

Smith, Margaret, Ritual Abuse, San Francisco, CA., Harper, 1993.

Unger, Merrill F., Biblical Demonology, Chicago, IL., Scripture Press, 1955.

Wagner, Peter, Wrestling With Dark Angels, Ventura, CA., Regal Books, 1990.

Engaging the Enemy, Ventura, CA., Regal Books, 1992

Dr. Boehm is Available to Speak
To your Church or Organization

Revivals & Evangelistic Meetings

Having preaching revivals and evangelistic meetings in the United States, Cuba, and Haiti, Dr. Boehm is well qualified. If you would like more information and a tape please contact Dr. Boehm.

Pillars of a Passionate Marriage

A Biblically based seminar for married couples and those contemplating marriage. Included in the presentation are such subjects as: respecting your mate; sharing responsibility together; enjoying recreation together; keeping romance in the marriage; being resolved in the marriage; and healthy Biblical sex and sexuality in a marriage. Typical presentation is a minimum 4 hours in length. A great seminar for a Saturday program.

Children in Danger

A Biblically based presentation designed for adult and youth functions

Adults: The topics arte designed to educate and heighten awareness of dangerous activities our children and teens are constantly being tempted by the world around them to be involved in, why these activities are dangerous, and what can be done. Typically plan on 1 ½ hours not including a time for questions at the conclusion.

Youth: For youth two sessions are recommended which would include a general presentation of approximately 1 to 1 ½ hours. Then the participants would be asked to fill out an anonymous *Spiritual Experience Inventory* which would be compiled. A second session would then be scheduled to discuss specifics related to the experiences of the particular youth group. These sessions could be conducted on the same day.

Our children are playing with fire. On the average, when Christian High School students are surveyed we find these startling results:

45% say they have experienced a "presence" in their room that scared them.

60% say they have harbored bad thoughts about God.

40% find it mentally hard to pray and read their Bible.

70% report hearing "voices" in their head, like there was a subconscious voice talking to them.

20% say they frequently entertain thoughts of suicide.

Both adult and youth presentations would be designed into the time frame of the church or group making the request.

Spiritual Warfare Seminar

A Biblically based presentation designed for church laity

Session topics include: Basic Understanding of Spiritual Warfare; Can a Born Again Believer be demonized?; Spiritual Warfare and the Family; Children in Danger; Problems in Homes, Churches, and other Buildings; Our Victory in Jesus Christ.

Dr. Boehm will tailor presentations to fit your church or group's time schedule and requests. Suggested scheduling might include four evenings 7pm-9pm, or weekend seminar.

All presentation titles can also be presented individually. Dr. Boehm speaks primarily on a love offering basis plus travel and accommodation expenses when out of the area.

For more information or a tailor made presentation or seminar for your church contact:

Dr. Roger Boehm

(321) 269-0404   FAX: (321) 269-8173

E-mail: cfcc@lwol.com

www.ingramcontent.com/pod-product-compliance
Lightning Source LLC
Chambersburg PA
CBHW051724260326
41914CB00031B/1728/J